African Psychology in Historical Perspective and Related Commentary

African Psychology in Historical Perspective and Related Commentary

Edited by
Daudi Ajani ya Azibo

AFRICA WORLD PRESS
TRENTON | LONDON | CAPE TOWN | NAIROBI | ADDIS ABABA | ASMARA | IBADAN | NEW DELHI

AFRICA WORLD PRESS
541 West Ingham Avenue | Suite B
Trenton, New Jersey 08638

Copyright © 1996 Daudi Ajani ya Azibo

First Printing 1996

All rights reserved. No part of this publication may be reproduced, stored in a retrieval system or transmitted in any form or by any means electronic, mechanical, photocopying, recording or otherwise without the prior written permission of the publisher.

Book design: Jonathan Gullery
Cover design: Linda Nickens

Library of Congress Cataloging-in-Publication Data

African psychology in historical perspective and related commentary / edited by Daudi Ajani ya Azibo.
p. cm.
Includes bibliographical references and index.
ISBN 0-86543-292-9 (cloth). -- 0-86543-293-7 (pbk. : alk. paper)
1. Afro-American--Psychology. 2. Blacks--Psychology. I. Azibo, Daudi Ajani ya.
E168.625.A386 1996
155.8'496073--dc20 95-50998
CIP

CONTENTS

This book is dedicated to the cause of the destruction of white supremacy, Arab supremacy, and all other forms of African (Black) oppression. To that end, I wish to acknowledge all the Africans, past and present and future, known and unknown, who qualify in Marcia Sutherland's terminology as "authentic strugglers"—dedicated to the corporate African self, fallen in love with the Black Race, striving consistently for the psychological, economic, cultural, social, spiritual, and political progress of Africans. Also, the contributions of whites and other non–Africans dedicated to justice are acknowledged, especially those like John Brown and Henry David Thoreau. These two must be held up as examples of white role models and "responsible white leadership."

Preface

This book is devoted to the discipline of *Africentric Psychology*. The chapters that are included do not exhaust the subject matter of the discipline. That would require several volumes. What is offered here is cogent discourse from carefully selected chapters on carefully selected issues that are fundamental and foundational to the existence and application of Africentric Psychology. Several of the chapters have never before been published, some having been written and painstakingly edited specifically for this book. Some have been available only to a limited circle of scholars and one is reprinted from a scholarly periodical. Thus, most of the offerings in this volume are "fresh."

It is anticipated that by exploring several basic issues the discipline itself will be further substantiated. Two byproducts of such substantiation, it is hoped, will be (a) the recognition of the sheer worth and potential of Africentric Psychology and (b) the adoption, refinement, and embracing by psychological professionals of the theory, research, and practice that emanates from Africentric Psychology. The realization of these two byproducts is the necessary springboard to psychological redemption, rebirth, and recoupment for Africans in particular as well as to the enhancement of the psychological orientation of all human groups in general.

This anthology begins by addressing the most fundamental aspect of any discipline, its own history. The first chapter, written by your Editor, aims to anchor the reader in what Africentric Psychology is, how it is defined, where it came from, and where it is going: an exploration into history and systems. It also explains why African (Black) Psychology is synonymous with Africentric Psychology. The title of the anthology is taken from the title of this chapter, because historical grounding and the perspective one attains from it are crucial to an understanding of African psychology, contemporary developments within the field, and the field's destiny.

The next section delves into the nature–of–human–nature question, perennialy an issue for psychological inquiry. Na'im Akbar's profound statement on the nature of human personality seen through the prism of Africentric analysis is the leading piece for this section. Akbar addresses the nature of human nature as it is understood in African thought. This is a fundamental work for understanding personality as conceived by the Sages of old Africa and passed on in the African worldview. In the third chapter, I address the nature of mental health and, in a painstakingly precise and systematic discussion, define mental health Africentrically. This unprecedented contribution will, I hope, be a welcome addition to psychological literature. Eurocentric psychology has yet to advance a cogent definition of mental health. I am especially proud to have authored this chapter.

Having attended to African–centered perspectives on mental health and human nature, the next section critically examines the psychological condition of Africans in the United States. In chapter 4, Kobi Kambon (also known as Joseph Baldwin) addresses the peculiar psychological predicament of the African of the United States of America. He elucidates how oppression's detrimental psychological consequences obtain and he provides direction on how they can be overcome. The analysis he offers is readily generalizable to other diasporan and continental African populations victimized by alien oppression. In chapter 5, Olomenji also analyzes the oppressed psychological state of the African of the United States. Emphasizing one of the major mental disorders peculiar to African (Black) personality called mentacide, Olomenji explicitly links this psychological malady and the impending genocide of U. S. Africans. Success in resisting genocide demands "National Vision," a view to sovereignity for U. S. Africans that requires a psychological reorienting of the African toward mental health defined Africentrically. Olomenji's chapter explicitly takes us to the border of Africentric political psychology. (The bulk of contemporary African Psychology interfaces directly with political psychology, albeit implicitly.)

Clearly, we must be concerned with what mental health professionals can do when working on the African's psyche. Chapter 6 discusses an Africentric psychotherapy in terms of theory and implementation. Not only does Africentric psychology explain the nature of human nature and the maladaptation of Africans to oppression, it provides efficacious treatment modalities. Only one is presented in this volume, NTU psychotherapy. Fred Phillips developed NTU psychotherapy and, with his clinical staff colleagues, has practiced it extensively with positive results. NTU psychotherapy is one example of a specific psychotherapy based in Africentric thought.

Africentric Psychology must address the need to properly develop and educate African children. Although volumes of work are needed in these two areas, the next section provides an exciting, provocative chapter for each. These two chapters, 7 and 8, can serve as excellent bases for an eventual articulation of Africentric developmental and educational psychologies, respectively. Regarding development, Neferkare Abena Stewart has, for the first time in a single essay, collected and synthesized detailed research findings on the early and advanced sensorimotor development of continental and diasporic African neonates. The *data*, as opposed to intellectual speculation, strongly implicate the genetic influences of melanin. (The ancient Kamites were melanin scholars and left literature on the psychological influences of melanin.) Stewart lays out the astounding implications for infant development and assessment. The editing required for this chapter was considerable, but the fruits of the labor are well worth it. The reader is invited to dine well, as valid knowledge about melanin is critical for African people's psychological diet. Amani na Uwezo ya Ukombozi (also known as Michael McMillan) has succinctly and devastatingly deconstructed the insulting and pernicious—but nonetheless predominant—thesis in educational psychology that integrated education is good for Africans of the United States. He shows that this entrenched idea is untenable in both its theoretical underpinnings and social psychological data. Although it is too late to undo the 1954 Brown *vs.* Topeka Kansas decision which relied on this erroneous idea to the detriment of the education of Africans, Ukombozi's analysis can henceforth be used to arrest and contain its implementation. Also, it provides the necessary space within which African Psychology and educational activists must articulate and usher in an Africentric educational psychology. Like Olomenji's chapter, the ramifications for political psychology are clear.

The field of community psychology is treated in the next section. As practiced Eurocentrically, it is well established. However, it has proven of dubious value to the Africans of the United States, correlated and implicated as it is with the disarray of the African community. In chapter 9, Na'im Akbar, Rashaad Saafir, and Dorothy Granberry–Stewart present a treatise on the concept of community psychology that is based in Africentric assumptions. It also salvages worthy notions extant in the Eurocentric version. The chapter is highly practical and readable and provides required reading for community mental health workers, especially administrators. Through the application of the ideas found in this chapter, the dubious role of community psychology in the African community could be reversed.

The next section focuses on science and methodology, which are crucial parts of the field of African psychology. It is implied in Wade Nobles' famous statement that Black psychology is not the darker dimension of White psychology that the *discipline* of African Psychology must have its own methodology based upon *its peculiar approach* to science (as does Eurocentric Psychology, I might add). The three essays which appear in this section number among the major statements on science and methodology. In chapter 10, Jacob Carruthers, one of the African world's contemporary sages, has provided an exegesis of the bases of Eurocentric science. Sublimely, he deconstructs it and lays bare its inherent oppressive character. Eurocentric science is necessarily oppressive because it derives from the oppressive Eurocentricworldview. Additionally, Carruthers, not at all the iconoclast, points out how Eurocentric science can be used to further African liberation. Moreover, he asserts that it is out of the collective wisdom of African people, i.e., the African worldview/African culture, that contemporary Africentric science (like its ancient predecessor) can only/must be developed.

Leachim Semaj's articulation of the concept of cultural science in chapter 11 demonstrates that this task may not be as difficult as it first appears (due to our conceptual incarceration in Eurocentric cultural science, I might add). Semaj enumerates criteria that will structure Africentric social science. Consequently, his chapter outlines specific methods for conducting research based in a science that is liberating for Africans.

In chapter 12, which I first published in the *Western Journal of Black Studies*, your editor takes the further step of articulating an actual research framework in which the "quantitative researcher" can conceive of research that is not only methodologically sound but culturally appropriate as well. At this point, we have put theory into practice. I call my research approach the *theory–derived steady state approach*. It is superior to the comparative approach and more appropriate and more functionally liberational than the cross–cultural approach. Students will find that they can use this approach successfully in conducting graduate theses, and professionals will at long last have an extant culture–specific research framework from which to work. (No more excuses!)

Of course, the foundations laid by the chapters in this book must be taught, and teaching African (Black) Psychology must be done correctly. To that end the last section is devoted. Chapter 13 by Charlyn Harper–Browne provides a most informative and lucid discussion addressing pedagogy in Africentric Psychology. Her discussion on how curriculum development can enhance the teaching of African psychology is a major contribution to the field. In chapter 14, Kobi Kambon provides an example of how a psychology department might be run. The department at Florida A & M University grants Bachelor's and Master's degrees. The opinion may be widespread that the FAMU psychology department is the mecca and fountainhead for psychological training that is *explicitly and curricularly* Africentric in the United States (and probably the world). The approach to training used there can be considered a beacon for other departments, especially historically Black colleges and universities in the United States. The continental and other diasporan African countries should seriously consider replacing their current programs which are modeled in the Eurocentric tradition with the "FAMU Model." These last two chapters make a fitting close to this anthology and complement the beginning historical essay: knowing the discipline's origin, what it has been through, and where it is going must effectively be translated into pedagogy. These chapters are timely and instructive.

In general, the authors use both terms "African" and "Black" in designating the people and their psychology. The terms are interchangeable with no explicit or implied difference as far as I can discern. Therefore, no editing of this terminology for clarity has been deemed necessary.

Daudi Ajani ya Azibo

Acknowledgements

I cannot thank the contributors enough for responding to my call and for being patient as the project was nursed along. Several external factors sidetracked this project from time to time, so I must express my gratitude to publisher Kassahun Checole for his sustained support. My deepest *"asante sana"* is extended to Nadia Kravchenko who diligently and expertly typed the various drafts of these chapters. To my graduate research assistant Ampufowaah Owusu–Ansah I am deeply indebted for her word processing and varied assistance. Finally, my wonderful wife, Muthy Fatama, provided as per usual the encouragement and support needed to complete this project.

CHAPTER 1

African Psychology in Historical Perspective and Related Commentary

Daudi Ajani ya Azibo

AFRICAN PSYCHOLOGY IN HISTORICAL PERSPECTIVE AND RELATED COMMENTARY

> Any discipline must begin with the study of its own history. — Maulana Karenga

This essay will not deliver a definitive and comprehensive history of African psychology, a worthy task that to date goes undone. Rather, we shall attempt here to provide an overview of the origin, essence, and consequent destiny of African psychology, which actually is unfolding right before our eyes (Azibo, 1990; Myers, 1988; Nobles, 1986a). As our discipline advances, taking care to be historically grounded in its tradition and intellectual heritage is imperative. As Dr. Maulana Karenga pointed out at the first National Council for Black Studies' Summer Institute in 1989, "any [and every] discipline must begin with the study of its own history."

THE IMPORTANCE OF ORIGIN, ESSENCE, AND DESTINY

A comprehensive appreciation of what African psychology is about requires knowledge of three things: its past, its present functioning as it is related to its past, and its future prospects as discernible from both its past and its present functioning. These are the issues of origin, essence, and destiny. The questions of destiny ask where African psychology is going and what its future will be. It must be understood that the essence of a thing defines its destiny. For African psychology, then, its destiny can only be as great or as lame, as enduring or as short-lived, as central to human life or as peripheral to human life as is the inherent capacity of its essence to carry it. The questions of essence ask what African psychology is, what constitutes African psychology, and what its mission is. These are fundamental issues of definition, scope, content, and purpose. It must be understood as well that a thing's essence is, in turn, defined by its origin. The questions of origin ask when, where, and under what circumstances African psychology originated.

A comprehensive historical perspective of African psychology can be achieved within this origin-essence-destiny conceptual framework. I shall build upon Dr. Naim Akbar's (1979) sublime observation that to know the destiny of a thing, you determine its essence, which is necessarily found in its origin. Logically, we begin with the questions of origin from which essence and destiny subsequently derive. Four dates can be posited for the origin of African psychology, each differing from the date of origin of Eurocentric psychology. From each of these five distinct dates of origination, corresponding essences and destinies necessarily derive. Fleshing this out will be indispensible for historical perspective. Table 1 contains the five dates of origin and corresponding essences and destinies.

Table 1. YEARS OF ORIGIN, WITH CORRESPONDING ESSENCES AND DESTINIES OF AFRICAN AND EUROCENTRIC PSYCHOLOGY

Origin	Essence	Destiny
African Psychology I: Ancient Kemet (Egypt), circa 3200 B.C.E.*	Cultivation of the human soul, emphasis on human illumination	Inherently unlimited, a self-perpetuating Africentric enterprise
Eurocentric Psychology II: Wilhelm Wundt, 1879, Father of Eurocentric Psychology	Scientific study of behavior inclusive of Psychoanalytic depth processes, emphasis on control of behavior	Will be maintained wherever the Euro-centric idea predominates
African Psychology III: Francis Cecil Sumner, 1920, Father of African-U.S. Psychologists	Same as Euro-centric psychology (capitulation), plus a reactive thrust of refuting racist and pejorative theory and research on Africans emanating from Eurocentric Psychology	Capitulation to Euro-centric psychology, or perpetual reaction against its white-supremacy-maintainance views of Africans that are endemic to Eurocentric theory, research, and practice
African Psychology IV: Founding of the Association of Black Psychologists in 1968	Same as African Psychology III (capitulation, reaction), plus two proactive camps: the pro-Black (which dotes on the authenticity of the African-U.S. experience), and the Africentric, which rests in the African cultural deep structure (African philosophy) and thereby returns to African Psychology I.	Same as African Psychology III (capitulation or reaction), plus principled disputation between the pro-Black and Africentric camps (Author's perspective is that the Africentric camp is achieving preeminence.)
African Psychology V: Wade Noble's publication on the African Philsophical basis of African Psychology, 1972	Same as Africentric proactive camp in African Psychology IV: African cultural deep structure is the base, a return to African Psychology I	Same as the Africentric proactive camp: steady propogation of the Africentric view.

* See in text discussion on dating, as this date will ultimately be pushed back further into antiquity. Note: The acronym B.C.E. (Before the Christian Era) is equivalent in time to B.C.

A Multiplicity of Origins, Essences, and Destinies

I. Africentric Psychology

Origin. The original African psychology has to be traced to that point in time when the Blacks of Africa produced an *organized system* of knowledge (philosophy, definitions, concepts, models, procedures, and practice) concerning the nature of the social universe from the perspective of African cosmology (see definition below). This predates the European Renaissance and even the founding of Greece, the first European nation. This carries us at least as far back as ancient Kemet (the Blacks' Nile Valley civilization of what today is Arab-conquered Egypt) where it can be demonstrated that "the entirety of the Kemitic cosmology is actually a comprehensive description of the Psyche of man." Indeed, "those concepts of human development . . . of Ancient Kemit . . . define . . . the genesis and implied potentialities of man" (Akbar 1985a: 121, 131). It is of utmost importance to understand that an *organized system of knowledge* is being dealt with here and not just lofty speculations on life and the cosmos. As such, this Kemetic system incorporated theory (ideas) and practice (applications). Techniques to guide the human in transformation to an ultimate state of development, which has been termed correct psychological and behavioral functioning (Azibo 1989a), were in use in this original African (indeed, original human) psychology (see Gilbert 1980; Hilliard 1985, 1986; James 1976; King 1985).

Even though this system of knowledge was clearly in place in ancient Kemet (Akbar 1985a; Hilliard 1985, 1986; King 1985; Nobles 1986b), Chancellor Williams (1976) has reminded us that Egypt is Ethiopia's oldest daughter. That is, the single empire known variously as Ta Seti (Hilliard 1988), Cushite (Houston 1985), and Ethiopian (Means 1980) established Kemet as a colony. Therefore, since Kemet inherited the older Cushite knowledge it is likely that the origination date for African psychology will have to be pushed back into this earlier period. For now, however, and with this caveat in mind, it is sufficient to date African psychology's origin to the time of ancient Kemet's political establishment, tentatively 3200 B.C.E. This date actually was Eurocentrically derived for the purpose of maintaining white supremacy; when calculated Africentrically, the date is pushed further back into antiquity, though Africentric scholars have yet to reach consensus on a particular date (Amen 1987, Appendix; ben-Jochannon 1986; Carruthers 1984:27–30). Nevertheless, there can be little doubt that the intellectual seedbed of African psychology predate its origin by millennia, given the antiquity of African high thinking (e.g., Jackson 1980).

The circumstances under which this African psychology began might be characterized in sum as "Southern Cradle": "existence was so easy in the valley of the Nile, a veritable Garden of Eden . . . a collective, sedentary, relatively easy, peaceful life" (Diop 1974:230). Human illumination achieved through self-realization was the articulated societal motif, as opposed to the human control achieved through domination that is found in the origins of Eurocentric psychology.

Essence. The Kamites practiced the cultivation of the human psyche or soul and the attendant higher mental faculties as part of a holistic, complex approach to the social universe that meshed "the understanding of man [with] . . . religion, science, . . . mathematics . . . and government" (Akbar 1985a 123). A field of psychology distinct and separate from this holistic system has not been identified. It follows that no Kemetic definition of psychology *per se* is advanced at this time. However, the definition articulated by Dr. Joseph Baldwin in 1986 is so fundamentally correct that it captures the psychological activities of the ancient Kamites:

> African (Black) Psychology is defined as a system of knowledge (philosophy, definitions, concepts, models, procedures and practice) concerning the nature of the social universe from the perspective of African Cosmology [meaning that] . . . African (Black) Psychology is nothing more or less than the uncovering, articulation, operationalization, and application of the principles of the African reality structure relative to psychological phenomena. (243)

Thus, it can be seen that "all human life processes, including the spiritual, mental, biological, genetic, and behavioral [and] . . . all human groups—Africans, Arabs, Europeans, Asians, and so on" (Azibo 1989b: 307) constitute the scope and content of African psychology. It should be equally clear that African psychology is by definition an Africentric enterprise. Thus the terms African and Africentric psychology may be used interchangeably.

Since by all legitimate accounts Kemet is described mainly as a technologically advanced and morally upright society (ben-Jochannon 1981, 1986; Diop 1974; Jackson 1980; Tarharka, 1979), it can be inferred that the purpose of this original African psychology was to propagate just such a way of life. Human development, societal justness, and scientific applications and study went hand-in-hand (Carruthers 1984, ch. 3).

Destiny. First, the fact that in 1996 C.E. we are seriously entertaining scholarly discussion of a psychology that began at least 5196 years ago (in 3200 B.C.E.) attests to the longevity of African psychology (Africentric psychology). Second, from Carruthers (1984), Gilbert (1980), James (1976), Karenga and Carruthers (1986), and many others it is clear that the scope and content of inquiry afforded by the Kemetic system of knowledge is of a vastness that is unlikely to be exhausted in several lifetimes. Akbar (1985a, 123) is instructive on this point:

> The wisdom of ancient Kemet is like a vast tapestry of amazing complexity. . . . As Schwaller de Lubicz (1977) observes . . . [there is] "abundant material. . . . An encyclopedic amount of work is available to the researcher. . . [that] Nevertheless . . . remains unknown in terms of its . . . contingent psychospiritual knowledge" . . . . The task that we have set for ourselves is an impossible one for even the Egyptologist of advanced knowledge.

Third, as I stated elsewhere (Burlew 1989:5), presently the field of African psychology "has [a] substantial scholarly tradition that underlies its [contemporary] revitalization" (G. Jackson 1979; Karenga 1982, ch. 8; Nobles, 1986a).

Based on these three points, it would seem safe to say that the destiny of Africentric psychology is inherently unlimited. It shall prevail among those practitioners of psychology who employ the African system of knowledge in their work (not just in their heart or social orientation; we speak of an actual praxis here that withstands non-Africentric hegemony). Its concepts shall indeed dominate the conceptual underpinnings of the professional ideations of these practitioners. African psychology will, additionally, continue to perpetuate itself through the production of student apprentices and by winning over non-Africentric psychologists by the sheer and compelling force of its essential and special truth.

II. EUROCENTRIC PSYCHOLOGY

Origin. According to the Eurocentric tradition, psychology formally began as late as the establishment of Wilhelm Wundt's laboratory in 1879 C.E. The significant intellectual seedbeds are said to be in the so-called Greek philosophy and the European Renaissance (Murphy and Kovac 1972). In both circumstances Europe was attempting to extricate itself from backwardness and propel itself into world domination.

Essence. Applying the questions of essence to this Eurocentric psychology, it is seen that the predominant definition for this psychology is the scientific study of behavior. There is a bias toward *observable* behavior even though Sigmund Freud's influence has made unconscious, depth processes a viable part of the scope and content. The less observable cognitive processes (implicit psychology) have also become a major content area. The concepts that constitute the scope and content of this psychology either derive from European-centered thought or are recast therein. The mission in truth is to explain and to predict behavior in order to *control* (dominate) the behavior of people, contemporary articulation of humanitarian goals notwithstanding.

Destiny. The destiny of this psychology, so constituted and originated that it can only be called Eurocentric (European, Euro-American, Euro-Australian, White, etc.), is that it will be maintained wherever the Eurocentric idea predominates. The destiny of Eurocentric psychology might be altered for the better if it were simply to adopt or to infuse with integrity intact non-Eurocentric psychological concepts. However, because the Eurocentric view perpetuates itself by either excluding concepts originating in "other-centric" thought from the universe of ideas or by recasting these concepts Eurocentrically, any substantial alteration in its destiny is unlikely. (It should be noted that the character of the Eurocentric recasting often incorporates outright thievery, expropriation, and plagiarism of concepts germinated in the centric thought of other people.) It appears that the post-Eurocentric period will only come about by the sheer force of non-Eurocentric scholarly production. Indeed, *the reemergence of the nascent, contemporary, and compelling Africentric psychology* since 1968, which itself is a harbinger of the post-Eurocentric period, *has come about as a direct result of Africentric scholarly production*. This shall become clear as we examine the psychological era ushered in with the establishment of the National Association of Black Psychologists in 1968. Prior to that era, however, was the era of the early African American (U.S.) psychologists.

III. 1920: DR. FRANCIS CECIL SUMNER

Origin. Guthrie (1976) showed that the first African in the Americas to achieve the Ph.D. degree in psychology was Francis Cecil Sumner in 1920. Guthrie honored Sumner with the title Father of Black American psychologists. Karenga (1982) followed Guthrie's revelation and located in time the beginning of African psychology with Dr. Sumner's historic feat, accomplished, to be sure, against all odds.

In 1920 in the United States anti-Africanism was rampant and openly practiced and promulgated. Eurocentric psychology was one of the leading social sciences in legitimizing the ideas of white supremacy and African inferiority. So steeped in anti-Africanism was Eurocentric psychology and psychiatry that "*Even the [laboratory] Rat was White*" (Guthrie 1976; Thomas and Sillen 1972). Under these oppressive and horrific circumstances did African psychology so-rationalized originate.

Essence. Clearly, African psychology so-rationalized is void of any inherent Africentric conceptualizations. The originating atmosphere permitted no space for the advancement of such conceptualizations because of the necessity for maintenance of Eurocentric hegemony. Thus, the definition of this African psychology so-rationalized is the same as Eurocentric psychology. Its scope and content are the same too, except that many of the early African psychologists add to this overarching Eurocentric essence a *reac-*

tive thrust, refuting and disputing the anti-African, racist claims and evidences that issued forth from the Eurocentric psychology.

It should be understood that the milieu of full-blown white supremacy did more to determine the essence of this African psychology than the lack of a proactive Africentric conceptual system on the part of the early African psychologists. They and this psychology so-rationalized must be seen in proper historical context. The fact that many of the early African psychologists reacted in defense of Africans, devoting major work to overturning the psychological white-supremacy onslaught, is testimony to an honorable orientation. It is conceivable that such reaction during those early hegemonic times may have been a proactive feat. Certainly it was a necessary precursor to proactivity under these circumstances.

Although reaction is predominant in the essence of this psychology so-rationalized, some overcame this. For example, the efforts of Dr. Herman G. Canady to establish a professional organization of African psychologists that potentially could proactively advocate for the Race as far back as 1938 (Guthrie 1976) is noteworthy.

Destiny. Because the essence of this African psychology so-rationalized is dependent upon the essence of the Eurocentric psychology which circumscribes it severely, its future holds only two options: (a) a neverending reaction to Eurocentric analyses since the culture of white supremacy and its attendant Eurocentric psychology remain in place; or (b) an intentional or unwitting capitulation to and participation in the hegemony of Eurocentric psychology.

Fundamental Eurocentric hegemony—and, I daresay, Arab-centered hegemony where *it* is in place—thoroughly stymies Africentric fields (Semmes 1982), as the impoverished and abject destinies of this African psychology so-rationalized illustrate.

Taking this rationale to the limit. Using the achievement of the first African to attain the Ph.D. in psychology for establishing the origin of African psychology so-rationalized could lead to an African-Caribbean psychology, an African-Australian psychology, an African-Dravidian psychology, a continental African psychology, *ad infinitum*. Each would have a non-Africentric essence deriving from an alien group. This state of affairs would doubtlessly produce a host of psychological obscurities masquerading as African psychology data. The valid African psychology data would be obfuscated. A reading of Baldwin's (1986) analysis suggests that this is indeed the case in the United States.

There is nothing to recommend this rationale as a way of establishing origin. Rather, it has proven useful in pinpointing an era or *Zeitgeist*. With Dr. Sumner we do not get a new psychology discipline, but rather the onset of a colorful and significant era that occurs within the parameters of Eurocentric psychology. At the same time, the realization of such an era reactively engenders the space needed for a future proactive paradigm shift (return) to Africentric psychology. It is likely that other eras of historical importance could be documented on the continent and throughout other parts of the diaspora using this rationale.

IV. 1968: The Association of Black Psychologists

Origin. The Association of Black Psychologists (ABP) was established in San Francisco in 1968 by thirty-three persons.[1] At first the organization did not separate itself from the Eurocentric psychological association called the American Psychological Association. However, the desirability and necessity of organizational independence for the ABP, coupled with the stark realization that the ethic of white supremacy was apparently endemic to and not abating in Eurocentric psychology as such (and the psychologists therein) motivated an ideologically diverse ABP membership to sever organizational connections with the Eurocentric psychological association. The spirit of the times was that of the 1960s—rebellion against and protest of white authority; pride in being Black; and the rediscovery of Africa. Ruth E. King (1977-1978), Warfield-Coppock (1984), and Williams (1974) provide detailed information on the history of the ABP. A related essay on the historical development of African psychology by G. Jackson (1979) should be consulted also.

There is substantial merit to the rationale that the nascent, contemporary, reemerging African psychology begins with the founding of the ABP in that African psychology's very emergence in our time is a direct result of the activities carried out under the auspices of the ABP. The most noteworthy of these activities are the quarterly publication of the *Journal of Black Psychology* and the annual national (moving toward international) ABP convention. These continue to be the two most important forums for the articulation of what African psychology is about.[2]

The rationale of Eurocentric psychology *and* that of arbitrarily fixing on the date of Dr. Sumner's feat as African psychology's origin alike preclude the existence of Africentric psychology before Wilhelm Wundt. In contrast, the rationale just given for the founding of the ABP as the inception date for a *re*emerging African psychology *requires* a preexistent African psychology. However, many (and perhaps most) significant psychologists who participated in this ABP-engendered African psychology movement neither entertained nor accepted the fact of a preexistent African psychology. Baldwin (1986) pointed out that many of these psychologists did not even conceptualize African psychology as an independent enterprise separate from Eurocentric psychology. This seeming paradox is addressed in the following discussion of essence.

Essence. Nsenga Warfield-Coppock (1984) has captured the multifaceted character of the essence of this ABP-engendered African psychology. The ABP, she says,

> was born of a vision to reclaim our African humanity and develop tools to assist our people in that rediscovery. This vision, from our earliest days took on the look of protest against those racist forces which appeared to control us and our full development as African American people and psychologists. . . . In asking the question, `How does one create, nurture and maintain the healthy Black/African mind/personality,' critical analysis of Euro-centric psychological models and theories, and their impact on Black/African people were foremost. Through our middle or adolescent years, we see more and more departures from Euro-centric models with an increasingly fruitful understanding of the African world, [African] models, . . . [and] our tasks as Black/African American psychologists and defining our relationship to Africa.

The point to be taken is that this ABP-engendered "African (Black)

Psychology is proactive as well as reactive, and it is most certainly political. . . . its thrust is clearly toward proactivity, that is, self-definition and self-determination" (Baldwin 1986, 246).

We can discern that there are distinct camps here that articulate divergent views on the definition, scope and content, and purpose of African psychology. There is a camp that continues to be enmeshed in reactive protest to the fallout that Eurocentric psychology visits upon Africans. Actually, this is a manifestation of the continued perpetual reaction that is destined in the African psychology rationalized to originate with Dr. Sumner in 1920! Also living out the same destiny as the reactors is a camp who have capitulated to the overarching Eurocentric hegemony and "do not conceptualize it [African psychology] as an independent enterprise separate from Western Psychology" (Baldwin 1986, 236), notwithstanding that such capitulators may reactively protest too.

There are two proactive camps that have vied for preeminence, the pro-Black and the Africentric. The former has mainly focused myopically on the African-United States diaspora using the nomenclature "Afro-American," "Black," or "African-American" psychology/experience. The proactivity of the pro-Black camp is seen in its correct insistence and propounding that the *social and cultural milieu of an African* (a) affords the best understanding of his or her psychological functioning and (b) is therefore a legitimate, viable, and preferred springboard to psychological inquiry regarding said African.

This has to be seen as an advance over capitulation to and reaction against Eurocentric hegemony. Seminal and major contributions to this pro-Black, proactive camp were made by Dr. Joseph White (1970, 1972, 1984). Unfortunately, however, *the conceptual view and vision of the pro-Black camp was stifled.* Although these contributions expanded discourse in the areas of scope, content, and purpose, none of the scholars in this camp freed themselves from the Eurocentric hegemony in psychological ideas. Baldwin explains this state of affairs:

> rather than operating as intellectually independent scholars-scientists . . . [the non-Africentric camps] follow the obscure . . . "European mentors" . . . by either employing directly some existing European models to explain Black

> people's psychological reality, or by attempting to "Blackenize" these same models in some obscure way to give them false appearance of being relevant . . . [thereby] failing to look to our own `African' historical, philosophical and cultural reality to give intellectual direction. (1985b:16)

Thus did—and do—the bounds set by Eurocentric psychology stifle the pro-Black camp, notwithstanding either its acknowledged acceptance and praxis of what it calls "the Black or Afro-American experience" as a springboard for its expanded scope, content, and purpose. To use contemporary Black Studies terminology (Azibo 1992), the pro-Black camp is *oriented* properly (i.e., recognizing and employing the African's own authentic experiences as the base for psychological inquiry) but not properly *located* (i.e., not employing the African cultural deep structure to provide the patterns for interpreting the reality of authentic African experiences).

On the other hand, the Africentric proactive camp has burst the bounds imposed by the hegemony of Eurocentric psychology by taking the position that African philosophy is the critical component that must anchor psychological conceptualization (Baldwin 1986; G. Jackson 1979; Nobles 1972). Thus the myopia of the pro-Black camp's "Afro-American experience" view was overcome by the Africentric camp. Also, from this springboard the hegemony of Eurocentric ideas was precluded because it is not possible for such ideas to be applied (either inadvertently or purposefully) in the guise of African psychology. It was at the time that this basic position coalesced in the works of the various Africentric camp scholars that African psychology was *reclaimed*, that is, that the field returned formally to the source. Consequently, the essence of African psychology for the Africentric proactive camp is ultimately the same as for the original, ancient African psychology. This camp, then, is both *oriented* and *located* properly, unlike the pro-Black camp.

Destiny. Since the psychologists who remain in the reactive and capitulation camps are merely continuing the line of their predecessors from the era ushered in by Dr. Sumner's feat, how could their destinies be any different? Perpetual capitulation or reaction are the only possible destinies for these camps. Goodman (1976) judged that to be reactive is to be nonproductive.

However, the two proactive camps, the pro-Black and the Africentric, share a common destiny of healthy intellectual combat and debate for preeminence in the field. That is, psychologists in each camp will attempt to propagate their positions. These positions will be substantiated or undermined on the basis of critical analysis. Mere fiats on the part of either camp or individual psychologists must be regarded as null and void. This disputation, when principled, is healthy for African psychology because its upshot is growth and substantiation of the field. Although life under white supremacy has engendered a testiness, a sensitivity to African-on-African critique, that actually is at variance with the African's heritage of rhetorical and oratorical discourse (Asante 1986; Smitherman 1977), a frequent utterance by Maulana Karenga might be taken to heart: "Truth that is not born of struggle [disputation] is not truth at all; it is just mindless agreement."

This part of African psychology's destiny is unfolding before our eyes. It is happening right now. My assessment of the situation is that the Africentric proactive camp has supported and sustained its positions more than the pro-Black proactive camp, over which it is fastly achieving preeminence. My assessment is based on chapters 5, 6, and 7 of Nobles' *African Psychology* (1986a), which show the culmination to date of the "disputation." Overall, it appears that the paradigm shift to the ancient African view is in full swing. For example, in recent works that may prove influential, Linda Myers (1988) and this author (Azibo 1989a) base and begin our psychological renderings in the Africentric view. Additionally, the pro-Black vs. Africentric debate and emergence of the Africentric paradigm shift are reflected in articles by Cedric Clark (1972), Cedric X, et al. (1975), and Baldwin (1976, 1986). Also, regarding my claim of the preeminence of the Africentric camp, it is important to take note of a trend that seems to be occurring. This author has observed that able scholars of the generation of African psychologists coming to maturity right in the midst or aftermath of the pro-Black vs. Africentric camp disputation who have not been reared in the Africentric camp theories and perspectives are finding themselves drawn to it. (Note that this does not mean that they *ipso facto* comprehend and handle them correctly.) An excellent example is Thomas Parham (1989: 196) who has worked extensively with an influential theory that comes from the pro-Black camp (Cross' "Negro-to-Black" conversion theory). However, Parham has recently altered that theory with original formulations of his own such that *now* it "is intended to be theoretically consistent with these positions" (the Africentric camp positions of Kobi Kambon [a.k.a. Joseph Baldwin] and Wade Nobles that the core of African personality is African in nature).

Finally, in a fair and hard-hitting reproach of African- American psychologists' activities, Baldwin (1985b) makes it clear that shortcomings are directly linked to non-Africentric praxis and, conversely, meaningful advancement of the field requires the implementation of positions that derive from the Africentric proactive camp. My assessment is neither intended to nor does it close the point about which proactive camp is currently preeminent.

V. 1972: AFRICAN PHILOSOPHY ARTICULATED BY DR. WADE NOBLES

Wade Nobles formulated his critical ideas while under the tutelage of professors D. Philip McGee and Syed Khatib (then Cedric X Clark). Wade Nobles' *African Philosophy: Foundations for Black Psychology* (1972) deserves special mention in our historical perspective. This article may have been the first one published in the context of the United States diaspora (perhaps the world) that articulated the basis in African philosophy upon which the discipline of African psychology rests. Moreover, it remains a seminal essay that has had enormous impact. It provided the underpinnings for the rationales put forth by the entire Africentric proactive camp. In a very real way, it can be argued that this contribution by Nobles represents the inception of the reemergent, nascent discipline of African psychology. Still, Nobles was a founder of the ABP and his work doubtlessly both affected and was affected by that movement. Thus his famous essay of 1972 shares the same *origin* as the ABP-engendered African psychology and the same *essence* and *destiny* as the Africentric proactive camp.

While this work was essential to the scholars of the Africentric camp, and, hence, to the reclamation of ancient African psychology, it was (and is) *not dealt with* by many in the non-Africentric camps. Many of these persons were prominent within the ABP and the Eurocentric-run psychological world. Consequently, the sheer prominence of these persons, who we might say represented psychological establishmentarianism among the African-U.S. psychologists, served to stymie the appreciation of students and less prominent psychologists for the Africentric view of the field. The result was that the Africentric camp, a relatively small cadre of scholars who were largely younger than the established psychologists, was more or less isolated within the general African-U.S. psychological community. Profound and seminal contributions like the work on African philosophy by Nobles (1972), the "Voo Doo or IQ" article on African psychology by Cedric X et al. (1975), as well as the penetrating and provocative articles by Baldwin (1976) and Clark (1972), were dismissed on ideological grounds. From the late 1970s through the mid 1980s, it was not uncommon to hear this camp pejoratively and derisively referred to as the African wing, as promoting romantic Africanity, and other such implied criticism.

However, special mention must be made of one prominent psychologist who made the transition from the pro-Black to the Africentric camp, Dr. Robert L. Williams (1981). Persuaded of the correctness of the Africentric view, Dr. Williams lent his considerable talents and prestige to the cause of the Africentric camp. Identifying this as a paramount event in African psychology's *reascension* is not too strong an assertion. Williams' promotion of Africentric camp notions in his theoretical work and public commentary helped to establish "face validity" for them. As a result, the general community of African-U.S. psychologists was more prone to entertain the positions advanced by the Africentric camp, which as I contended above is now preeminent.

The fundamental position of the Africentric camp is the employment of a conceptual system that is centered in African thought. Centric thought, a subject that is critical in its own right (Azibo 1992), plays a vital role in the formation of schools of African psychology.

THE FUNDAMENTALITY OF CENTRIC THOUGHT

Culture consists of deep and surface structures. Nobles (1982) and

Nobles, Goddard, and Cavill (1985) have defined culture as patterns for interpreting reality that give people a general design for living. In the beginning, African psychology was based on the African's answer to the issues of cosmology, ontology, axiology, world view, ideology, and ethos. These answers actually underlie African thought. Taken together, these issues comprise the deep structure of culture. Patterns for interpreting reality come from the answers to these deep-structure issues. That is, how the world is construed by a people depends upon the characteristic response that their cultural-racial group (distinct peoplehood as opposed to current geopolitical reality) made to the deep structure component of culture. This statement is foundational to the very humanity, peoplehood, and essence of the people who make it. *It is their centric thought base*, these answers to the cultural deep-structure issues. It is also enduring. It is their cultural statement forever, to the end of time. Even if a people unconsciously or by conscious choice reject their foundational cultural statement (their characteristic centric thought base), it remains their only cultural statement; any other cultural orientation that they might take on could never represent *their* cultural statement. Rather, it can only represent their operation under the duress, hegemony, or adoption of an alien way.

Now, whether or not a people operate from their own characteristic cultural statement or from an alien one, their general design for living is an outgrowth or upshot of the underlying cultural statement. Language, behavior, folkways, customs, and so on make up the cultural surface structure that can be seen as the general design for living. A people who follow an alien cultural statement may, nevertheless, frequently and systematically manifest unconsciously in their cultural surface structure "holdovers" that derive from their characteristic cultural deep structure and the sheer persistence of their indigenous cultural surface structure.

Interpretations of a people's functioning must be based in their peculiar deep and surface structures of culture in order to be valid and free of transubstantive error.[3] Thus, to explain (and prescribe) African psychological functioning adequately, the psychologist has to employ a psychology based in Africentric thought.

Schools of African psychology. A group of people who take a particular position on a given matter of doctrine make up a school of thought. African psychologists who take particular positions on the existence and essence (definition, scope and content, purpose) of African psychology comprise distinguishable schools of African psychology, the largely political concerns of Nobles (1986a, ch. 5) notwithstanding. As the historical perspective surveyed above and Nobles' own review show, the emergence of schools of African psychology, as we know them now, is an inescapable consequence in the developmental process of the struggle of African psychologists for *Kujichagulia* (self-determination) within the post-Wundt context of Eurocentric psycho-political hegemony. Again, when the struggle is principled and the strugglers are mature, the resulting disputation can lead to synthesis rather than division.

Bearing this in mind, we can discuss three schools of African psychology as described by Karenga (1982, ch. 8). This author sees his classifications as cogent and meeting the criteria for schools of thought. Karenga's categories are not definitive but are adequate as a first attempt to identify schools. The schools are distinguishable in their doctrinal positions on the existence and essence of African psychology. The fundamental discrepancy in these positions appears to derive from divergent centric thought bases.

The *Radical School* was born of the Africentric camp in the ABP epoch. It explicitly embraces Africentric thought as its intellectual foundation. It recognizes that spirit is a content area of psychology and that non-Africans are to be analyzed from the African reality structure. Africentricity serves as its social theory as well. The *Traditional School* was born in the epoch of the early Black psychologists ushered in by Dr. Sumner. It uses the Eurocentric thought base, and its psychological theory, research, and practice are derived thence. The inherent constraints and limitations are obvious. Dangling as it were between these two schools is the *Reform School*. It too was born in the ABP epoch, but in the works of the reactive and pro-Black camps. Its intellectual base is sometimes Eurocentric and frequently an admixture of Eurocentric and non-Africentric pro-Black concepts. Never, to date, has its intellectual base been Africentric thought. However, it is possible that a Reform School psychologist who is making a transition to becoming a Radical School psychologist might attempt to synthesize Reform notions with Africentric-based notions. Our historical perspective suggests that we should begin to see much more of this at this point in time (eventually giving way to a pure Africentric-based praxis). Regarding social theory, it is intriguing that many psychologists in the Reform School appear to maintain an inordinate concern over establishing and maintaining professional (and perhaps personal) African-European relationships. As Karenga (1982, ch. 8) pointed out, such concerns are absent in the Radical School (at least in the context that the Reform School raises them).

On the topic of African-European relationships, some writers have suggested that African psychology is a third great tradition in or plays some type of a "noble" role regarding Eurocentric psychology (Cook and Kono, 1977; White, Parham, and Parham 1980). Any such notions are not only inaccurate but possibly debasing as well. The historical perspective presented here makes the following presuppositions: (a) African psychology predates Eurocentric psychology; (b) African psychology is based in Africentric thought whereas Eurocentric psychology obviously is based in Eurocentric thought; and (c) these two centric thoughts are antithetical (Baldwin 1980, 1985a). The Africentric thought base has been called "optimal" whereas the Eurocentric is politely considered "sub-optimal" (Myers, 1988). Additionally, hegemonic Eurocentric thought (which is typical), as opposed to nonhegemonic (which is a theoretical possibility), has four peculiar characteristics that contrast markedly with Africentric thought: it projects itself as universal rather than as particular, as standard rather than as relative, it is exclusionary rather than inclusive of other-centric thought, and, as the American Indian cultural nationalist Russell Means (1980) pointed out in a profound statement, it is defensive rather than inviting of scrutiny.

However, practitioners of Eurocentric psychology will steal Africentric and other non-Eurocentric knowledge, then package and produce it as their own contribution to humanity. Such plagiarism is tantamount to what Williams (1981) defined as cultural racism. The term "expropriate" might capture more fully the essence of this sort of theft of knowledge, considering: (a) the postulated necessity of maintaining white supremacy (Welsing 1974); (b) the fact that in the words of Chancellor Williams (1976), whites are the implacable foe who have never come in peace; and (c) the value of owning knowledge in world conquest acknowledged by the Greek Alexander and his tutor Aristotle (Nobles 1986a, ch. 1) and evident in the practice of scientific colonialism (defined in Nobles 1976). The Machiavellian value orientation of the Eurocentric culture, opposed to *Ma'at* of the Africentric culture (Asante 1986; Carruthers 1984), combined with Eurocentricity's defensive and exclusionary character and the manifest proclivity of Europeans for psychopathic behavior toward Africans (see Wright 1985) continually feed this time-tested practice of knowledge expropriation.

It is apparent that the characteristic make-up of Eurocentricity precludes the inclusion of an authentic African psychology within the history and systems of Eurocentric psychology. (Marimba Ani's [1994] recent groundbreaking analysis of Eurocentric thought supports my position.) Plus, surely, the younger Eurocentric psychology must be considered relative to the preextant Africentric psychology. If truth be told, Eurocentric psychology actually represents a devolved paradigm shift away from the original human psychology which is Africentric psychology. The devolution "has its roots in the Greek mutation of ancient African thought . . , [which] is the core basis . . . of the current inadequacies of western [Eurocentric] psychology" (Nobles 1986a, 22). As the various schools of thought in Eurocentric psychology jockey for paradigmatic preeminence, the paradigm debate in African psychology is ultimately much more profound: whether to return to the original view of human nature espoused in Africentric thought or to continue to operate within the devolved conceptual parameters imposed by Eurocentric thought.

The fundamental factor underlying the differences between the three schools of African psychology is their divergent centric thought bases. This is not to be confused with the different approaches to psychological inquiry that African psychologists have historically used.

Approaches to psychological inquiry. The constructive/constructionist approach is the initial way that African psychology was practiced. In the ancient days, the priests, priestesses, and scribes developed psychological knowledge using Africentric cultural concepts. That is, what we today call psychological constructs and concepts, such as the *Sakhu* (*psyche*, soul, spirit), the *Heru* (Horus/Christ) consciousness, spirituality, and the ontological principle of consubstantiation, to name a few, were produced using the Africentric thought base. Thus, historical perspective reveals that the constructive approach is the oldest approach, not the most recent. It is only recently that psychologists of the Radical School have explicitly employed this approach (Azibo 1988a; Jackson 1979). Others may back into or otherwise employ the constructive approach covertly.

The deconstructive/deconstruction approach refutes, falsifies, or otherwise renders void anti-African theses and research findings that prevail in Eurocentric psychology (Banks 1982). In other words, when African psychologists produce work that literally debunks the historical and continuing anti-African theory and research that is clearly part and parcel of Eurocentric psychology (e.g., Azibo, 1993; Bulhan 1981; Guthrie 1976; Nobles 1986a, ch. 1; Thomas and Sillen 1972), they are employing the deconstructive approach. The approach often entails empirical falsification, but pejorative views can be countered conceptually as well. Also, the views to be debunked need not be anti-African (although they usually are), they may be simply at odds with African reality.

The reconstructive/reconstructionist approach revises Eurocentric psychological theory and practice *vis-à-vis* Africans and its views of Africans to better fit or jibe with the African cultural reality. Reconstructive efforts have often amounted to little more than a "Blackenizing" of Eurocentric psychology. Revamping some Eurocentric psychology might have some merit, but the psychologist must proceed with the attitude expressed by Nobles (1972) that African psychology is more than Eurocentric psychology's darker dimension if he or she is to get beyond Blackenizing. This approach is prone to mistakes of meaning: pseudoetiç errors (Triandis 1972), category mistakes (Ryle 1949), and transubstantive errors (see note 3 below).

Nobles (1986a, ch. 5) reviewed the deconstructive, reconstructive, and constructive literatures with characteristic insight. To conclude my discussion of these approaches, two points should be noted. First, the deconstructive approach has a place in African psychology only as a consequence of its contemporary unfolding. That is, it is a necessary reaction to the sheer hegemony of the Eurocentric psychological views of Africans. Otherwise, it is without merit and would not enjoy the prominent role it has had. African psychologists must be clear that the deconstructive approach is justified solely in African psychology's political confrontation with hegemonic non-African psychologies, not at all in scientific dogma. The science of the matter is really nonessential here, but the politics are central. Second, the deconstructive and reconstructive approaches serve two major functions: (a) as Nobles pointed out, they correct the faults in Eurocentric psychology, and (b) they often bridge to the constructive approach as modern African psychologists liberate themselves from Eurocentric shackles.

CONCLUDING REMARKS

Riding on the back of the Africentric camp's rise to preeminence is the paradigm shift *back* to Africentric thought. Scholars have called for this return (e.g., Akbar 1985b; Azibo, 1992). This paradigm shift is as important as any that has occurred in the physical and social sciences over the last millennium. The Africentric view may yet rescue the world tomorrow from its Eurocentric-plotted course of destruction, even as it beaconed, via Kemet, European Greece from nothingness and propelled a resistant Europe from its "Blight" Ages into its Renaissance, courtesy of the African Moorish culture. Eurocentric consciousness is, however, presently running rampant throughout the earth and the worst part of the problematic is that it is usually implicit rather than explicitly stated. All peoples of the earth have had their character laid waste and devolved by the Eurocentric consciousness. Now, here counterposing itself is Africentric thought, especially African psychology, as the way to human liberation (Azibo, in press).

The historical perspective presented shows that the practitioners of African psychology are rapidly becoming a genuine counterpoise to Eurocentric thought and its psychology. Though the recognition and respect that are required for legitimacy (Clark

1973) have not yet been attained, the discipline of African psychology is well on the way to *revitalization*. Karenga (1982) has substantially facilitated the field's legitimacy (recognition and respect) by providing its first platform as a recognized discipline in his internationally circulated textbook. Perhaps it will not be too long before continental and other diasporic African psychologists can effectively link with African-U.S. psychologists under the revitalized, nascent, Africentrically rooted African psychology. After all, historical perspective reveals an unlimited destiny, if our shoulders are broad enough, our arms strong enough, our intellect keen enough, and our observance of our duty diligent enough to carry on in the work started by our ancestors.

NOTES

1. The founding members of the ABP are Calvin Atkinson, Joseph Awkard, Ronald Brown, J. Don Berney, Ed Davis, Harold Dent, Jim DeShields, Ross Evans, George Franklin, Bill Harvey, Reginald Jones, Al Goins, Roy Jones, Luther Kindall, Robert L. Green, Thomas Hilliard, George Jackson, Mel King, Mary Howard, Walter Jacobs, Delores Minot, Jane Fort Morrison, Leon Nicks, Wade Nobles, Lonnie Mitchell, Sylvia O'Bradovich, Bill Pierce, David Terrell, Joseph White, Charles Thomas, Shirley Thomas, Mike Ward, and Samuel Winslow (Warfield-Coppock, 1984).
2. The National Association of Black Psychologists annually sponsors a scholarly and gala convention. Networking, Association business, Africentrically principled discourse (for the most part), and spiritual rejuvenation are its hallmarks. Personal observation suggests that typically four hundred to six hundred persons attend. However, attendance should typically range between 1500 and 2000. A substantial number of African-U.S. psychologists refuse to attend for two ill-conceived and bankrupt reasons. First, many manifest an abhorrence of integration within their own Race first (an issue Chancellor Williams [1976] analyzed), opting instead for (dis)integration at the Eurocentric (white American) Psychological Association convention. Second, many make the conscious "political" assessment that not attending the ABP convention and attending the Eurocentric organization's convention will facilitate tenure and job security. The same rationale is offered for publishing in Eurostream journals. These shrewd politicians reason that once tenure is obtained, after a

five to seven year period, they will participate in the ABP. Now this is easily seen as an absurdity and a rationalization since the question is open as to whether African psychologists in largely white psychology departments get tenure on the first try anyway! Even if and when tenure is achieved, there is the looming pressure of promotion that still militates against any meaningful participation in the ABP by the wayward African psychologist. Being out of the fold for so long impedes the return as well. Although I disdain it and refuse to play it, those African psychologists who opt to play this political game could at least participate in the ABP's convention every other year and submit some of their superior scholarship to the *Journal of Black Psychology* (and other quality Africana Studies journals).

3. Transubstantive error is defined by the African Psychology Institute as "taking the cultural and psychological norms of one group and applying them in establishing the meaning of the cultural and psychological functioning of another group" (Azibo, 1988b:86).

REFERENCES

Akbar, N. African Roots of Black Personality. In *Reflections on Black Psychology*, ed. W. Smith, K. Burlew, M. Mosley, and W. Whitney Washington, D.C.: University Press of America, 1979.

Akbar, N. Nile Valley origins of the science of the mind, In *Nile Valley Civilizations*, ed. I. van Sertima, New Brunswick, N.J.: Journal of African Civilizations Press, 1985a.

Akbar, N. Our destiny: Authors of a scientific revolution. In *Black Children: Social, Educational and Parental Environments*, ed. H. McAdoo and J. McAdoo, Beverly Hills: Sage Publications, 1985b.

Amen, R. The original African calendar and calendar history. In *The Calendar Project*, ed. R. Amen and D. Reese New York: The Hunt Printing Co., 1987.

Ani, M. *Yurugu: An African-centered Critique of European Thought and Behavior*. Trenton, NJ: Africa World Press, 1984.

Asante, M. The Egyptian origin of rhetoric and oratory. In *Kemet and the African Worldview*, ed. M. Karenga and J. Carruthers. Los Angeles: University of Sankore Press 1986.

Azibo, D. A. Personality, clinical, and social psychological research on Blacks: Appropriate and inappropriate research frameworks. *Western Journal of Black Studies* 12, 4 (1988a):220-33.

—— Understanding the proper and improper usage of the comparative

research framework. *Journal of Black Psychology* 15, 1 (1988b): 81-91.
—— African-centered theses on mental health and a nosology of Black/African personality disorder. *Journal of Black Psychology* 15, 2 (1989a):173-214.
—— Pitfalls and ameliorative strategies in African personality research. *Journal of Black Studies* 19, 3 (1989b):306-19.
—— Advances in Black/African personality theory. *Imhotep: An Afrocentric Review* 2, 1 (1990): 22-47.
—— Articulating the distinction between Black Studies and the study of Blacks: The fundamental role of culture and the African-centered worldview. *The Afrocentric Scholar* 1, 1 (1992):64-97.
—— Eurocentric psychology and the issue of race. *Word: A Black Culture Journal*, 2, 1 (1993):43-57. *Liberation Psychology*. Trenton, NJ: Africa World Press I (in press).
Baldwin, J. A. Black psychology and Black personality. *Black Books Bulletin* 4, 3 (1976):6-11, 65.
Baldwin, J. A. The psychology of oppression. In *Contemporary Black Thought*, ed. M. Asante and A. Vandi, Beverly Hills: Sage Publications, 1980..
Baldwin, J. A. Psychological aspects of European cosmology in American society. *Western Journal of Black Studies* 9, 4 (1985a):216-223.
Baldwin, J. A. The role of Black psychologists in Black liberation. *Association of Black Psychologists Newsletter* 17, 1 (1985b): 16-20.
Baldwin, J. A. 1986. African (Black) Psychology: Issues and synthesis. *Journal of Black Studies* 16 (3): 235-249.
Banks, W. C. Deconstructive falsification: Foundations of a critical method in Black psychology. In *Minority mental health*, ed. E. Jones and S. Korchin, New York: Praeger Press, 1982..
ben-Jochannon, Y. *Black man of the Nile and his family*. New York: Alkebu-lan Books, 1981.
ben-Jochannon, Y. *Abu Simbel-Ghizeh: Guide book manual*. New York: Alkebu-lan Books, 1986.
Bulhan, H. Psychological research in Africa: Genesis and function. *Race & Class*, 23, 1 (1981):25-41.
Burlew, A. K. Journal of Black Psychology preview. *Psych Discourse: ABPsi Newsletter* 20, 3 (1989):4-5 [an interview of Daudi Ajani ya Azibo].
Carruthers, J. *Essays in ancient Egyptian studies*. Los Angeles: University of Sankore Press, 1984.
Cedric X (S. M. Khatib), D. P. McGhee, W. W. Nobles, and Luther X (Naim Akbar). Voodoo or IQ: An introduction to African

Psychology. *Journal of Black Psychology* 1 (1975):9-29.

Clark, C. (now S. M. Khatib). Black Studies or the study of Black people? In *Black psychology*, ed. R. Jones, 1st ed. New York: Harper and Row, 1972..

Clark, C. The concept of legitimacy in Black psychology. In *Race Relations: Current Perspectives*, ed. E. Epps, Cambridge, Mass.: Winthrop Publishers, 1973..

Cook, N. and Kono, S. Black psychology: The third great tradition. *Journal of Black Psychology* 3, 2 (1977): 18-28.

Diop, C. A. *African origins of civilization: Myth or reality*. Westport: Lawrence Hill & Co, 1974.

Gilbert, G. Journey into the secret life. *Black Books Bulletin* 7, 1 (1980):9-12, 25.

Goodman, J. Race, Reason, and Research. In *African Philosophy: Assumptions and Paradigms for Research on Black Persons*, ed. L. King, V. Dixon, and W. Nobles Los Angeles: Fanon Research and Development Center, 1976.

Guthrie, R. *Even the rat was white: A historical view of psychology*. New York: Harper and Row, 1976..

Hilliard, A. G. Kemetic concepts in education. In *Nile Valley civilizations*, ed. I. van Sertima New Brunswick, N.J.: Journal of African Civilizations Press, 1985.

Hilliard, A. G. Pedagogy in ancient Kemet. In *Kemet and the African worldview*, ed. M. Karenga and J. Carruthers Los Angeles: University of Sankore Press, 1986..

Hilliard, A. G. *Free your mind, Return to the source: African origins (The transcript)*. East Point, Georgia: Waset Educational Productions, 1988..

Houston, D. D.. *Wonderful Ethiopians of the Ancient Cushite Empire*. Baltimore, Md.: Black Classic Press, 1985.

Jackson, G. G. The origin and development of Black psychology: Implications for Black Studies and human behavior. *Studia Africana* 1, 3 (1979): 270-293.

Jackson, J. G. *Introduction to African civilizations*. Secaucus, N.J.: Citadel Press, 1980.

James, G. G. M. *Stolen Legacy*. San Francisco: Julian Richardson Associates, 1976.

Karenga, M. 1982. *Introduction to Black studies*. Inglewood, Calif.: Kawaida Publications.

Karenga, M. and Carruthers, J. *Kemet and the African worldview*. Los Angeles: University of Sankore Press, 1986.

King, R. The symbolism of the crown in ancient Egypt. In *Nile Valley civilizations*, ed. I. van Sertima New Brunswick, N.J.: Journal of African Civilizations Press, 1985.

King, R. E. Highlights in the development of ABPsi. *The Journal of Black Psychology* 4, 1 (1977-1978): 9-24.

Means, R. Fighting words on the future of the earth. *Mother Jones*, 1980 (December):24-31, 38.

Means, S. *Ethiopia & the missing link in African history*. Harrisburg, PA: The Atlantis Publishing Co, 1980.

Murphy, G. and J. Kovac. *Historical introduction to modern psychology*, 3rd ed. New York: Harcourt Brace Jovanovich, 1972.

Myers, L. *Understanding an Afrocentric world view: Introduction to an optimal psychology*. Dubuque, Iowa: Kendall/Hunt Publishing Co, 1988.

Nobles, W. W. African philosophy: Foundations for Black psychology. In *Black psychology*, ed. R. Jones, 1st ed. New York: Harper & Row, 1972.

Nobles, W. W. Extended self: Rethinking the so-called Negro self-concept. *Journal of Black Psychology* 2 (1976):15-24.

Nobles, W. W. The reclamation of culture and the right to reconciliation: An Afro-centric perspective on developing and implementing programs for the mentally retarded offender. In *The Black mentally retarded offender: A wholistic approach to prevention and habilitation*, ed. A. Harvey and T. Carr New York: United Church of Christ Commission for Racial Justice, 1982.

Nobles, W. W. *African Psychology: Toward Its Reclamation, Reascension and Revitalization*. Oakland, Calif.: Black Family Institute, 1986a.

Nobles, W. W. Ancient Egyptian thought and the development of African (Black) psychology. In *Kemet and the African worldview*, ed. M. Karenga and J. Carruthers Los Angeles: University of Sankore Press, 1986b.

Nobles, W. W., L. Goddard, and W. Cavill, III. *The KM EBIT Husia*. Oakland, CA: Institute for the Advanced Study of Black Family Life and Culture, 1985.

Parham, T. Cycles of psychological Nigrescence. The *Counseling Psychologist* 17. 2 (1989):187-226.

Ryle, G. *The concept of mind*. London: Hutchinson & Co, 1949.

Semmes, C. E. Black studies and the symbolic structure of domination. *Western Journal of Black Studies* 6 (1982):116-122.

Smitherman, G. *Talkin and testifyin: The language of Black America*. Boston: Houghton Miflin Co, 1977.

Tarharka. *Building of civilization by the Black man of the Nile*. Washington, D.C.: University Press of America, 1979.

Thomas, A. and S. Sillen. *Racism and psychiatry*. Secaucus, N.J.: Citadel, 1972.

Triandis, H. *The analysis of subjective culture*. Brooks/Cole

Publishers, 1972.

Warfield-Coppock, N. An organizational history of the Association of Black Psychologists. In *History, by-laws and ethical standards of the Association of Black Psychologists*. Washington, D.C.: Association of Black Psychologists, 1984.

Welsing, F. The Cress theory of color-confrontation. *Black Scholar* (1974):32-40.

White, J. Guidelines for Black Psychologists. *Black Scholar* (March 1970): 52-57.

White, J. Toward a Black Psychology. In *Black psychology*, ed. R. Jones, 1st ed. New York: Harper & Row, 1972.

White, J. *The psychology of Blacks: An Afro-American perspective*. Englewood Cliffs, N.J.: Prentice-Hall, 1984.

White, J., W. Parham, and T. Parham. Black Psychology: The Afro-American Tradition as a Unifying Force for Traditional Psychology. In *Black psychology*, ed. R. Jones, 2nd ed. New York: Harper & Row, 1980.

Williams, C. *The Destruction of Black Civilization*. Chicago: Third World Press, 1976.

Williams, R. L. History of the Association of Black Psychologists: Early Formation and Development. *Journal of Black Psychology* 1 (1974).: 9-24.

Williams, R. L. *The collective Black mind: An Afrocentric theory of Black personality*. St. Louis, MO: Williams & Associates, 1981.

Wright, B. *The psychopathic racial personality and other essays*. Chicago: Third World Press, 1985.

CHAPTER 2

African Metapsychology of Human Personality

Na'im Akbar

One of the many benefits of an African psychology model is that it affords an effective alternative to prevailing ways of viewing personality functioning. The models of personality which have emerged from the European perspective are either that of a mechanistic system which operates as an automated program of inputs and outputs or that of a meaningless cataloging of the infinitude of possible personality traits. Both approaches rob the human personality of its dignity and fail to provide any real insight into the highly refined functioning of the human being.

Freud's devastatingly popular postulates of a conflict-ridden psyche have rationalized several generations of meaningless human conflict—both internally and externally. Freud viewed the dynamism or movement of human personality as resulting from the bombarding confrontation of incompatible energies and impulses. The Behaviorists saw no movement at all, just a passive adaptation to a precarious and sinister environment. The humanist, in an attempt to rescue the human being from such dehumanizing trends of thought, exalted the man to an isolated island of abstract "becoming" but left him there without appointment.

PERSONALITY AS CONCEPTUALIZED IN AFRICAN PSYCHOLOGY

African psychology, however, offers some genuine alternatives to all of these crippling perspectives. African psychology views personality as purposeful in its emergence, harmonious with its ecology, and consistent with the laws of life. The human being is neither a passive agent shaped by his environment totally, nor is he an exalted isolated god with goalless freedom. The African sees a continuity and harmony between nature and himself. Though consistent with nature in his orderly being, he stands above the lowly nature in his capacity for will, choice, knowledge, and self-government. To comprehend the laws governing his nature, man has always looked to the laws governing his living environment. He has sensed the peacefulness of the heavens, the orderliness of the earth, the predictability of the cycles of time, and the continuity of life as an insight into unknown qualities of his own life. The ancient African people of the Nile Valley saw these forces of the environment as little gods or angels that they called "Neters." These Neters were the prototypical teachers of nature. They were often personified as immortal beings operating throughout time.

With nature in her pristine purity as a model we should be able to postulate a model of human personality which is both meaningful and universal. Such a model, hopefully, would be free of the ethnocentric assumptions so destructively evident in the Euro-American conception of personality. (Though we prefix our model with African, it is not an attempt to claim an exclusive corner of the universe; it merely identifies the environment out of which these universally applicable notions have emerged.) Such a model would offer the very universe itself as a laboratory for testing our assumptions. One would expect to find in such a model some absolutes about the human form. The current conceptions of the human being emerging from the West say, in essence, that a normal human being is one who is not abnormal.

Western psychology is a pathology-oriented psychology.

Because of the absence of vital universal assumptions or values regarding the human being, there is no absolute standard of defining a human being. Normal behavior is simply the ability to conform to the predominating patterns of behavior. Abnormal behavior is the inability to conform to such patterns. However, there are no universals or generalizations that can be made regarding the human being's functioning.

We believe that the African's model of nature affords us an avenue for being able to infer a universal standard for adequate human functioning. An effectively functioning human being should basically agree in form to the definition of any successful life form. At all levels of life, the one pervading motif that defines life is the tendency that life forms have to preserve themselves. From the one-cell organism to the very galaxy, the entire life process is geared toward maintenance of itself. Certainly, the human being is no different in this regard, in fact (s)he represents the highest evolution of this self-preservative process.

THREE COMPONENTS OF BEING: PHYSICAL, MENTAL, AND SPIRITUAL

Let's look at the human being at his/her three levels of being. These levels of the physical, mental, and spiritual self, so alien to Western psychology, form the unquestioned structure of the human being in African and Asian worldviews. The African views the person as spirit in his/her essence with the physical and mental components as tools of spiritual development. The human personality is a composite of these factors finding expression in the environment. The Akan view of the *Okra*, as the guiding spirit of man (Abraham, 1962) is viewed as being present before birth and continuing after death. The African people of the Nile Valley in their advanced culture and concepts saw the human being as *ka* (body) and *ba* (soul), with a variety of related qualities of a spiritual form (Akbar 1986). Spiritual language and its intangible quality presents discomfort only for the heavily encumbered Western mind which is unable to comfortably conceptualize outside of the physical and observable. The very prominence of spiritual considerations in African American life should tell the observer that any science which precludes the spiritual is alien and irrelevant to understanding people of African descent and how they understand all forms of life.

THE PHYSICAL COMPONENT.

This self-preservative model can be viewed at each of the three aspects of human life. The observable physical manifestations of the survival orientation can allegorically point to similar processes at the unobservable but more powerfully motivating levels of mental and spiritual life. Certainly, the most prominent characteristic of the physical organism is its orientation to survive. The basic equipment, motivationally and instinctively, which the human being is born with is geared towards the preservation of the life of that body. The newly born infant immediately responds to hunger, thirst, and pain. Hunger and thirst are drives of such magnitude that the human infant instinctively responds in an unlearned panic reaction when these needs are aroused. Equipped with little more than a powerful set of lungs, the infant insistently provokes the environment to respond to its need.

The infant's demand for food is the untaught recognition that this input is necessary for survival. The magnitude of the response communicates how critical the input is to the life of that organism. Similarly, it doesn't take any lessons in "becoming a person" to experience genuine pleasure in having that hunger alleviated. The response to pain is very similar. To the extent that pain is a danger signal of physical damage, we can see the self-preservative disposition operative in the response to pain.

Even in ways outside of voluntary control the body is programmed for its own maintenance. The homeostatic process is automatic though connected by alarm signals to the conscious being to assist at times of danger. Increases in body temperature which endanger the organism automatically activate the cooling system of perspiration. Decreases in body temperature automatically activate a shivering reaction which generates body heat. Short supplies of oxygen activate yawning and so on for hundreds of unconscious (autonomic) physical processes which maintain a balanced state within the physical organism. The same process of homeostasis activates the subjective experience of hunger when essential nutrients are deficient.

The body is also equipped with a highly sophisticated defense system. The autonomic nervous system is programmed for immediate and assertive defense behavior. Under conditions of danger the physiological response is so considerable that people are capable of feats of strength far in excess of their ordinary physical abilities. With the release of adrenaline into the blood stream, every system of the body becomes mobilized for defense. So critical is survival for the human body that it has a defense system so elaborate that it can literally mobilize every cell of the body for "fight or flight."

Even at the microscopic level, dramatic processes go on constantly within the body which ensure its survival. Highly sensitive microorganisms called antibodies maintain a ready army against any alien intrusions into the body. The liver, kidneys, intestines, and nearly every other organ in the body are equipped with self-maintaining life systems. The writers from ancient Egypt (Kemit) have left us the wisdom: "As below, so above." This informs us that we can find operating at the "micro" level, the same processes which exist at the "macro" level.

In the same way that the body operates to preserve its individual self, it also is motivated to preserve its generic self. To this end, we find the powerful sex drive. Contrary to Freudian interpretation of this drive, we attribute the power of this drive to the urgency of the self-perpetuating motive in the life process. Rather than the hedonistic pleasure-seeking attributed to this drive in the Freudian hypothesis of libido, we see a much more profound implication in this drive. Despite the surface incompatibility of Freudian and Behaviorist assumptions, they both attribute a kind of hedonism to the primary rewarding nature of these life-preserving drives. The power of the sex drive as a motivator of human behavior is a coded message of the human's need to perpetuate self and as a consequence, preserve self in perpetuity. We shall see how this function expresses itself on higher planes in our discussion below.

The point is that this is the prototype of a normal human being from a physical perspective. There are certainly higher mental and spiritual survival motives which can override these physical drives, but taken in isolation, it is simple to describe the physically normal (healthy) human being as one whose self-preservative functions are operative. A physician has no difficulty diagnosing dysfunction or abnormality when he finds any of these functions impaired. The premature infant is placed in an incubator because it cannot maintain a safe body temperature. The anorexic person causes concern because his or her natural hungers are dysfunctional. Societies have major constraints and taboos on abandoned sexual indulgence because the process of self-perpetuation requires careful protection and maintenance. Cancer is such a deadly disease because the malignant cell fails to respond to the naturally preservative control in its nature. In some forms of cancer, the cells which should protect the organism from alien intrusions begin to attack the life-giving cells. No physician has any philosophical problems in identifying a condition in which the body is destroying itself as being a disease. The deadliness of AIDS is a result of a breakdown in the defense system of the human body and its ability to appropriately preserve itself against invasion and attack from destructive influences. A recognition of the signs of stability and the absolute norms of the human body has greatly advanced medical science. Psychology or the science of the mind can be equally advanced when similar absolutes are recognized in human mental and spiritual functioning.

From an absolute perspective and assuming the absence of more powerful survival motives from the mental or spiritual sphere, any behavior that is intentionally self-destructive is abnormal (or sick) behavior. At an unconsciously instinctual level, the body responds by revulsion to toxic substances which are introduced into it. The respiratory system automatically activates to expel smoke entering the lungs. The throat, the taste sensors, and the stomach initially respond in a repulsive way to expel alcohol when it is introduced into the body. The same is true for all kinds of physically destructive activities. There is some sign that the body gives to indicate the danger of any type of toxic agent. Because of the body's adaptive capacity, it fairly quickly accommodates to the insistent intrusion and begins to activate other systems which seek to neutralize the destructive influences. For example, the body's vitamin C supply is utilized to neutralize the nicotinic acid from smoking, which lowers the body's supply of this important nutrient.

Another dramatic—and disastrous—example of the body's submissive accommodation to unnatural conditions is seen in the variety of psychophysiological stress disorders. Hypertension, an adaptive response to conditions of stress, becomes a condition for coronary attacks and strokes if allowed to persist. In unnatural environments (of a social or psychological type), people respond to sustained stress by a condition of constant mobilization for defense. The very survival process can be subverted into a death process in an environment of unnatural conditions. We can effectively operationalize our concept of natural and unnatural as those conditions which foster or interfere with the life processes. The environment that leads to the kind of sustained stress that subverts to destructiveness the body's survival strategies is an unnatural environment. An environment that permits effective survival-oriented behavior and responses is a natural environment.

We could pursue this argument, if space permitted, to demonstrate a wide range of behaviors which according to this criteria of self-preservation are sick or disordered. This is a value argument, but it is demonstrable at the most basic value level, i.e., the value of the survival of the organism. Such a position is able to call for testimony every life process in the universe as evidence of the sanity (health) of self-preservation and the insanity (sickness) of self-destruction. The normal human being is the one who is cautious and protective of his life in all of its dimensions.

Let us hasten to say that we are not suggesting a Darwinian analysis of human behavior that hypothesizes a kind of cold-blooded "survival of the fittest." Though we speak of survival as an essential value, we also accept the African notion that survival for the human being is much more than the preservation of his body. Though preservation of the body is basic, it is only a means of preserving a higher life which inhabits that body. To the extent that that physical body is the womb and medium for the growth of the higher life within it, then preservation and survival of that body does become a crucial value. Let us now turn to those higher dimensions of life.

THE MENTAL COMPONENT: SURVIVAL OF THE MENTAL LIFE.

In the Western psychological conceptualizations, we generally do not think of the intelligence as actually constituting a life or world. We wish to suggest that the intelligence is a system, world, or life which operates according to the same principles as does the physical system of life. The mental or intellectual life is too often equated with the physical instrument panel called brain. Such an inept equation is like attributing the musical genius of Coltrane to his lips or his lungs. In any event, we introduce here the assumption that the intelligence or mental sphere is a dimension of life and that we can evaluate its effectiveness by the degree to which it preserves and perpetuates itself.

As the body manifests a natural hunger for food in order to maintain itself physically, the mind has a parallel hunger. This hunger which feeds and perpetuates the mind is the nutrition of enlightening knowledge. Knowledge which brings light, guidance, direction, discrimination, and effectiveness to the human being is the food of the mind. Not unlike the body, the mind is naturally equipped with a hunger for such knowledge.

The mind's hunger is initially manifested in curiosity. The two-month, six- month, year-old child is most demonstrative of this hunger for knowledge. So avid is the youngster's appetite for knowledge that it is actually difficult to get it to go to sleep. The child seems to be literally propelled by the hunger for knowledge. As soon as the physical comforts are attended (and often, even before) the eager young mind is off and exploring. In the early months, any novel stimulus fascinates and engages the young mind. It seems that acquisition of mobility is propelled by the desire for wider exploration. The initial discovery of the child's own body rapidly gives way to the ability to lift it up and turn it over. The greater exposure that these skills give propel the child after several months to begin to drag that body around, then crawl, then pull up, and eventually walk. The fuel for this phenomenal acquisition of locomotion is the hunger for knowledge. The greater is the mobility, the wider the field of exploration, and, ultimately, the more knowledge that the developing person is able to acquire.

Much of the infant's early behavior can be shown, rather meaningfully, to be geared toward this hunger for knowledge. Another important observation made by Freud is the prominence of oral activity during the early months of life. In Freud's preoccupation with hedonism, he saw this behavior as being primarily motivated by sensual pleasure. Freud's conviction that sensual pleasure was the lowest level to which human behavior could be reduced blinded him to the intangible essence of human life. His victimization by the physical-mindedness of his time and culture thoroughly impaired his spiritual vision. The early oral preoccupation of the child could more usefully be interpreted as the prototype of incorporation or internalization of the external reality. Perhaps, the child in its natural reasoning intuitively makes the connection between the incorporation of physical food for the physical body and the incorporation of mental food for the mental body. Perhaps, the child rather wisely extrapolates from one process of survival to the next level. In the light of such an inference, it is not surprising that the next most powerful hunger is fed through the same channel as that which satisfies the physical hunger. The automatic connection of seeing a new object sends it directly to the mouth if it can be grasped. The mother of a young toddler told me recently that her young son was very upset and frustrated one day because he couldn't swallow the wall. As ludicrous as that sounds to our adult knowledge, the child's hunger for knowledge (internalization of the external) is so intense that such frustration is conceivable for the recent arrival into our vast world of experience.

The oral exploration of the young infant is undoubtedly an indication of his rapidly growing appetite for knowledge. He wants to be fed information about his world. He wants to take in the enlightenment that brings consciousness and light to the untapped waters of mind. So curiosity is hunger of the mind. It fuels the development of mobility which affords an ever-expanding menu for the mind. The oral preoccupation is the child's initial effort to internalize his world or take in knowledge, using the metaphor of physical hunger and the mode of its satisfaction.

Another component of the hunger of the intelligence is the desire for order. The discovery of patterns usually affords the child moments of delight as they find that one action predictably leads to another. This delight is the mental life's appetite for ordered experiences. Relationships and patterns represent the real meat of knowledge. Such orderliness and knowledge of relationships give the human being a sense of mastery over an environment which becomes more predictable as knowledge increases.

The mental life has safety valves, as do the satiation levels of the body. Boredom signals the need to move into new arenas of knowledge. Imbalances in the knowledge diet trigger the need to pursue new directions. Curiosity and interest continue as appetites which guide the mind to everincreasing horizons of knowledge.

The normal, living mind seeks knowledge naturally. The very nature of the intelligence is to seek enlightenment in much the same way as the body seeks nourishment for itself. Only a mind robbed of its natural dispositions (a common phenomenon in this society) actively seeks unconsciousness, ignorance, or mental death. This writer has some serious objections to the arguments which suggest that children must be stimulated or externally motivated to learn. It is certainly difficult to believe that a young mind that was so eager to be enlightened only months previously is suddenly incapable of being stimulated once it enters public school (a most serious problem in the United States). Some serious questions must be raised about what happens to that mind between the time of that early enthusiasm and the alleged apathy in the early grades. We are suggesting that some powerfully destructive force has altered the natural intellectual curiosity which characterizes the human mind.

Knowledge of one's world and knowledge of oneself is the foundation for the self-mastery to which the human being is naturally disposed. The early examples of physical mastery dramatically illustrated in the child's acquisition of balance and walking skills are only prototypes of the inner self-mastery to which the human being aspires. We are suggesting that there is no discontinuity in human growth. The accomplishments at lower dimensions simply find greater expression at higher levels. Learning to propel one's body is the birth of the desire to propel one's world and life. Knowledge of how one works and of the characteristics of one's environment is the objective of enlightenment. The intelligence of mental life is naturally attuned to receive that data. Without knowledge of one's human capabilities and with ignorance of one's environment, one is rendered essentially blind in the mental world. More consistent with our analogy from above, it leaves the person mentally starved and subject to immediate death.

Similar to the self-perpetuating function of the physical life reflected in reproduction, there is a similar urge in the mental life.

This urge to express and perpetuate one's knowledge is seen in the basic desire for communication. As with the early curiosity drive, the child very early manifests the desire to spread what he knows. He delights in the response he gains from his babbles. He eagerly begins to incorporate language as he recognizes its capacity to propagate what he knows, and later he discovers that it can also feed his knowledge. Speech or communication is to the mental life what sex is to the physical life. It is the vehicle of self-perpetuation through expression of one's ideas and knowledge. It is also the basis for contact between mental worlds, the vehicle which brings two minds together as sex brings two bodies together.

We described above the body's natural revulsions to poisons. Similarly, the mind has a natural revulsion to ignorance, unconsciousness. Again, this is illustrated in the young child's revolt against sleep, once he has been excited by wakefulness, and his revolt against being locked away from a point of curiosity. The numerous "why's" that characterize the conversation of the three-year-old tells us of his need to have full understanding of the order around him. Under normal circumstances the mind naturally seeks greater consciousness and awareness of itself. (Given the destructive job that has been done on the human mind, I can only offer this as an hypothesis in the light of only limited evidence in the adults of our contemporary world.)

As the human body can rapidly accommodate to ingested poisons despite the initial revulsion, the human mind is capable of even greater adaptation or adjustment. The broader capability of the mental life than the physical life permits greater flexibility of the intelligence. Though its dispositions are systematically marked out, as is illustrated by the early mental thrusts of the mind coming to life, it is very susceptible to perversion. The intelligence can be systematically molded in a distorted form by the early impressions which are made on it. Rather than seeking consciousness, it can be perverted to seek unconsciousness. Rather than seeking knowledge, it can seek ignorance. Rather than the intelligence striving for self-mastery, it can seek self-indulgence. The signs of mental death from intellectual starvation are not as obvious as are the signs of physical malnutrition and starvation. In fact, mental death can occur in a body which persists in carrying on its physical life functions for some time after mental death has occurred. However, one does not have a human being under these conditions, only a living corpse.

The demand for unconsciousness through alcohol, drug abuse, and general apathy which has come to be the predominant mental disposition in our society today is evidence of distorted human material rather than the true form of the human being. The mental life's natural urge for enlightenment and nourishment has been fed on such a continuous diet of artificial ingredients that the natural appetites have accommodated themselves into nonrecognition. The artificial diet has been one of opiates, fantasy, and falsehood.

As we have described above, the unnatural environment can subvert survival processes and turn them against the life of the organism. This is, of course, dramatically illustrated in the psychophysiological disorders of ulcers, hypertension, and other deadly diseases. It can be demonstrated that the entire array of mental disorders results from a subversion of the intellect's efforts at survival. For example, the painful and debilitating rationalizations and intellectualizations of the obsessive-compulsive, rather dramatically demonstrate the subversion of intellectual processes. The withdrawal into fantasy—i.e., unreality or ignorance—seen in schizophrenics is the most severe form of subversion of the mental life. What is, in fact, adaptive withdrawal away from consciousness or reality under conditions of stress becomes a persistent style under conditions of an unnatural environment.

We can see from these brief examples how such a model of natural human life begins to give us a universal standard for assessment of mental as well as physical disorders. Cultural context notwithstanding, these are universally identifiable characteristics which affirm human physical, mental, or spiritual survival. Those characteristics are healthy, sane, normal, or similarly designated. In contrast, there are identifiable patterns which are destructive to human survival. Those patterns are sick, crazy, abnormal, and so forth.

THE SPIRITUAL COMPONENT: NATURAL HUNGERS OF SPIRITUAL LIFE

Nearly all writers on the African worldview maintain that the human being is intimately tied with the supreme force in the universe through his spiritual life. This spirit represents the human potential for perfectibility from before birth and through his eternal essence which continues after death. As strange as this language may sound to scientific Western psychology, it has only been very recently that the world's most advanced scientists ever chose to speak of order without affirming supreme processes and a Supreme Being. This writer submits that the difficulty in Western science is its neglect of these supreme and divine processes in the universe. Certainly, the overwhelming failure of psychology to remedy the severe mental turmoil of the contemporary Western world is its failure to recognize the spiritual essence of the human being.

The African student of mind has never neglected the reality that the human being at his highest and in his most enduring form is ultimately spirit. Be it the *Okra* as described by the Akan of Ghana (Abraham 1962), the *nyama* as described by the Dogon (Forde 1970), or *nommo* as described by the Bantu (Jahn 1961), the pervasive African conception is that man is essentially spirit. Therefore, survival of the spirit represents the ultimate survival of the human being.

This message of spiritual survival has, unfortunately, been left to the religious institutions alone. This is unfortunate because in the Western world, religion has been separated from the daily life experience, and the human being has been fragmented. The African, on the other hand, according to Mbiti (1970) is caught up in a religious drama from long before birth and until long after death. The psychologist has attempted to attend to the mental life often to the disregard of the physical life and almost invariably to the complete neglect of the spiritual life. The physician has usually attended the physical life to the exclusion of the mental and spiritual lives the religious practitioner has too often attended the spiritual life to the utter disregard of the physical and mental. The human being is a unity and can only be distorted by a fragmentary approach to his adjustment. According to Pierre Erny (1973): "the African cosmos is like a spider web: its least element cannot be touched without making the whole vibrate." Certainly if this is true of the African cosmos, it must be true of the human microcosm.

The spiritual life, not unlike the physical and mental, has innate survival processes as well. In fact, the survival orientation of the physical and mental planes or dimensions of being are for the ultimate purpose of spiritual survival. The physical and mental spheres operate as vessels for the transmission and growth of the spiritual life. The relationship of the physical and mental self to the spiritual self is not unlike the relationship of organs or senses to the physical body. The hand has no life without the body though the body is capable of sustaining itself without a hand. The eye is a source of knowledge into the mind, and the eye has no function without an active mind, though knowledge still comes with no eyes at all. Similarly, physical life and mental life supply the spiritual life, though the spiritual life is capable of maintenance in the absence of either or both of them.

How can we characterize the hunger of the spirit? It is actually a metaphysical hunger—a hunger for the infinite. The body hungers for finite ingredients—physical food, sensual experience, physical reproduction, etc. The mind hungers for knowledge, enlightenment, order, communication. The spiritual life hungers for the universal, for the transcendent—for God! It is the strong desire in all people that has led to the establishment of religion and a conceptualization of God. It is the drive in the human being which pushes him to seek goals higher than material, higher than partisan ideology, higher than himself. It is the drive in the human being that guides him to conceive of the Eternal and of a Supreme and Divine Power and plan. The very universality of these concepts of the spiritual life is evidence of its force in the life of the human being. Only societies in which human beings have fallen into the most base debauchery and have become less than human is there a lack of evidence of a concept of a transcendent Being. Those societies which have reached the highest levels of human refinement, sensitivity, and cultural dignity are the ones with a widely accepted and powerful image of God.

The force of the spiritual life has been described as: "a force within you that wants something at the expense of every other force in your body, to work with it to accomplish its goal. It is struggling trying to get everything else in your makeup to agree with it so that it can get something done for you in your lifetime" (Muhammad 1975). It is the transcendent self that potentially is intended to rule over the lesser human appetites. It restrains hunger from becoming greed, self-perpetuation from becoming lust, knowledge from becoming arrogance, and order from becoming tyranny. It is the voice of conscience.

Conscience is the voice of the spirit. We suggest, in line with African philosophy, that moral sense is indigenous to the human being. As the *sunsum* in Akan metaphysics (Abraham 1962) is the basis of character, the conscience is an innate force which also lies at the foundation of the personality. It is, according to the Akan, the educable part of the personality which is the foundation of personal and moral responsibility. This force may be shaped by experience, but, as an instrument of moral force, it is innate to the human being. This position stands in sharp contrast to the Western (particularly Freudian) precepts which view moral conscience as a socially imposed entity having no genuine foundation in basic human makeup. We suggest that the force of self-restraint, self-regulation, and perfectible aspiration is actually more basic to human life than physical hunger. In fact, physical hunger operates in the service of raising human life to a higher plane of experience.

The spiritual life is the force in the human being that fights human degradation. It is the voice of frustration that cries out when people become encapsulated by material wishes and preoccupations. It is the force that drives the human being above lustful inundations—the force of dissatisfaction with sensual pleasure. It is the force that pushes the bum to brush himself off when he spots his humanly degraded appearance in the mirror. It is a force which gives the human being the desire and power to rise above any condition which robs him of his God-given potential for growth and human progress.

The physical life yearns for self-perpetuation. On the mental plane, the same yearning is in communication. And, spiritually, the highest form of this yearning is for oneness and immortality. It is a desire for harmony, fusion, and peace with all things. It has been called "heaven" by the Christians, "paradise" by the Muslims, and "Nirvana" by the Hindus. Every religious group has an analogous concept that describes this state of universal harmony and peace. Though it is described in physical allegories, it speaks to a spiritual state beyond the visible world. It has remained the utopian dream of all times and all societies. It represents the highest wish of the human being to be fused into the eternal harmony of the Conductor of creation—the Creator. The desire to know the essential reality versus the illusionary reality prods the intelligence and refines the mental life. The universal oneness is the ultimate discovery from the struggles of diversity, polarity, and conflict which have characterized the lower stages of life.

As the survival forces can become distorted on the physical level with the psychosomatic disorders or on the mental plane in insanity, the spiritual forces can also become similarly perverted. The improperly developed being will seek transcendence in human tyranny or oppression. The voice of conscience will become cruel inhibition, self-flagellation, and elitist self-exaltation. The desire for the universal can be distorted into a mystical superstitious tyranny that locks human beings into a world of fears. This is literally the diabolical. These are the forces which deliberately operate to destroy human life and block human development. The spiritually dead are those who have lost the motivation to be human.

CONCLUSION

One might characterize the foregoing discussion as a Metapsychology of Human Personality. It describes the human personality not in terms of its actions, behaviors, or observable dimensions, but in terms of its purpose or teleology. It focuses on the ultimate unity and goal orientation of human life. Though it describes the human being as manifesting life on several planes—physical, mental, and spiritual—it also describes the unity of those strivings.

It presents a model of human life which is absolute. It is culture-free, ethnicity-free, society-free. It describes the universality of the highest human potential which when subjected to unnatural influences can become corrupt, degraded, oppressive, even subhuman. Many periods in history have shown human life in this lowly condition. Certainly, the conceptions offered here are consistent with the African philosophical view of humans and life. This model offers a yardstick by which the adequacy of human life can be evaluated in any context. Despite the variability of the behavior which may characterize the disorder, insanity and inhumanity can be identified in any cultural context given the criteria of human-life-survival suggested in this discussion.

We can see the potential self-destructiveness of any of these survival mechanisms if they are perverted by unnatural environments. By looking for human outcomes reflective of the highest human potential, we can assess the effectiveness of the human environment. Though the human form is potentially quite malleable or subject to assuming almost any form, its nature is to acquire the distinct and quiet dignity reflected in the being whose spiritual being has come to life and stands as a master force over the lower stages of human evolution within the human makeup.

REFERENCES

Abraham, W. E. *The mind of Africa*. Chicago: Univ. of Chicago Press, 1962.

Akbar, N. Nile Valley origins of the science of the mind. In *Nile Valley Civilizations*, ed. I. van Sertima New Brunswick, N. J.: Journal of African Civilizations Press, 1986.

Erny, P. *Childhood and cosmos*. New York: New Perspectives, 1973.

Forde, D. *African worlds*. New York: Oxford Univ. Press, 1970.

Jahn, J. 1961. *Muntu*. New York: Grove Press, Inc.

Mbiti, J. S. *African religions and philosophy*. Garden City, N. Y.: Doubleday, 1970..

Muhammad, W. D. The Crown of Creation. In *Muhammad Speaks* (October 1975).

CHAPTER 3

Mental Health Defined Africentrically

Daudi Ajani ya Azibo

CULTURE AND THE MENTAL HEALTH IDEA

The idea of mental health, like most concepts of social behavior, is culturally bound. That is, the limiting form of what mental health is is defined by culture. Therefore, when behavior or psychological orientation violates the parameters of mental health as defined by Culture X, then the behavior is definitely inappropriate, lies outside of mental health, and represents and demonstrates behavior that reflects unhealthy mental functioning, from the perspective of Culture X. Under no circumstances could such behavior be construed under the conceptual universe of Culture X as appropriate or within the context of mental health.

Now, since Culture X may differ significantly from other cultures, it is axiomatic that whether a given psychological orientation or behavior is illustrative of healthy mental functioning is relative to the patterns for interpreting reality that arise from Culture X's cultural deep structure. That cultural deep structure, in turn, gives the people of Culture X their general design for living.

If Culture X is Eurocentric, then the limiting form of what mental health is and the definitions offered for mental health will fall right out of (i.e., derive directly from) the European world view. The same holds if Culture X is Africentric, Arab-centric, and so forth.

TOWARDS THE DECONSTRUCTION OF THE EUROCENTRIC DEFINITION OF MENTAL HEALTH

Proof of this point abounds. Regarding Eurocentric culture, for example, Akbar (1985) has shown that in Eurocentric psychology the limiting form for mental health is the set of culture-bound characteristics prototypical to the white male. (These are affectlessness, individualism, competitiveness, control, and future orientedness.) It has to be this way for two reasons: (1) since the European world view is ingrained with a tremendous patriarchal orientation arising from the "northern cradle" evolution of whites (Diop 1978; Wobogo 1976), the male orientedness is overdetermined; (2) since the European cultural deep structure dictates separateness and independence, materialism, conflict, the imposition of order by the mightiest, and the relentless mastery and control of nature as its prominent patterns for interpreting reality (Baldwin 1985), it can promote, promulgate, and project *only* its own image and selfish interests.

Additionally, *the European worldview can be seen as the determining factor of what the concept of mental health is in Eurocentric psychology*. What it is is an elusive and ill-defined concept because, drawing on the deep structure of their culture, the powerful Europeans decide what order is in accordance with their needs. *Ma'at*, a notion and value orientation of inherent orderliness (Carruthers 1984; Karenga 1984), does not rule and is precluded as a stable concept. Therefore, an *a priori*, inherent notion of order cannot be attained in the European worldview. This is the underlying reason why determining what mental health is is problematical in Eurocentric psychology.

Lacking an *a priori* model of sanity or mental health, Eurocentric psychology infers sanity by the absence of insanity, infers mental health by the absence of mental illness: "Now that's insane to me" remarked Na'im Akbar (1981b). Even the views of Eurocentric psychology on mental illness can be directly traced to the European worldview. The medical, statistical, psychological, and absolute models are representative (Calhoun 1977; Ukombozi 1981). The *medical model* posits that mental illness results from organic dysfunction and reflects overreliance on and encapsulation in material ontology. The *statistical model* sees mental illness as behavior deviating from the average, normative functioning. In other words, mental health or normalcy is behavior that is prevalent and approximating what most or many people do in the sense of a statistical norm, according to the statistical model. From this view, Kunta Kinte's behavior and orientation represented mental illness whereas Fiddler's represented normalcy!* The behavior and orientation of spectators and perpetrators of lynchings of Africans (Ginzburg n.d.) do not represent mental illness under the statistical model. Besides being based in the object-measure/counting-measuring epistemology, which itself has been shown to be intrinsic to the European worldview (Baldwin 1985; Carruthers 1995; Dixon 1976; Myers 1988), the statistical model belies any concept of *a priori* order. Rather, it reflects the accommodation in the European worldview to order determined by the mighty. Therefore, when the social planners and the "movers and shakers" of white culture deem it in the best interest of "white genetic survival" (to use Dr. Frances Welsing's most *apropos* terminology), they simply redefine order, the population masses follow accordingly, and *presto*, there is a statistical base for the "normalcy" of this behavior that has been redefined as order. The *psychological model* construes disorder as a result of an intrapsychic personality process gone awry. It assumes the existence of an orderly or organized intrapsychic personality process. The *absolute model* postulates disorder to be the lacking of some nonarbitrary standard. Even though it might be argued that both the psychological and absolute models posit an a priori concept of order and disorder, the point to be taken is that every idea of order/disorder generated under these models in Western psychology is based on concepts derived from the European worldview. Since this worldview is inherently anti-African (Baldwin 1985), it is expected that maltreatment of Africans would prove to be the norm under the Eurocentric mental health system (Azibo [in press], ch. 6; Nobles 1986a, ch. 1; Thomas and Sillen 1972).

DECONSTRUCTION BRIDGING TO CONSTRUCTION

The preceding discussion has somewhat deconstructed the concept of mental health as defined by Eurocentric psychology. (Deconstruction refers to the falsification, refutation, voiding, literal debunking of the social science edifice of anti-African theory, research, and practice that emanates from a Eurocentric psychological base.) Consequently it appears safe and necessary to proceed on the grounds that it is neither theoretically nor practically appropriate to apply the mental health concept as conceived Eurocentrically to Africans. Indeed, doing so might be endamaging. These are most important points for *every* African psychological worker because at present *all* mental health training in the Western academies is grounded in European worldview concepts. (The exception is Florida A & M University's psychology department under Dr. Joseph Baldwin's chairmanship. See both Baldwin's chapter on the FAMU model and Harper-Browne's chapter in the present volume on how to teach African psychology.) Consequently, the African psychological worker is usually a miseducated and conceptually incarcerated product, especially by the time s/he attains a doctoral degree. Given this reality, it is often necessary to deconstruct first in order to facilitate the understanding of psychological conceptualizations constructed from the African worldview. (Construction refers to developing psychological knowledge using Africentric cultural concepts.) This supports my contention (Azibo 1995) that the main value of deconstruction lies in its bridging to construction.

MENTAL HEALTH DEFINED AFRICENTRICALLY

Consubstantiation and self-extension are paramount among the principles that comprise the patterns for interpreting reality arising from the deep structure of the African culture. These principles are crucial to an understanding of what mental health is. They are also inseparable. Consubstantiation stands on the cosmological assumption of holistic interconnectedness and interdependence of all entities within the universe. It also relies on the ontological assumption that the Divine spirit underlying creation is the same spiritual energy underlying human conception. (Thus every

Figure 1

AFRICAN'S EXTENDED-SELF CONCEPT

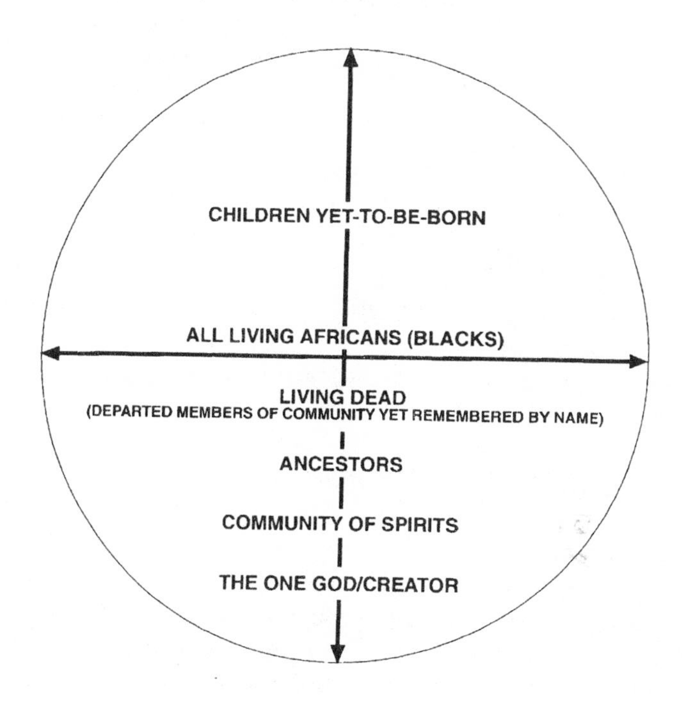

woman's conception is Immaculate, not only that of Auset/Isis/Mary/Maryum.) Now, since the African is the original human being, the consubstantiation principle states "'we [Africans] are one people, we are of [we share] the same [spiritual] essence' . . . transmitted biogenetically at conception" (Azibo 1989, 175). This shared spiritual essence is the basis for the African self-extension principle: the contemporary African person is a direct extension of the (presumed) Divine (Creator, One God, etc.) by virtue of begetting through the Ancestors and the immediate line of progenitors. Her or his progeny are equally and likewise extended into the past through him or her as s/he is equally and likewise extended into the distant, infinite future through the required continuation of progeny. Taken together, since they are inseparable, the consubstantiation and self-extension principles give rise to the African *extended-self concept*. Part and parcel of the self of every contemporary African are all other living Africans and all Africans who have entered the realm of the Ancestors and all African Progeny yet to be begotten. Thus, the "self" for Africans has to be understood *a priori* as extended (Nobles 1976), as an unbroken circle (Richards 1989) encompassing an infinite past, an infinite future, and all contemporary Africans. Figure 1 illustrates the idea.

(The reader should note that the extended-self concept is not even remotely congruous with the "reference group orientation" concept [Cross, Parham, and Helms in press]. The latter is actually a Eurocentric construct that has been injected into African psychology discourse. Consequently, it serves as a rampart for the realization of the specter of an entire, visible literature based on transubstantiation. Transubstantiation is the interpretation and explanation of African reality using non-African meanings. Nothing could be potentially more regressive and arresting of African psychology's contemporary revitalization.)

What mental health is under Africentric conceptualizing must reflect the dictates that derive from this African concept of self, most notably *race maintenance*. "Own-race maintenance" has been postulated from an evolutionary perspective "as a natural human imperative for the sustentation of organisms of biogenetic commonality. . . . [that] would be manifested to greater degrees for organisms of biogenetic commonality relative to organisms of lesser biogenetic commonality" (Azibo 1983; 1990: 30; 1991: 185; in press). Is it "only natural" that an organism would be so oriented? Apparently the answer is yes, if Akbar's (1981a) assertion that all life forms tend to preserve themselves is accurate. In his Africentric theory of Black personality, Baldwin (1981, 1984) postulates the existence of an innate, natural propensity for organismic survival maintenance, i.e., race maintenance. In looking at individual differences in responses to oppression, Marcia Sutherland (1989) pointed out that (what we might call) the authentic manifestation of the African personality consistently strove for African race maintenance.

Clearly, these statements bearing on what mental health is are imbued with the idea that the natural order has determined *a priori* that order is inextricably linked to self (remember, self is extended) maintenance. The emphasis on natural order itself derives from the African culture's deep structure position on worldview. Consequently, the definitions of mental health that might be constructed under this conceptual universe may appear to fall within the absolute or psychological models discussed above. Here, as well as discussed above, the point is that the concepts are culture bound. Those used here come out of (derive from) the African worldview.

Definitions. Mental order is defined as "the state at which mental processes are self-preserving [in the extended sense] in accordance with Universal Principles [as conceived Africentrically]" in the *African Psychology Institute Training Module Handbook* (1982:15). According to Nobles (1986a:94-95; 1986b), ordered "Black human conduct is . . . the behavioral representation of African thought [African worldview manifested in behavior]. . . . Thus to be normal is to be consistent with the dictates of one's Ka" (spiritual essence). With some reflection, we see that these definitions are suggestive of the idea that the African's *ka*, with its inherent dictates of consubstantiation and self-extension into and out of eternalness, compels the African's mental life to orient his or her behavior towards race maintenance. Adjusting Welsing's (1981:29, 35) definition of mental illness might produce this definition of mental health: patterns of perception, logic, thought, speech, action, and emotional response—whether consciously or unconsciously determined—that reflect personal and extended self-respect and personal and extended self-affirmation. This is perfectly consistent with the two preceding mental health definitions and underscores the idea of race maintenance also. Additionally, this definition explicitly incorporates the notion of the development of one's personal being as part of mental health. Note, however, that the definition *does not separate* personal and extended self-development but *yokes* them. This is implicit in the first two definitions as well: universal principles discernible in the African worldview reveal that the dictates of the African person's *ka* are fundamentally "participation in the supreme Force" which is "the Ka of God" (Nobles 1986a:55). What this means is that there is a natural, innate propensity in the African person to develop herself or himself into a goddess or god by achieving a transfiguration with the One God (Azibo 1989). Stated differently, one's personal *ka* is endowed with an inherent capability and orientation to join, link, or otherwise be participatory with the universal Force or Spirit that underlies creation and existence and compels development of the extended self. This suggests then that the personal *ka* is motivated for growth and development to realize its full cosmological nature of interdependence and interconnectedness. Thereby does personal *ka* development of this sort serve the collective to which it is inextricably linked.

Contained in these definitions and in this elaborative discussion of mental health are explicit and implicit notions of the nature of the original human being, the nature of the African. Also, the discussion has relied on interpretations and explanations from the African cultural deep structure. Figuring prominently in all of this has been the idea of race maintenance or survival thrust. It would appear warrantable, in conclusion, to offer a definition of *what mental health is* in a manner that succinctly crystallizes all of these points:

> mental health is that psychological and behavioral functioning that is in accord with the basic nature of the original human nature and its attendant cosmology and survival thrust. (Azibo 1989:177)

NOTES

* As portrayed in Alex Haley's *Roots*, Kunta Kinte strove to maintain his African identity and resisted enslavement; Fiddler internalized and followed the dictates of the United States slavery system.

REFERENCES

African Psychology Institute Training Module Handbook. Atlanta: African Psychology Institute, 1982.

Akbar, N. Mental disorder among African-Americans. *Black Books Bulletin* 7, 2 (1981):18-25.

Akbar, N. Transcript of lecture given at the Social Learning Laboratory Seminar Series, Educational Testing Service, Princeton, N.J., 1981b.

Akbar, N. Our destiny: Authors of a scientific revolution. In *Black children: Social psychological and educational environments,* ed. H. McAdoo and J. McAdoo, Beverly Hills, Calif.: Sage Publications, 1985.

Azibo, D. A. *African (Black) personality theory, status characteristics theory, and perceived belief similarity: Which is predominant in dominance/reactance behavior?* Ph.D. diss., Washington University, St. Louis, Mo, 1983.

Azibo, D. A. African-centered theses on mental health and a nosology of Black/African personality disorder. *Journal of Black Psychology* 15, 2 (1989):173-214.

Azibo, D. A. Advances in Black/African personality theory. *Imhotep: An Afrocentric Review* 2, 1 (1990):22-47.

Azibo, D. A. An empirical test of the fundamental postulates of an African personality metatheory. *Western Journal of Black Studies* 15, 2 (1991):183-195.

Azibo, D. A. African psychology in historical perspective and related commentary. In *African psychology in historical perspective and related commentary*, ed. D. Azibo, Trenton, N.J.: Africa World Press, 1995.

Azibo, D. A. *Liberation psychology: An introduction to the African personality construct.* Trenton, N.J.: Africa World Press (in press).

Baldwin, J. Notes on an Africentric theory of Black personality. *Western Journal of Black Studies* 5 (1981):172-179.

Baldwin, J. African self-consciousness and the mental health of African-Americans. *Journal of Black Studies* 15, 2 (1984):177-194.

Baldwin, J. Psychological aspects of European cosmology in American society. *Western Journal of Black Studies* 9, 4 (1985):216-223.

Calhoun, J. *Abnormal psychology: current perspectives.* New York: Random House, 1977.

Carruthers, J. *Essays in ancient Egyptian studies.* Los Angeles: University of Sankore Press, 1984.

Carruthers, J. Science and oppression. In *African psychology in historical perspective and related commentary*, ed. D. Azibo Trenton, N.J.: Africa World Press, 1995.

Cross, W., T. Parham, and J. Helms. Nigrescence revisited. In *Advances in Black psychology*, ed. R. Jones Oakland, Calif.: Cobb & Henry Publishers (in press).

Diop, C. A. *The cultural unity of Black Africa.* Chicago: Third World Press, 1978.

Dixon, V. World views and research methodology. In *African philosophy: Assumptions and paradigms for research on Black persons*, ed. L. King, V. Dixon, and W. Nobles Los Angeles: Fanon Research and Development Center, 1976.

Ginzbergh, R. *100 years of lynchings*. Lancer Books (n.d.).

Karenga, M. *Selections from The Husia*. Los Angeles: Kawaida Publications, 1984.

Myers, L. *Understanding an Afrocentric world view: Introduction to an optimal psychology*. Dubuque, Iowa: Kendall-Hunt, 1988.

Nobles, W. W. Extended self: Rethinking the so-called Negro self-concept. *Journal of Black Psychology* 2 (1976): 15-24.

Nobles, W. W. *African psychology: Toward its reclamation, reascension and revitalization*. Oakland, Calif.: Black Family Institute Publications, 1986a.

Nobles, W. W. Ancient Egyptian thought and the development of African (Black) psychology. In *Kemet and the African worldview*, ed. M. Karenga and J. Carruthers, Los Angeles: University of Sankore Press, 1986b.

Richards, D. *Let the circle be unbroken*. New York: Black Studies Dept., Hunter College, 1989.

Sutherland, M. Individual differences in response to the struggle for the liberation of people of African descent. *Journal of Black Studies* 20, 1 (1989):40-59.

Thomas, A. and S. Sillen. *Racism and psychiatry*. Secaucus, N.J.: Brunner-Mazel, 1972.

Ukombozi, A. *To Blacktualize or not to Blacktualize: Toward a comprehensive Afrocentric framework of mental health for Afrikan people*. Typescript:1981.

Welsing, F. The concept and color of God and Black mental health. *Black Books Bulletin* 7, 1 (1981):27-29, 35.

Wobogo, V. Diop's 2-cradle theory and the origin of white racism. *Black Books Bulletin* 4, 4 (1976):20-29, 72.

Chapter 4

The Africentric Paradigm and African American Psychological Liberation

Kobi K. K. Kambon

Introduction: The Africentric Approach to Cultural Reality

The Africentric paradigm in social science, as it has evolved over the past twenty years, represents no less than a scientific revolution in African American scholarship (Akbar 1984, 1985; Asante 1980, 1988; Baldwin 1976, 1985a, 1986; Karenga 1982; Nobles 1980a, 1986). This paradigm consists of at least four basic characteristics: (a) it generates the construction of African social reality from the framework of the history, culture, and philosophy of African civilization; (b) it recognizes and articulates the basic continuity of the African worldview throughout the diverse African populations around the globe; (c) it recognizes and articulates the basic distinctness and independence of the African worldview (relative to any other, such as the European worldview); (d) it projects the African survival thrust as the center of African social reality.

From these basic characteristics of the Africentric paradigm, several major propositions regarding cultural reality (i.e., multicultural reality) may be delineated: (1) Each culture generates its own peculiar view of the world or approach to reality/existence, which we might call its *worldview or cosmology*. (2) This worldview/cosmology naturally evolves from and reinforces the *survival maintenance* of the culture: it reflects its *survival thrust*. (3) Culture varies with race, such that different racial groups generate different cultures, peculiar to their group's distinct biosocial histories and experiential realities. (4) There are fundamental differences between the African and European worldviews, just as there are fundamental biophysiological differences between them, in terms of their distinct survival thrusts. (5) Under normal/natural conditions, Africans (Blacks) operate/function in terms of the African worldview, and Europeans (Whites) operate/function in terms of the European worldview. Therefore, any substantive deviations from these normal/natural relationships represents unnaturalness and abnormality or pathology, as defined by the natural order.

WORLDVIEW CLASHES AND PSYCHOLOGICAL OPPRESSION IN AMERICAN SOCIETY

Based on this perspective, a worldview system can be regarded in terms of its racial-cultural definition. Hence, the African worldview or social-cultural reality and the European worldview or social-cultural reality define the distinct survival thrusts of the African (and African American) and European (and European American) communities, respectively. What then constitutes the basic nature of these worldviews and their fundamental distinctness from one another?

THE AFRICAN/AFRICAN AMERICAN WORLDVIEW

The basic assumption underlying the African American worldview reflects the notion of humanity-nature unity or oneness (Baldwin 1980, 1985b; Carruthers 1984; Dixon 1976; Nobles 1980a, 1980b). In this worldview, the human-nature relationship is defined as an interdependent, inseparable whole. Humanity, then, is inextricably connected to nature or the natural order; they are in fact one in the same phenomenon. The ethos reflective of this assumption is that of "oneness" or "harmony with nature" and "survival of the group" (Nobles 1980a, 1980b). The harmony-with-nature principle emphasizes that the basic striving of human life is toward seeking to maintain balance or harmony among the various aspects of the universe, a striving to maintain a complementary coexistence with the universal order (Carruthers 1984; Dixon 1976). The dominant emphasis in the principle of the survival of the group is placed on the prioritizing of the maintenance/survival of the corporate whole (family, community, nation, and all of humanity) above the individual or special segment. Deriving from this ethosic order are the values and customs that emphasize inclusiveness, cooperation, and collective responsibility, cooperateness and interdependence, spiritualism, complementarity, and understanding. The derivative psychobehavioral modalities reflect an operational emphasis on groupness, sameness, commonality, and humanism/religion.

The European/European American Worldview

The basic assumption underlying the European American worldview is that of a human-nature dichotomy, organized in conflictual-antagonistic relationship (Baldwin 1980, 1985b; Carruthers 1972; Diop 1974; Dixon 1976; Nobles 1980b). That is, the universe is separated into two major components, humanity or (self) consciousness and nature or phenomenal experience (Dixon 1976). It is assumed that humanity-nature conflict and strife are inevitable and natural. Reflecting this basic assumption is the ethos of "control over nature" or "humanity versus nature" and "survival of the fittest" (Baldwin 1980, 1985b; Nobles 1980b). Nature is seen as life threatening and hostile. Thus, in order to survive, humanity must intervene into nature to gain control over, dominate, suppress, and alter the natural arrangement of objects (Baldwin 1985b; Bradley 1981; Carruthers 1972; Richards 1979, 1980). The thrust of this ethos, then, is toward achieving mastery and control over nature. The principle of the survival of the fittest refers to the basic notion that those people (individuals, races, etc.) who achieve the greatest degree of mastery or control over nature are regarded as the most fit to survive. They are defined as the superiors, the most competent, or the "fittest" among the human community (Baldwin

1985b). Fittest, then, represents the highest status of human achievement, attained through competition and aggression, and is indexed by object control or the amount of distance/ separation one is able to establish between the self and nature (i.e., the degree to which one has gained effective manipulative power or dominance over nature).

Deriving from this ethosic order are several basic values and customs that reflect an emphasis on exclusion and dichotomy, competition and individual rights, separation and independence, and materialism and aggression or intervention. The psychobehavioral modalities deriving from these values and customs reflect an operational emphasis on individualism, differences, and European supremacy/racism. These basic differences between the African and European worldviews are contrasted in Table 1. Beyond the basic nature of these differences of worldview that have already been elaborated, it should be clear from Table 1 that these differences are also incompatible and more or less oppositional.

PSYCHOLOGICAL OPPRESSION

Given the multicultural nature of American society, it would therefore seem to be inevitable that conflict between these oppositional worldviews would occur. It would also be expected that the racial-cultural group with the greater amount of social-political power in America would ultimately gain control over those basic societal institutions defining the American social reality (Baldwin 1980).

The thrust of this analysis thus proposes that the basic ideological and philosophical character of American society, as reflected in its basic institutions, is essentially defined by the European worldview. This is because the European American community effectively controls all of the basic institutions which formally define the American social reality. As I have argued elsewhere (Baldwin 1985b), the basic philosophy, values, customs, and standards inherent in the European worldview form the core or frame of reference for the American social reality. The American social/cultural reality, then, is "Eurocentric" in its basic nature. It projects European people, their history, philosophy, culture, etc., as the center of the universe. The American situation in which these two worldviews confront one another, therefore, poses some of the most serious psychological and mental health implications imag-

Table 1
COMPARISON OF WORLDVIEWS

African American Worldview		European American Worldview
Human-Nature Oneness	BASIC ASSUMPTION	Human-Nature Dichotomy
Harmony with Nature	ETHOS	Control/Mastery over Nature
Survival of the Group Inclusiveness/ Synthesis		Survival of the Fittest Exclusiveness/ Dichotomy
Cooperation and Collective Responsibility	VALUES AND CUSTOMS	Competition and Individual Rights
Corporateness and Independence		Separateness and Interdependence
Spiritualism and Circularity		Materialism and Ordinality
Complementarity/ Understanding		Intervention/ Oppression
Groupness Sameness Commonality Humanism/ Religion	PSYCHOBEHAVIORAL MODALITIES	Individualism Uniqueness Differences European Supremacy/ Racism

inable for the African American community (Baldwin 1980, 1984, 1985a, 1985b).

This analysis further argues that to the extent that the European American community effectively controls American society, it has been able to superimpose its worldview on other, non-European American communities (Baldwin 1980). This is a particularly dangerous situation for the mental health of African Americans, given that the European American worldview opposes the African

American worldview, and is, therefore, "antiAfrican" in its basic nature. Thus, to the extent that the African American community has come under the control of the European American worldview, it has influenced Blacks to perpetuate a survival thrust that is "antiBlack" (antiself) and contradictory to their survival as African people (Baldwin 1984, 1985b; McGee 1973; Nobles 1976; Williams 1976; Woodson 1969).

This process of Eurocentric cultural/psychological oppression of African Americans results in a condition of gross psychopathology among Blacks, which is defined as normal and functionally healthy by the European American worldview. I have labeled this dangerous condition of mental disorder among African Americans as "Psychological Misorientation" (Baldwin 1980, 1984, 1985b). *Psychological misorientation* refers to a condition in African Americans whereby the individual, in his or her own mind, is neither confused about his/her identity nor dysfunctional in his/her behavior according to the standards prescribed by the European American worldview. This is because the (African American) person is operating in the manner of a European American. The African American so defined obviously holds an *incorrect and contradictory* psychological orientation according to the African American worldview. Yet, at the same time, it is regarded as correct and quite functionally adaptive within the framework of the European American worldview. The social cues and institutional support systems of American society reinforce African Americans operating in such a disordered manner (Baldwin 1980, 109).

In short, the condition of psychological misorientation refers to the acquisition of a pseudoEurocentric self-consciousness by African Americans, which is regarded as functionally normal in the American social reality because it only reinforces the European survival thrust. While this condition can affect individuals in varying degrees, from minimal to severe, in all cases it represents *a grossly psychopathological condition in African Americans masquerading as functional normalcy* (Baldwin 1984).

Manifestations of the operation of the European worldview among African Americans (i.e., psychological misorientation) are pervasive in African American community life. I have given various examples of this pervasive situation elsewhere (Baldwin 1984, 1985b). Suffice it to say here that the areas of African American religious, educational, economic, and social activities reveal some of the most blatant illustrations of the great dangers posed by the condition of psychological misorientation.

This analysis, of course, is not meant to overlook the fact that African Americans, by and large, also exhibit widespread expressions of the African worldview in their daily lives. Some illustrations of these manifestations are the widely practiced extended family system among African Americans, along with the highly popular emphasis on annual family reunions extending out to very distant degrees of kinship. Expressions of the African worldview also are evident in African Americans' socializing-affiliational emphasis and the "shared-participation" ritual that occurs in all viable and intense social situations and settings (e.g., secular, sacred, etc.); in the emphasis on respect for and continued involvement of the elderly in the everyday life of the community; in the fervent practice of religion and morality; and in the strong shared feelings of victory and defeat in virtually all public displays of "Black *versus* White" competition.

The problem, however, is that these pervasive expressions of the African worldview are "unconscious" rather than conscious expressions (Baldwin 1980). The conscious expressions of African Americans, as was noted earlier, are Eurocentric/psychologically misoriented in nature. Hence, psychological oppression among African Americans manifests itself as a basic psychological condition of "contradiction": that is, there are antithetical or paradoxical conscious and unconscious psychological strivings coexisting within the African American psychological system (Baldwin 1984). The *conscious Eurocentric* (misoriented) psychological striving, therefore, gives rise to a constant manifestation of functional contradictions—*contradictory behaviors*—among African Americans (Baldwin 1984, 1985b). The most blatant example of this paradoxical phenomenon is the widespread manifestations of "antiBlack" and self-destructive behaviors among African Americans that are regarded more or less as "normal" (or at least as "non-"psychiatric/pathological) by the general American social reality (Baldwin 1979, 1980, 1984, 1985b).

AFRICAN SELF-CONSCIOUSNESS AND PSYCHOLOGICAL MISORIENTATION

What is proposed here, then, is that African Americans who are victimized by Eurocentric cultural/psychological oppression have indeed lost the authentic affirmative orientation toward themselves that is so vital to their survival as African people. More specifically, these African American victims place little or no priority on any of the following vital Africentric dispositions: (a) awareness of their African American identity and their African cultural heritage, and valuing the pursuit of self-knowledge; (b) African American survival priorities and the necessity for societal institutions which affirm African life; (c) active participation in the survival, liberation, and affirmative development of African people; (d) defending uncompromisingly their dignity, worth, and integrity as people of African descent. It is noteworthy that the opposite of these self-negating strivings/ tendencies in the psychologically misoriented person constitute the critical Africentric dispositions in the operation of what I have called "African self-consciousness" (Baldwin 1981, 1984).

African self-consciousness is a construct in the Black personality which defines and directs self-affirming/self-fortifying behaviors among African American people. Thus, psychological misorientation represents in effect a severe weakening or distortion of the African American person's African self-consciousness. This model enables us to localize the core of the problem of psychological misorientation within the African American personality system (Baldwin 1984) and, therefore, gives focus to the needed intervention and preventive measures.

A MODEL FOR AFRICAN AMERICAN PSYCHOLOGICAL LIBERATION

Given the nature of African American psychological oppression as it has been interpreted herein, what is the appropriate approach to resolving this pervasive threat to African American survival? Based on this analysis, one critical focus of preventive-intervention strategies must involve the reconstruction and reinstitutionalization of *Africentric institutions* throughout all areas of African

American community life. This is necessary in order to sever the African American community's enormous and pathogenic allegiance to the European worldview and to reestablish their full (conscious) allegiance to and practice of their indigenous African worldview.

The operation of Africentric institutions would focus on the history, culture, philosophy, basic needs, and social priorities of African American people. African American survival and cultural advancement thus becomes the primary objective of Africentric institutions. African American activities, therefore, are defined in terms of their ability to facilitate the Africentric objectives of respect for African American life, the securing of African American physical and psychological survival, and the full development-affirmation of the African American community. Africentric institutions articulate and reinforce the African worldview in African American people, thereby affirming African Americans as "African people," having an African commitment, responsibility, and destiny.

Perhaps the most critical area of Africentric institutionalization in African American community life is *education*. This is because education is such a vital instrument of indoctrination and advanced socialization of the people. The African American community must begin to develop *independent educational institutions* that are grounded in Africentric philosophy of education (Akoto, 1992; Asante 1980; Baldwin 1979; Du Bois 1933; Williams 1976; Woodson 1969) and are controlled *by* African Americans *for* African Americans. In other words, African Americans need an educational policy grounded in their cultural history and contemporary social priorities. Additionally, the African American community must begin to exercise rigid scrutiny over the media influencing its people, especially the electronic and print media. Radio, although often overlooked, has long served as a dominant instrument of indoctrination and social conditioning of African Americans, and, of course, television has assumed the dominant position in contemporary times. These two mediums, in particular, comprise the primary instruments of psychological oppression supporting the major societal institutions of education and religion. Thus, African American children especially, and the adult population as well, spend far too much time exposed to these Eurocentric-controlled media and institutions to overlook them in developing effective preventive-intervention/liberation strategies. The African American community must definitely gain *control* over these vital mediums through *redefining* them according to the Africentric framework.

As I have further noted elsewhere (Baldwin 1985b), the practice of the "Nguzo Saba," the observance of the *Kwanzaa* holiday (Karenga 1977), as well as the incorporation of many other traditional Africentric customs (i.e., libation/ancestor acknowledgement and reaffirmation of individual responsibility to the collective, etc.) into their regular ceremonial practices (e.g., birth, marriage, and funeral ceremonies, etc.) should become a basic part of everyday African American community life. In addition, the taking of traditional Africentric names, especially for the children, should become a basic practice in African American community life. The African American community must not continue to allow generation after generation of its children to grow up without personal labels that link them to their great African heritage. Such a practice would undoubtedly have a revolutionary impact on the subsequent psychological/cultural development of the future African American community.

Finally, and just as importantly, African Americans must begin to incorporate the Africentric philosophical principles (Asante 1980, 1988; Baldwin 1981, 1984; Carruthers 1981, 1984; Nobles 1980a, 1986; Williams 1976) not only into their practice of education, but also into religion, economics, and politics. African Americans must remove the Eurocentric/Caucasian images and symbols from their religious concepts and practices (Welsing 1981) and replace them with traditional Africentric concepts, symbols, and practices that derive from the framework of the African worldview (Asante 1980; ben-Jochannon 1971, 1976; Carruthers 1984; Karenga 1984). The adoption of Africentric economic and political principles and practices based on African self-respect, cooperation, and collective responsibility is also a necessary step toward liberation and self-determination for African Americans.

CONCLUSION

Overall, this analysis has attempted to show the critical importance of understanding the construct of *worldview* to our being able to grasp the vital role of the Africentric paradigm in the psychological liberation of African Americans. It is this author's view that the major impediment to our mounting an effective liberation struggle has been the failure of the masses of African American scholars and educators to comprehend this fact of multicultural reality and to appreciate our sociopolitical plight within it. Although this analysis is focused on the African American condition, the reader should recognize that it can be applied to the condition of Africans around the globe (Fanon 1968; Memmi 1965, 1968; Sofola 1973, 1988; Williams 1976). We in Black/African Psychology are committed to generating a substantive data base supportive of this view (Baldwin 1984, 1987; Baldwin and Hopkins 1990; Curry 1984; Nobles and Goddard 1984). Hopefully, the analysis advanced herein will contribute to our arriving at the final solution to this problem.

REFERENCES

Akbar, N. Afrocentric social science for human liberation. *Journal of Black Studies* 14, 4 (1984): 395-414.

Akbar, N. Our destiny: Authors of a scientific revolution. In *Black children: Social, educational and parental environments*, ed. H. McAdoo and J. McAdoo Beverly Hills: Sage Publications, 1985.

Akoto, K. A. *Nationbuilding: Theory and practice in Afrikan centered education.* Washington, DC: Pan Afrikan World Institute, 1992.

Asante, M. K. *Afrocentricity: The theory of social change.* Buffalo: Amulefi Publications, 1980.

Asante, M. *The Afrocentric idea.* Philadelphia: Temple University Press, 1988.

Baldwin, J. A. Black Psychology and Black personality: Some issues for consideration. *Black Books Bulletin* 4, 3 (1976):6-11, 65.

Baldwin, J. A. Education and oppression in the American Context. *Journal of Inner City Studies* 1, 1 (1979):62-85.

Baldwin, J. A. The psychology of oppression. In *Contemporary Black Thought*, ed. M. Asante and A. Vandi Beverly Hills: Sage Publications, 1980.

Baldwin, J. A. Notes on an Africentric theory of Black personality. *Western Journal of Black Studies* 5, 2 (1981):172-179.

Baldwin, J. A. African self-consciousness and the mental health of African Americans. *Journal of Black Studies* 15, 2 (1984):177-194.

Baldwin, J. A. The role of Black psychologists in Black Liberation. *Association of Black Psychologists Newsletter* 17, 1 (1985a):16-20.

Baldwin, J. A. Psychological aspects of European cosmology in American society. *Western Journal of Black Studies*, 9, 4 (1985b):216-223.

Baldwin, J. A. African (Black) Psychology: Issues and synthesis. *Journal of Black Studies* 16, 3 (1986):235-249.

Baldwin, J. A. African Psychology and Black personality testing. *Negro Educational Review* 38, 2-5 (1987):56-66.

Baldwin, J. A., and R. Hopkins. African-American and European-American cultural differences as assessed by the world views paradigm: An empirical analysis. *Western Journal of Black Studies* 14, 1 (1990):38-52.

Ben-Jochannon, Y. *Africa: Mother of western civilization*. New York: Alkebulan Publications, 1971.

Ben-Jochannon, Y. *Black man of the Nile and his family*. New York: Alkebulan Publications, 1976..

Bradley, M. *The iceman inheritance: Prehistoric sources of western man's racism, sexism and aggression*. New York: Warner Books, 1981.

Carruthers, J. H. *Science and oppression*. Chicago: The Kemetic Institute (1972 or see chapter 11 of this volume.)

Carruthers, J. H. Reflections on the history of the Afrocentric world view. *Black Books Bulletin* 7, 1 (1981):4-7, 13, 25.

Carruthers, J. H. *Essays in ancient Egyptian studies*. Los Angeles: Timbuktu Publications, 1984.

Curry, A. O. *An examination of traditional attitudes and values of Black/African people: A study within an African worldview*. Paper presented at the 17th Annual Convention of the Association of Black Psychologists. Washington, D.C.: The Association of Black Psychologists, 1984.

Diop, C. A. *The African origin of civilization: Myth or reality*. Westport, Connecticut: Lawrence Hill & Company, 1974.

Dixon, V. J. Worldviews and research methodology. In *African philosophy: Assumptions and paradigms for research on Black Persons*, ed. L. King, V. Dixon, and W. Nobles Los Angeles: Fanon R & D Center, 1976.

Du Bois, W. E. B. The field and function of the Negro college. In *Education of Black people: Ten critiques, 1906-1960, by W. E. B. Du Bois*, ed. H. Aptheker, New York: Monthly Review Press, 1973 [*1933].

Fanon, F. *Black skin, White mask*. New York: Grove Press, 1968.
Karenga, M. R. *Kwanzaa: Origin, concepts, practice*. Los Angeles: Kawaida Publications, 1977.
Karenga, M. R. *Introduction to Black studies*. Los Angeles: Kawaida Publications, 1982.
Karenga, M. R. *Selections from the Husia: Sacred wisdom of ancient Egypt*. Los Angeles: Kawaida Publications, 1984.
McGee, D. P. White conditioning of Black dependency. *Journal of Social Issues* 29 (1973):53-56.
Memmi, A. *The colonizer and the colonized*. Boston: Beacon Press, 1965.
Memmi, A. *Dominated man*. New York: Orion Press.
Nobles, W. W. 1976. Black people in White insanity: An issue for Black community mental health. *Journal of Afro-American Issues* 4 (1968):21-27.
Nobles, W. W. African philosophy: Foundation for Black Psychology. In *Black psychology*, ed. R. Jones, 2nd ed. New York: Harper & Row, 1980a.
Nobles, W. W. Extended self: Rethinking the so-called Negro self concept. In *Black psychology*, ed. R. Jones, 2nd ed. New York: Harper & Row, 1980b.
Nobles, W. W. *African Psychology: Toward its reclamation, reascension and revitalization*. Oakland, Calif.: The Black Family Institute, 1986.
Nobles, W., and L. Goddard. *Understanding the Black Family: A guide for scholarship and research*. Oakland, CA: The Black Family Institute, 1984.
Richards, D. The ideology of European dominance. *Western Journal of Black Studies* 3, 4 (1979):244-250.
Richards, D. European mythology: The ideology of progress. In *Contemporary Black Thought*, ed. M. Asante and A. Vandi, Beverly Hills: Sage, 1980.
Sofola, J. A. *African culture and the African personality*. Ibadan, Nigeria:1973.
Sofola, J. A. *Cultural self-knowledge and cultural self-appreciation for true development in Nigeria*. 1973. Ilorin, Nigeria: University of Ilorin Press, 1988.
Welsing, F. The concept and the color of God and Black mental health. *Black Books Bulletin* 7, 1 (1981):27-29, 35.
Williams, C. *The destruction of Black civilization*. Chicago: Third World Press, 1976.
Woodson, C. G. *The Mis-education of the Negro*. Washington, D.C.: Associated Publishers, 1969.

CHAPTER 5

Mentacide, Genocide, and National Vision: The Crossroads for the Blacks of America (An Essay of Commentary)

Olomenji

OVERVIEW

The psycho-political condition of the Blacks of America (United States) is taken as the focal point for analyzing the mentacide construct. Prominent in the Azibo Nosology is the disorder of mentacide. Mentacide was defined by Dr. Bobby Wright as the deliberate and systematic destruction of an individual's or group's mind with the ultimate aim being the extirpation or elimination of that group. Within the logic of the Azibo Nosology, mentacide can be precipitative and predisposing of the other disorders. As its definition clearly states, the mentacide disorder is interlocked with genocide. This essay, written as commentary, explains the nature and technique of mentacide and explores its inseperable relationship with genocide (heretofore left to the reader's own power of discernment). What will inoculate both the individual and collective Black psyche against mentacide and enable meaningful resistance to its manifestation, I will argue, is a concrete psycho-political mentality of proactive national vision. The Black psychological worker must serve as an inoculator in this regard.

INTRODUCTORY REMARKS

There are two fundamental questions that will plague the Black nation in America for the remainder of the twentieth century. The first question is: Will Black people survive genocide by White America in the 1990s and beyond the year 2000? The second question is: Who will win the battle for the collective Black mind? Are we Black people capable and willing to change our slave mentality? Do we as Black people have the collective will to fight the enemies of our National interest? The battlefield in the '90s will be (as it was in the '80s) for the collective mind. It is a war that we must win. Whoever wins the collective mind and will of Black people will ultimately determine whether the physical war against the enemies of our race will be won, or if the Blacks of America will be destroyed.

Clearly, many of our problems lie in our slave mentality. I am not blaming the victims for the origin of their problems, but the victims must bear the burden of failure to resolve their problems. Who else can be held responsible for our survival but us? It is the intention of this government and of white people in general to destroy us. It is their intention to destroy our life-support systems. Without life-support systems, life cannot survive. But is it an issue of mere survival?

We as a people want more than just to exist on a physical level, like animals. There must be a higher level of existence. What is the ultimate meaning and purpose of life? As slaves, we survived. Now we must survive with a purpose, a vision, a national direction. This purpose for which we live must be a sovereign nation with borders and land and an army to protect and secure it. But these things cannot occur without a change in our mentality.

THE MENTACIDE CONCEPT

Mentacide, according to the late, great Dr. Bobby E. Wright (1985), is the systematic, deliberate destruction of an individual's or group's collective mind with the aim of group termination. Mentacide is the silent rape of a people's collective mind by the penetration and perpetuation of alien culture, values, belief systems, or ideas for the purpose of group destruction or for political use of the victim group. Mentacide's method is to control the behavior of the victim through mind control. Mentacide systematically utilizes the institutions which project *images, values, beliefs, and opinions*.

Mentacide creates an illusion which the victim believes to be real until it's too late. Black people are given the belief that they are citizens of the United States, yet the reality is that Black people are slaves in this country. Dr. Bobby Wright (1982, 1985) defined enslavement as follows: whenever the life-sustaining resources (food, shelter, water, etc.) of one group [the Blacks] are controlled by another group [the Whites, the Arabs]. Nevertheless many Black people believe that they are actually first-class citizens in America.

EFFECTS OF MENTACIDE

Our collective mind has been raped, violated and penetrated with white perceptions and white belief systems. Our behavior cannot help but be white-inspired. What other way do we know as a people? Unless Black people change their thinking, we will be phased out of existence, like obsolete equipment. Remember, we are neither needed nor wanted by the society at large. Machines provide the labor Black people used to do. Machines and computers are cheaper and less troublesome than people, especially Blacks.

The controllers of this society have made use of psychological warfare to erode and destroy the will and mind of Black people. This is Mentacide pure and simple.

Once the victims discover the truth, we are forced to change our lives. But, the victim fears change because the victim doesn't know where that change will take him or her. Indeed, we fear the unknown. The victim seeks to deny. But, denial of this reality is problematical because the victim is reminded everyday. The victim is caught in an internal double bind, damned if they don't, damned if they do.

The effects of mentacide begin to overwhelm the victim, causing survival fatigue. As the victimizer applies continuous, constant pressure, the victim begins to slowly die inside. As the victim loses the self, depression and fear set in, causing illness, death, etc.* What has the victim done to deserve this fate of a slow, tortuous death? The victim has lost hope and has learned to be helpless.

When the victims cease to see themselves as victims, but as a nation within a nation, then the victims regain themselves. The victims must reject the society's culture and values. Only then can the victims minimize the effects of mentacide. The victims must develop a new consciousness, based on truth, to replace the negative consciousness implanted by the victimizer. The victims must seize and develop their own institutions in order to reinforce and encourage their belief system and behavior. The key is that the victims must create a new generation of minds which have been brought into the new consciousness, to the point that it becomes a part of them. The "slave mentality," however,is a major impediment.

"SLAVE MENTALITY": A MEANINGFUL, USEFUL COLLOQUIALISM

The Black slave in America views the world through his master's eyes, which is why our belief system is not "ours," but rather that of the slave master. How a race perceives the world will determine what that race will think and believe about the world, which will determine what that race will *do* about the world. One of our greatest problems is this slave mentality that is made up of learned perceptions, learned belief systems, learned behaviors taught to us over 400 years of slavery. This mentality is an American-made product designed with the intention of controlling the Black slave. The African psychology literature uses the conceptual terms mentacide (defined earlier) and psychological misorientation (operating with a non-African belief system) to describe and explain this prevalent psychological state (see Azibo 1989;

Baldwin 1984). However, employing the colloquial "slave mentality" term when discussing mentacide-induced misorientations is appealing because it grounds the technical terms and the reader in the true reality of the Black condition: enslaved, slave mentality being prevalent.

Being free begins with our mentality, for there is no way we can become an independent people with our present slave mentality. Six factors were involved in creating this slave mentality (Harding 1981):

(1) The establishment of strict discipline over the captive African community in America; the development of "unconditional submission";

(2) The development within black people of a sense of personal inferiority, especially in relation to their African ancestry;

(3) The development of raw fear, "to awe them with a sense of their master's enormous power" (of course, behind the power of the master stood the power of the local and national governments);

(4) The establishment within the enslaved person of a sense that the master's welfare was really synonymous with his own;

(5) The creation of a willingness within the Afro-American captives to accept the slaveholders' standards of conduct as their own; and

(6) The development within the captive people of "a habit of perfect dependence" upon those who claimed to be their masters.

If we are to be free, then we must change this state of mind. We must reject everything in White Law Society because only through this rejection can the mind rebuild itself with new thoughts. This also gives time for the new thoughts to take root. These new thoughts must come out of the development of a collective race consciousness which is based in skin color *first*. That is, being Black is the first requisite standard for our collective race consciousness.

At first glance, the criterion of skin color might seem trivial. Actually, it is paramount. Bobby Wright stated the matter plainly:

> We are in a race war. We are the only people who don't know it [that we are in the midst of race war with whites]. And, *we are the only people who don't know what race we are*. (original emphases, Wright 1982)

(History supports Wright's observation of a continuing race war [Williams 1976]). Indeed, mentacide is effectively undermining Blacks' racial awareness, which is defined as "the knowledge of the visible differences between racial categories by which one classifies people into these divisions and, once such knowledge is cognitively achieved, the acceptance of it" (Azibo 1984:10). Without racial awareness Blacks cannot contemplate the social theory articulated by Marcus Garvey: *Race First* (Martin 1976).

The second standard upon which this collective race consciousness is built is that of laws and interests. Until a race knows its laws and interests, it can never become a force in the world. We must become Black Law conscious, for Black Law consciousness today means movement toward independence, sovereignity tomorrow. *Common interest + Common Laws = Common Destiny*. To be authentic, Blacks' interests and Blacks' laws have to be based on a sense of African-centered history and culture that is concretely applied to contemporary circumstances. The common destiny for Blacks resulting from this would reinforce Blacks' collective race consciousness. In turn, this would be enabling for a Black Law Society that is neither a reflection of nor solely a reaction against White Law Society to take root. There would be no room for the development or continuation of slave mentality. However, the perpetration of genocide on Blacks must be derailed and ultimately stopped if an effective Black Law Society is to be realized and sustained.

GENOCIDE?

Since through the efficacy of mentacide our collective race consciousness is underdeveloped, White Law Society has effectively maneuvered the Blacks of America into a genocide-prone position. Despite all of the available statistics on life chances and quality of life in the United States indicating that Blacks exist on the precipice of extirpation, many Blacks refuse to admit or believe it. However, it must be understood that it is normal behavior for the victim to disbelieve, since nowhere in the victim's "collective view" can it be imagined why any group would seek to destroy them. This is the mentality of the victims. Consider the following quotation from *Destruction of European Jews*:

> People do not easily accept the fact that they are going to be killed; if they have the know-how to resist, they will defend themselves as best they can. If, on the other hand, they have unlearned the art of resistance, they will repress their knowledge of the true situation and will attempt to go on as though life could not change. The Jews could not resist. In complying with German orders they therefore tried, to the utmost of their ability, to ignore all evidence of danger and to forget all intimation of death. They pretended that nothing unusual was happening to them, and that belief became so crucial that they did anything to perpetuate it.*

To overcome this denial we must first realize the reasons why America must destroy 30 million members of our race: Black people in America are no longer needed by industry. Black people are obsolete as a labor force. With the advent of automation, Black people have become expendable. Wilhelm's (1975) work is important on this point. For a time, the post-industrial white man was still dependent on human labor to run his machines. Now machines themselves have liberated him from that dependence. Machines run machines, making Black workers obsolete. This is the new social outlook of America. Thus, Wilhelm further elaborates,

> The black race is caught in a cross-fire of technological change. He is in the transition period. Once the solution to the white problem, today he is the white problem. Why? Because 1) machines produce more efficiently than people (less time and more work done), 2) it costs less to operate a machine in the long run, 3) machines create a greater profit, and 4) there is no longer a need for blacks because of the ultimate technological advances.

American wealth is limited and the economy is not growing as in previous years. Whites and Blacks must compete for the same resources. It becomes an issue of survival of the fittest. Americans will attempt to destroy the Black race rather than allow our people to acquire any resources because it is a White Law Society view that "a job for a black means one less for whites." White Law Society is in pursuit of its own interests.

Professor Andrew Hacker (1970) has stated the situation plainly:

> Those who preoccupy themselves with the immorality and irresponsibility found in slum society would do well to turn their attention to the new generations of youngsters being spawned in our ghettos this very moment. These infants will be adolescents 15 years hence and potential criminals, terrorists, and unemployed a decade thereafter. Having come into the world unwanted by their parents and unneeded by society, they stand only the slightest chance of knowing love or encouragement or even recognition of their humanity. In the process of creation right now are rioters and rapists, murderers and marauders, who will despoil society's landscape before this century has run its course. The time has come for some unwelcome candor; to admit that white America does not want to deploy its resources toward redeeming the black citizenry, [because] any meaningful amelioration of black America's condition would require money and effort, personnel and priorities—indeed, moral and emotional commitments—that the white society simply will not muster.

Hacker continued:

> White America's responses . . . will adhere to less costly alternatives. . . . Indeed, the white majority has already committed itself to a course whose effect, if not intention, will be to frustrate the most pressing of black aspirations. White wealth, white votes, plus the sheer preponderance of white numbers will be used to preserve the style of life white Americans have won for themselves in recent decades. The white population has nothing to gain and everything to lose by any significant alteration of the lines now separating the races.

The forthrightness of Hacker and Wilhelm may be disturbing and chilling to some, but nonetheless is simultaneously refreshing. The resolute anti-Blackness found in the Federal Violence Initiative (see Association of Black Psychologists 1995) and the placing of violence in the Black community as a public health issue (Walters 1994) is consistent with Hacker's and Wilhelm's arguments.

Role of the victim in genocide.

Blacks must understand that the white American nation will destroy us if we allow them to. How else can the process of genocide work except by the victim's decision to either consciously or unconsciously default on life. No matter what the grand strategies or well-laid plans, it is the victim who, in the final analysis, will determine the success or failure of the process of death. It is an interaction between the Black victim and the white victimizer: the victimizer being only as strong as the victim is weak, the victimizer being only as clever as the victim is stupid, the victimizer being capable of deceiving only as the victim is willing to be deceived.

The victim has the power to halt the process of destruction. That power is called *resistance*. The victim must not be deceived by the victimizer's projection of being all powerful and invincible. It is in the interest of the destroyers to continue the theme of the all powerful. Would it not be foolish to project otherwise?

We must resist White Law Society for clear and purposeful reasons, such as land with borders and a Black Law Government based on a sense of African-centered history and culture. It is for the sake of these things that we must resist; any other purposes would be foolish. We must acquire a national strategy to resist genocide. Elements of that strategy must be awareness, preparedness (physically, mentally, and spiritually), and a knowledge of who and what our enemies are. We must perceive that our victory is possible. We must believe our victory is probable. We must work to bring our victory into reality. We must begin each day remembering that what we do in our lives will decide how close or how far away victory for national independence will be.

National Vision

A mentality of proactive national vision must undergird our drive toward national independence. What is our national vision? Do we as a race have a National Vision? Are we just locked into the here and now? Where do we see ourselves by the year 2000? As used here, "vision" means being able to see mentally, in vivid clarity, what others dare not see, or are blinded to. Vision allows a people to see new possibilities, while others see only the impossibilities.

Vision is the balance between reality and dreams. Dreams are imaginations never carried out, ideas never materialized. The dream mentality is cheap and requires no price because it remains in the dreamer's mind. "Reality" as used here is simply what is now. Reality demands only to be lived for the moment. Each mentality carries with it its own behavior.

The slave mentality discussed earlier lives for the moment, seeing reality now, never daring to look beyond to a possible world of its own creation. The slave mentality never imagines the possibility of that ever happening. This mind set sees the reality of White Law Society as being absolute, unchangeable, and overwhelming. This mentality views reality as rigid. This mind set is not receptive to new possibilities nor can it perceive a notion of independence, borders, or a national Black Law Government. This mentality is limited, not just in thought, but also in direction. It tries the same old solutions that, frankly, have never worked for our people. This mind is locked into dead-end roads that are devoid of any creativity. This so-called realist cannot see beyond his nose. He fails to understand that reality can be made, changed, and brought into existence.

Then, there is the mentality of the dreamer who wishes, hopes, and prays that reality will go away, never giving of their time and energy in order to make the reality change into their dreams. The dreamer has "spaced" on reality and lives in a universe of fantasy. The dreamer is too pure to touch the contaminated tools of reality, to make his dreams a reality. This mentality has lost its balance and flexibility. The dreamers hope unreal hopes, pray for salvation, failing to understand that they are their own salvation.

Finally, there is the visionary who dares to look into the unknown, who dares to imagine the creation of a new Black world. It is imperative that the visionary embrace and actualize an African-centered cultural and historical frame of reference lest s/he engage in misguided action. This visionary uses reality as a tool to carve a universe of his own image. The visionary uses reality to ensure that his vision will exist. This visionary uses reality to create reality. This is dangerous to our enemies because the visionary ceases to see himself as a slave. Her/his mentality is one of balance and has no "hang-ups" implanted through mentacide. S/he is free mentally to think and grow to the highest level of his/her potential. Technically speaking, the visionary as described here reflects the Black personality states of correct orientation (Azibo 1989) and African self-consciousness (Baldwin 1984).

The visionary's task.

The greatest test of a visionary is whether or not s/he has the ability to sell that vision to the race. The masses of our race, through this vision, can acquire a higher level of consciousness. The masses of our people must believe in the vision, share it, and support it. The dedicated of the race must struggle to implement it. The races' thinkers, planners, and formulators must figure out how to bring the vision into existence.

The Blacks of America need a national vision which will become our national direction. We need a "Mantle of Heaven." All nations have a vision for tomorrow—a new world, a new life, a destiny. Dr. Chancellor Williams (1976) provided the race with a mighty foundation and blueprint from which to achieve our national vision and national direction. That our race has not effectively moved toward proactive national vision and direction reflects more the formidable grip that mentacide has on the psyche of Blacks, sustaining the slave mentality, than the inability to formulate the vision. Clearly, then, the Black psychological worker must run the gauntlet thrown down by our enemy and work to overcome mentacide so that our national vision can be realized. As Chancellor Williams (1976:329) documented, "The Black World [is] at the Crossroads": our current course leads to death by genocide; the successful course requires national vision.

Notes

* Olomenji is on to something here. The concept "survival fatigue" is related to depression, but more than that concept. Using the Azibo Nosology (see: D. A. Azibo "African-centered theses on mental health and a nosology of Black/African personality disorders," Journal of Black Psychology 15, 2 [1989]:173-214; See also: D. A. Azibo, Liberation Psychology, Africa World Press [in press]), it is clear that survival fatigue is a reactionary disorder. It is a similar condition to

and may indeed be related to psychological burnout, another reactionary disorder that affects Africans who consciously fight Black oppression, as a predisposing condition.

REFERENCES

Association of Black Psychologists. A holistic view of American violence: A position paper on the Federal Violence Initiative. *PsychDiscourse* 26, 3 (1995):8-13.

Azibo, D. A. Position paper: Racial images in the media *PsychDiscourse*, 19, 4 (1984):9-12.

Azibo, D. A. African-centered theses on mental health and a nosology of Black/African personality disorder. *Journal of Black Psychology*, 15 (2), 173-214.

Baldwin, J. 1984. African self-consciousness and the mental health of African-Americans. *Journal of Black Studies* 15, 2 (1989):177-194.

Hacker, A. *The end of the American era*. New York: Antheneum, 1970.

Harding, V. *There is a river*. New York: Harcourt, Brace, Jovanovich, 1981.

Martin, T. *Race first*. Dover, MA: The Majority Press, 1976.

Walters, R. The public health model of violence reduction: The back end of the paradigm. *BPA Quarterly*, 21, 1 (1994):10-12.

Wilhelm, S. *Who needs the Negro?* Cambridge, MA: Schenkman Publishing Co, 1975.

Williams, C. *The destruction of Black civilization*. Chicago: Third World Press, 1976.

Wright, B. *Dr. Bobby Wright: The man and his mission*. Videotape, The Atlanta Chapter of the National Association of Black Psychologists, 1982.

Wright, B. *The psychopathic racial personality and other essays*. Chicago: Third World Press, 1985.

CHAPTER 6

NTU Psychotherapy: Principles and Processes

Frederick B. Phillips

INTRODUCTION

NTU is a root word from the Bantu tribe of Central Africa. It refers to the cosmic universal force that is manifested in all life and things. NTU is the basic element which unifies the universe and, as such, it is the *essence* of life and living. NTU is the force in which Being and beings coalesce, and, insofar as human beings are concerned, NTU is both immanent and transcendent. In the context of NTU psychotherapy, NTU refers to the natural healing force, the force that is oriented toward harmony, balance, and health.

NTU psychotherapy emphasizes the spiritual-intuitive process over the rational-scientific, though NTU aims to integrate both systems within the person. The goal of NTU therapy is to assist people and systems to become authentic and balanced within a shared energy and essence that is in alignment with natural order. Natural order implies a unity of mind, body, and spirit throughout life. It also implies that the relationships within and between life are purposeful and orderly and, at base, spiritual. Natural order implies that our lives and our relationships have a purpose and a direction, and, consequently, it is our ongoing life task to be in tune with natural order. Further, good mental health springs from being in tune (in harmony) with natural order; healing is therefore a "natural" process.

NTU psychotherapy is based on core principles of ancient African and Afrocentric world view, nurtured through African American culture, and augmented by Western conceptualizations of humanistic psychology. Some of the core principles of NTU psychotherapy are harmony, balance, interconnectedness, cultural awareness, affective epistemology, and authenticity.

CORE PRINCIPLES OF NTU PSYCHOTHERAPY

HARMONY

NTU psychotherapy is spiritually based. That is, it maintains a vibrant belief that there is a spiritual force to all of life and that the spiritual dimension is the connective link to the mental and physical spheres of human kind. The NTU core belief in the ubiquity of spirituality is extremely important since spirituality provides a value system, a focus, and a direction to human endeavor. And, through NTU psychotherapy, spirituality provides a base assumption as well as a therapeutic direction and purpose.

The overriding focus of life from a NTU therapeutic perspective—indeed, the goal of the mentally healthy person—is to be in harmony with the forces of life. When we are in harmony with our minds, bodies, and spirits, we are experiencing confluence or the act of aligning ourselves from within (immanent) and from without (transcendent). When we are confluent, we are experiencing a oneness with life and are "in tune with life." When we are harmonious we are "at peace," whether or not the external forces surrounding us are fragmented, because being in harmony depends more on our abilities to adapt through a clear process of organizing the disparate parts into a meaningful whole. When in harmony, we are NTU.

BALANCE

The concept of balance is strongly related to harmony in that balance and harmony are different sides of the same concept. The base meaning of "balance" is that all life is a dynamic process of energy fields and forces and that our life task is to balance these seemingly competitive forces in a manner that brings about a unified whole. Life is not dichotomous at base yet may often appear to be in its manifestations (for example, the socialized dichotomy between males and females). Rather, life from an Afrocentric world view is diunital: phenomena are a union of opposites, and our task is to unify our various internal and external forces.

INTERCONNECTEDNESS

NTU is cosmic universal force, the essence of life and things which never occurs apart from its manifestations. Further, it is only modern rationalizing thought which attempts to separate or abstract NTU from its manifestation. NTU is the connecting link among all phenomena. It is that which binds all of the universe. NTU psychotherapy emphasizes the interconnectedness of human beings from within and from without. That is, there is a spiritual network that binds all of life, and it is this NTU that is the bridge on which successful therapeutic intervention is accomplished.

CULTURAL AWARENESS

Maintaining a balanced and authentic awareness of one's cultural self is an important principle of NTU psychotherapy. To be aware and accepting of one's cultural self is a psychological imperative. It is a given that the key psychological question "Who Am I?" contributes fundamentally to one's definition of self. Similarly, the connection to one's cultural self is likewise fundamental to one's full and healthy awareness of self.

The structure of an appropriate cultural awareness has been addressed by a growing number of Black psychologists. It has, for instance, been developed as the African self-consciousness by Joseph Baldwin (1981, 1984, and 1985) and as psychological Blackness by Daudi Azibo (1983, 1988, 1990, and in press). Even though these and other psychologists have descriptions which differ slightly, the core principle is clear—that an Afrocentric paradigm conceives of healthy Black behavior as being in harmony with the authentic needs and social priorities of the African community, i.e., towards affirmation, enhancement, survival, positive development, and fulfillment of its potential as a community (Baldwin 1984). Joseph Baldwin has cogently argued that normal (healthy) Black behavior is neither negatively energized nor is it merely reactive to negative and adversative environments. Normal (healthy) Black behavior, to the contrary, is positively energized under normal conditions and proactive in its thrust toward the affirmation and enhancement of African American life (Baldwin 1981, 1984, 1985).

The preceeding description of healthy cultural self-awareness can be extended to measure the relative healthy balance of cultural self that individuals within other ethnic groups might attain. A key to this human principle is that the person must be authentic and in harmony with the natural order in order to establish his cultural self properly. The relationship of an authentic and balanced cultural identity to good mental health is a universal principle.

AFFECTIVE EPISTEMOLOGY

"Epistemology" relates to the nature and basis of knowledge while the term "affective" speaks to the quality of one's feeling or emotional being. Affective epistemology, then, refers to the process and belief system of a people discovering knowledge and truth (i.e., awareness) through feeling or emotion. This feeling orientation to knowledge is highly representative of African peoples and is recently experiencing a reawakening among many progressive Western thinkers and health professionals (Davies 1983; Capra 1983).

What, however, is the meaning of an affective epistemology for NTU? Simply stated, it is that people, certainly African people, come to awareness of and process reality through both feeling experience and verbal, cognitive interaction. NTU psychotherapy, therefore, is both spiritually-intuitive as well as rational-scientific and aims to help a person integrate both aspects of the self. The feeling experience integrates knowledge and brings information into reality. Therapeutically, we are able to achieve access to awareness, belief, and truth through the feeling component of the person and not just through "talking." We are directed to have the client become an active participant in the therapy process, and, therefore, NTU therapy is an active, participatory therapy.

Authenticity

Within the Afrocentric world view, the highest value lies in the interpersonal relationships between people. Prioritizing the value of the relationship places a premium on the authenticity of the person. The relationships that we build within the larger family/community of people are accorded prominence. It is our connectedness with the essence (NTU) of others that brings fulfillment. The authenticity of any particular person is colloquially referred to as his or her "Realness." That is, as a community we ask that a person "Be For Real," and it is this authentic essence that becomes the basis for effective and satisfying relationships. It is similarly true in the NTU therapeutic encounter that the degree of realness that is experienced influences the direction and depth of psychological movement.

Authenticity is both a state and a process. That is, while we may be able to acknowledge its presence in ourselves and in others and thereby take a mental snapshot of it, the quality of authenticity is always shifting and growing. A mentally healthy person is continuously gaining in his or her authenticity as he or she becomes more closely connected to his or her spiritual self. We must nurture this quality whether we express it in ourselves or experience it in others because the very process of nurturing authenticity is itself an authentic act.

Being authentic implies spontaneity. A mentally healthy person/system is more able to respond and interact with the environment in a natural, effortless manner. There is less emphasis on thinking as such and more priority on responding holistically. Being spontaneous facilitates more trust in ourselves and in our connection to others. Because we are in harmony, then our intentions are trustworthy, and we can feel freer to respond naturally to our ongoing, ever-changing environment. When we are spontaneous, authentic, and harmonious, then our natural healing and problem-solving mechanisms are functioning properly. We are NTU.

GOAL OF NTU PSYCHOTHERAPY

The goals of NTU psychotherapy are twofold. The first is to assist the client to function harmoniously and authentically within himself or herself and in his or her relationships within the context of natural order. The second major goal is for the client to function within the guidelines of *Nguzo Saba*, the seven principles of *Kwanzaa*.

In regards to the first goal, when a person-system is functioning harmoniously and authentically then it is felt that the natural healing forces are functioning properly. Not only can the person-system resolve the present psychological difficulty, but s/he also has a system in place for effective resolution of future issues. Harmony implies that a person or family is aware of itself and its contact boundaries with others. To be fully aware a person must be in contact with himself or herself mentally, physically, culturally, and spiritually as well as be confluent in his or her interaction with the world. To have clear crisp contact with oneself and one's environment demands an open, receptive stance towards the world where one's psychological defense mechanisms are utilized appropriately.

When we are harmonious, we have appropriate respect for ourselves and others. We are in tune with our own needs as well as sensitive to the needs of others. We are able to feel the continuity of and interconnectedness with the relationships between ourselves and others. We are, therefore, able to realize our interdependence with all of life while being cognizant of our individuality. Having made this realization we then must follow through by providing satisfactory nourishment to ourselves as well as our relationships. We grow, in part, through the process of sharing ourselves with others. A person or system that is authentic is trustworthy and reliable because they are being their true self mentally, physically, and spiritually. They are genuine because they are in tune with themselves and others. They are, in others words, to be believed.

The second major goal of NTU psychotherapy is to assist a client or client system to live within the *Nguzo Saba* or seven principles as developed by Dr. Maulana Karenga (1977). The *Nguzo Saba*, which are viewed as guidelines for healthy living, are:

Umoja (unity)—To strive for and maintain unity in the family, community, and nation.

Kujichagulia (self determination)—To define ourselves, create for ourselves,and speak for ourselves.

Ujima (collective work and responsibility)—To build and maintain our community together and to make our brothers' and sisters' problems our problems and to solve them together.

Ujamaa (cooperative economics)—To build and maintain economic enterprises and to profit together from them.

Nia (purpose)—To make as our collective vocation the building and developing of our community and to be in harmony with our spiritual purpose.

Kuumba (creativity)—To do always as much as we can, in the way that we can, in order to leave our community more beautiful than we inherited it.

Imani (faith)—To believe with all our hearts in our parents, our teachers, our leaders, and our people.

The principles of *Nguzo Saba* and, indeed, NTU psychotherapy itself are universal. That is, they are equally applicable to Africans throughout the diaspora since the concepts are based on a spiritual connection that human beings have with the life force. The values that *Nguzo Saba* espouses are human survival values that speak to the healthy promulgation of the human race. NTU psychotherapy is *culturally sensitive*, and the specific techniques are appropriately modified given the uniqueness of the person, his or her family and cultural background, and the overall therapeutic needs of the client.

ROLE OF THE THERAPIST

NTU psychotherapy places a premium on the relationship between the therapist and client for two important reasons. First, psychotherapy is a spiritual and sacred relationship; and second, the strong people-to-people orientation is primary to the Afrocentric value system. NTU psychotherapy recognizes that there is a spiritual dimension which is the basis of the therapeutic encounter. Further, NTU psychotherapy appreciates that the healing process is a natural process for mental health as it is for physical health. For example, when there is a small cut of the finger, the body marshals resources in order to close and eventually heal the wound. This is true only if one encourages the healing and does not interfere with this natural process. An example of such interference would be allowing the wound to become infected. Similarly with mental health, the ego may become bruised, and a natural healing emerges if one does not interfere or complicate his or her emotional matters with ineffective communication or low self-esteem.

The therapist's task is to assist the client to align himself or herself in an authentic and harmonious manner so that the natural healing force (NTU) can operate. The therapist appreciates that healing is natural. It is *through* the therapist, rather than being *caused* by the therapist, that healing occurs. This distinction is extremely important in that it relates to the proper use of therapeutic techniques. The NTU therapist realizes that he or she is in the service of a spiritual healing force and that he or she exists within a sacred relationship with the client. The fact that the therapist relationship is a sacred relationship and that the therapist must view it as such has many therapeutic and social implications. For instance, the sacredness of the relationship gives definition and answers to the question of confidentiality in therapy. When we as therapists are functioning with sacredness in mind, our clients can feel protected because we communicate that we have their best interests at heart.

PROCESS OF NTU PSYCHOTHERAPY

There is a general process to NTU psychotherapy which guides the therapist through the therapeutic journey by providing him a therapeutic road map. The phases of NTU therapy are (1) Harmony, (2) Awareness, (3) Alignment, (4) Actualization, and (5) Synthesis. These phases of psychotherapy must be considered within the context of circular—not strictly linear—time, so that the therapist perceives that all five phases can be occurring at one time or that, for example, the phases can occur "out of sequence." A technique can be utilized in one phase that has equivalent meaning for the client in another phase. The therapist when thinking circularly, not sequentially, understands that therapy is never out of any one phase altogether, rather that each phase has dominant needs which generally constitute the primary focus of the therapeutic moment. In other words, the phases are interconnected and continuous and form a complete gestalt. When we attempt to dissect and discuss them separately, the phases lose some of their identity and meaning. Although they will be discussed separately, the reader is advised to see them as holistic principles that occur interconnectedly.

HARMONY

Harmony relates to the initial phase of therapy in which the primary, though not exclusive, objective is to develop a shared consciousness or shared trust experience with the client. Through the development of a shared consciousness, a bond or therapeutic bridge is created upon which the mutual trust of client and therapist can rest. Harmonizing includes the process of mutual sharing of information by both the client and therapist. It is a joining by the therapist to the client and is a necessary first step.

AWARENESS

The second general phase of therapy encompasses the tasks of awareness. Awareness includes two related aspects. One is cognitive recognition whereby the client begins to recognize the presence and outline of destructive, unhealthy behaviors and patterns. The second is affective awareness wherein the client comes increasingly into contact with his or her own needs, wants, strengths, weaknesses, and emotions. The client begins to know who he or she is at successively deeper levels of meaning and to feel increasingly comfortable with himself or herself. Almost paradoxically, he or she can become clearer about himself or herself only while striving to reach his or her potential. Consider the familiar examples from the world of athletics in which a soccer player tests his limits by extending himself to catch a pass or a gymnast extends herself through increasingly intricate horizontal bar maneuvers. In both instances, the athlete has come to know his or her limitations through the process of striving for optimal functioning. They both come to learn more of themselves.

A basic task of this phase of NTU therapy is to help the client to uncover his or her base neurotic fear or anxiety. The client's or family's base fear or anxiety usually surfaces during the process of self-awareness. As the client becomes aware, he or she will often need strong therapist support as well as other environmental support. Typically base fears are usually stated in terms of "I'm afraid I'll go crazy" or "I might die (emotionally)" or some other catastrophic fear. The continuing objective of this phase is to assist the client with his or her boundaries, potential, and fears.

ALIGNMENT

The third phase of the therapy process is alignment. It is during this phase that the client or family must successfully overcome the fears, avoidances, etc., that have become clearer through the previous phase of awareness. This is commonly referred to as "working through" the issues of therapy. In Gestalt therapy this process is known as moving though the impasse. Although there are different references, the key element is consistent—awareness and information must be integrated in order to achieve psychological growth.

During the alignment phase, the client confronts his or her fear(s) in order to achieve the outcome of assimilation and reconciliation of these psychological anxieties into a maturing, confident, and harmonious self. The client feels more at peace whenever there is a successful completion of this phase. The client has integrated his alienated self into a harmonious whole, and his fears become appropriate to the stimulus. He becomes more self-assured and spontaneous which allows him to *respond* to his environment rather than *react* to it. The act or process of alignment implies taking responsibility psychologically for oneself and one's needs and actions. One cannot be fully aligned until acceptance and responsibility are connected with awareness of the total self.

Alignment can be accomplished in a number of ways, but the amount of emotion involved is usually in proportion to the amount of psychological energy that the person/family system is using to sustain its present maladaptive attitude and behavior. That is, there is often a release of anger, sadness, joy or other intense emotion as this immobilizing fear is confronted. The extent to which this anxiety is deeply rooted in the client personality is a major determinant of the level of emotional energy that will be released.

The phase of alignment is integrative since the objective of the phase is not necessarily to expel a fear but rather to come to terms with it. The process of coming to terms, i.e., of assimilating, may include confrontation, but the latter is the means and not the end. The goal of reconciliation, as has been stated, is to develop confidence by coming to terms with the actual or potential anxiety.

ACTUALIZATION

The fourth general phase of NTU therapy can be termed actualization since it is at this point that the client can begin to practice and experiment with new attitudes and behaviors in the context of his regular environment. The client takes his budding awareness into real or actual situations where he experiences himself differently even though his external environment may not have changed. What has changed, however, is the client's perception of himself and his environment, and, through his changing responses to and interaction with his environment, the client influences the behavior and attitudes within his environment.

The process of actualization can be as simple as a homework assignment for an adolescent or a vocational or other life change for an adult. The magnitude of the actualization may vary, but the internal psychological process is similar: the clients or family are able to witness their changing response to stress from the inside out and to receive validation and empowerment from the actual fact of being different in a small but noticeable manner.

SYNTHESIS

The last general phase of therapy can be called the synthesis phase. Herein, the client integrates his knowledge gleaned through the process of awareness/realization together with his experience from having put into operation in real life some of his changing attitudes and behaviors. This integration occurs simultaneously on physical, mental, and spiritual dimensions whenever the synthesizing phase is proceeding well. Effective integration is realized when the client has incorporated the problem process into his or her life so that, beyond the presenting or current difficulty, the client has an effective human problem-solving strategy which is readily available to him or her when presented with future life difficulties.

Table 1. NTU Psychotherapy: Phases and Techniques

Phase	Definition	Manifestation	Outcomes	Techniques
Harmony	A developing coherence or compatibility between therapist and client system such that the therapist is experienced as a positive extension of the client system.	Shared essence,belonging, nurturance, love, interdependence, developing trust, relaxation.	Shared consciousness, therapist "joins" with client system, "therapeutic bridge".	Being real/authenticity, self-disclosure, use of rituals, acceptance of where client is, therapist composure and relaxation, accentuation of the positive in all components of the client system.
Awareness	Having or showing realization, perception, or knowledge of self and of self in relation to others. Cognitive awarenes of issues allows a sensitivity to the "facts" and the definable aspects of a situation and makes available a process for definining or knowing reality. Affective awareness of issues allows a sensitivity to the subjective aspects or feelings generated by a sittuation or experience.	Differentiation between thoughts and feelings; process vs. content focused, clarification of discrepancy between realtity and expectation, acknowledgement, ownership of and respect for feelings. Developing feeling of NTU energy.	Identification and expression of thoughts and feelings. Clarification of significant factors which influence functioning.	Reframing, relabeling, visualization techniques, use of "I" statements, talking directly, awareness wheel, feedback of thoughts and feelings, present centered, empty chair, self-awareness.

Alignment	The synergism of being and of beings, material and psychic forces toward a central point of existence. The adjustment or arrangement of people and/or things in relation to each other so that healing force (NTU) becomes operative.	The sharing of feelings and experiences, introspection, role clarification, corrective recapitulation, catharsis, interconnectedness, restoration, and revitalization. The experience of NTU, appropriate responsibility for self and for system.	Restructured client system, reinforcement of and emphasis on indigenous strengths. New energy available to client system.	Peeling the onion, exploration of worst fear, owning projections,confronting fear, accepting responsibility, sharing self, taking risks.
Actualization	The materialization of potential. Utilization of new attitudes and behavior in a system's life space.	Identification of goals, tasks, roles, behaviors, processes and resources.	Increased confidence and problem solving abilities.	Practice new behavior, record new behavior, establish task/objectives, homework assignment.
Synthesis	The balancing, integration, and appropriate use of all functional resources available to the system including spiritual, psychic, and material. The delineation and availability of a problem-solving process indigenous to the client system.	Realistic expectations and goal setting, personalization of the problem-solving process, system stability and flexibility, proactive involvement and investment in systemic well-being.	Need fulfillment, empowerment, reciprocal nurturing, authentic and supportive relationship, a unified , resilient, and self-correcting system. The absorption of the NTU force throughout the system.	Q. How have you responded differently to life situations? Q. What do others say about you? Q. How do you resolve stressful situations? Q. What is your process for psychological problem-solving?

The five phases of NTU therapy (harmony, awareness, alignment, actualization, and synthesis) must be seen as a circular process. All five phases can occur during any one session, and the process even becomes a convenient guideline for therapy session review. Were all "bases" touched during the session? Was there a beginning, middle, and end? What synthesis occurred since the last session? What actual experiences did the client have? Or, for that matter, what synthesis did the therapist have that related to the client's process?

The phases of NTU psychotherapy have as their ultimate objective the empowerment of the client system in alignment with natural order. The client should leave the therapy process in control of himself, including the ability to express appropriate requests for termination. The client should be more keenly aware of self and others, engage life in a more authentic manner, and incorporate effective tools for clear identification, analysis, and resolution of future life difficulties.

SUMMARY

NTU psychotherapy is based on core principles of ancient African and Afrocentric worldview, nurtured through African American culture, and augmented by Western conceptualizations of humanistic psychology. NTU psychotherapy is both holistic and spiritually based and aims to assist people and systems to become authentic and balanced within a shared energy and essence that is in alignment with natural order. Further, NTU therapy utilizes the principles of *Nguzo Saba* as guidelines for harmonious living.

Basic principles of NTU therapy include: harmony, balance, interconnectedness, awareness, affective epistemology, and authenticity. The role of the NTU therapist is based on a spiritual relationship with the client, since NTU therapy recognizes that the healing process is a natural process in which the therapist assists the client to rediscover natural alignment. The five phases of NTU psychotherapy discussed under the heading of therapeutic process are harmony, awareness, alignment, actualization, and synthesis. Table 1 presents the five phases, the techniques, manifestations, and outcomes associated with each.

References

Azibo, D. A. Some psychological concomitants and consequences of the Black personality: Mental health implications. *Journal of Non-White Concerns* 11, 2 (1983):59-65.

Azibo, D. A. Personality, clinical, and social psychological research on Blacks: Appropriate and inappropriate research frameworks. *Western Journal of Black Studies* 12, 4 (1988):220-33.

Azibo, D. A. Advances in Black/African personality theory. *Imhotep: An Afrocentric Review* 2, 1 (1990):22-47.

Azibo, D. A. *Liberation psychology: An introduction to the African personality construct.* Trenton, N. J.: Africa World Press, in press.

Baldwin, J. Notes on an Africentric theory of Black personality. *Western Journal of Black Studies* 5 (1981):172-79.

Baldwin, J. African self-consciousness and the mental health of African Americans. *Journal of Black Studies* 15, 2 (1984):177-194.

Baldwin, J. Psychological aspects of European cosmology in American society. *Western Journal of Black Studies* 9, 4 (1985):216-23.

Capra, F. *God and the new physics.* New York: Surana and Schuster,

Davies, P. *The Tao of physics.* New York: Bantam Books, 1983.

Karenga, M. Kwanzaa: *Origin, concepts, practice.* Los Angeles: Kawaida Publications, 1977.

CHAPTER 7

Melanin, The Melanin Hypothesis, and the Development And Assessment Of African Infants

Neferkare Abena Stewart

The purpose of this chapter is to elucidate the role of melanin, a biochemical polycyclic polymer, in African infant development. Necessarily, the role of melanin in the human organism must be clarified. The popular contention that melanin is mainly a waste or insignificant product is contraindicated here by the melanin hypothesis. At its most general formulation, the melanin hypothesis argues that melanin is *fundamental* in the *functioning* of the human organism, both physiologically and psychologically. The chapter is arranged as follows: (a) information about melanin is provided so that the reader can understand its nature and exactly what it is; (b) literature on melanin and the central nervous system is reviewed; (c) the melanin hypothesis for infant development is articulated; and (d) infant development literature highlighting the implications for the melanin hypothesis is reviewed.

MELANIN: WHAT IT IS

A detailed description of the different pathways of production, transportation, structure, and the many physiological and psychological influences of melanin is far beyond the scope of this paper. A brief introduction to melanin, however, is necessary. For further and detailed information on the subject, the reader is referred to Kambon (1992, ch. 3), King (1979), Lerner (1955), Stewart (In press), and Wasserman (1974).

Melanin is a pigment which ranges in color from pale yellow to reddish brown to almost black. It is also in almost every major organ of the body. One of its many purposes is to shield and protect body tissues against radiation damage (Daniels 1959; Isenberg 1964). Dr. Phillip McGee explained that:

> Melanin is synthesized and dispersed by specialized cells which are called *melanocytes*. Melanocytes synthesize melanin through a series of biochemical reactions beginning with the consumption of the amino acid phenylaline. Each subsequent biochemical reaction in the chain is controlled by a specific enzyme. If all the essential enzymes are present, the pigment melanin is produced in considerable quantity. When this occurs, an individual has skin which is dark in color, hair which is black, and eyes which are brown. If any of the enzymes are relatively inactive, the individual manifests a pale skin color, hair which is light or blonde, and eyes which are blue. This occurrence defines a state of depigmentation—the genetic inability to produce sufficient amounts of melanin. It is worth noting, however, that all human organisms produce some degree of melanin. Variation occurs with regard to the specific level of melanin activity which takes place within the cytoplasm of the melanocyte. (McGee 1976, 218)

As mentioned by McGee, melanin can be synthesized through a series of biochemical reactions beginning with the consumption of the amino acid phenylaline. There are twenty different amino acids which are linked together to make up proteins. Phenylaline is one of those vital amino acids. When proteins from foods are eaten they are metabolized through a series of biochemical reactions. Specific enzymes are sometimes needed as catalysts in these biochemical changes. When biochemical pathways are not blocked, the phenylaline hydroxydose acts as a catalyst for this change. Tyrosinase is a copper-containing enzyme which catalyzes oxidation of tyrosine to dihydroxyinylanime (Dopa) and then to dopa quinone. The next set of metabolic changes are nenenymicilly formed and probably spontaneous: dopa quinone catalyzes oxidation of Leuko compound to Hoolachione (red) to 5, 6 Dehydroxyindole—2 carboxylic acid and then to melanin. It should be noted that this is only one metabolic pathway used to form melanin.

There is conclusive evidence that the enzyme tyrosinase and the precursor tyrosine are responsible for melanin formation in melanocytes. However, there is no conclusive evidence that melanin is only produced and transported by melanocytes. That is, melanin also has been found to be produced by mast cells; although the overall importance of melanin production in mast cells is still uncertain (Okum 1967). Further, it has been found that neuromelanin is produced without the aid of melanocytes (Dirchon, Fitzpatrick, and Seiji 1968). Neuromelanin is present throughout the central nervous system. Existing data suggest that neuromelanin is a true melanin although the cellular mechanisms for its formation are unknown at this time. Vander Wende and Spaerlein (1963) have asserted that neuromelanin may be formed from dopamine, adrenalin, serotonin, and thytamine.

MELANIN AND THE CENTRAL NERVOUS SYSTEM

Both melanocytes and nerve cells are embryologically derived (Langman 1969; Moore 1974). That is, they both develop in the neural crest of the developing human fetus.

> The fertilized egg divided rapidly, forming first a ball of cells called a morula; later this mass of cells develops a cavity and is termed a blastula. . . . With time three classes of cells can be distinguished in the embryonic germ dis of

> the blastula: the ectoderm or outside layer; the endoderm or inside lining; and the mesoderm, the cells between these surface layers. (Copenhagen, Bunge, and Bunge 1975, 68)

These three distinct layers are referred to as the germ layers of the developing embryo. The ectoderm, or the outermost layer, contains a collection of black pigments and is crucial to the development of the nervous system (Langman 1969; Moore 1974). That is, from the ectoderm layer develops the epidermis and epidermal tissues (nails, hair, glands of the skin), the brain and spinal cord (central nervous system), and the external sense organs (ears, eyes, etc.) (Copenhagen, Bunge, and Bunge 1975; Langman 1969; Moore 1974). The importance of the central nervous system and major sense organs developing from a group of pigmentated cells will become clear in later sections of this paper where I discuss melanin's influence on the development and functioning of the central nervous system.

The central nervous system (CNS) controls the sensory, neuromuscular, and hormonal organs in the body. Thus, damage to the CNS can impair the nervous activity essential to human sensitivity, movement, and consciousness. Melanin plays an information processing role which is essential for proper neurological and metabolic functioning (McGee 1976).

Melanin and the Eye

The retina is considered an active part of the central nervous system. It aids in the organization, interpretation, and transmission of light energy to the brain. Since melanin surrounds the retina of the eye, absorption and reflection of light energy is dependent on greater or lesser amounts of pigmentation. That is, how much and what kind of light energy is taken in through the eye is dependent on melanin levels. Melanin acts as a protective shield as it surrounds the retina of the eye. It can be found behind the retina making the pupil appear black. It can also be found in the iris layers. Eye color varies when greater or lesser degrees of melanin are present in the iris layers.

The eye serves two major functions: reception of light and vision. The metabolic rhythms and other important bodily functions are synchronized and directly influenced by light. The presence of light energy is crucial to the proper functioning and/or survival of plants, animals, and humans. The eye as a photoreceptor is most effective in providing such services. Although light sensitivity is an asset, it has been pointed out that too much sensitivity reduces the revolving power of vision in the eye, bringing us to the second function of the eye, vision.

Iris pigmentation and vision are related. Pigmentation of the eye retards the level of light sensitivity while it facilitates visual acuity. Melanin acts as a light shield which protects the area surrounding the pupil from an overabundance of light rays. An overabundance of light rays would reduce visual acuity if protection were not available. Ample evidence has been presented to support the fact that visual acuity is greater in people with hyperpigmentated eyes than for those with hypopigmentated eyes. Karpinas (1960) conducted a study which investigated visual acuity in a million American soldiers. The results indicated that 82% of the African American soldiers had 20/20 uncorrected vision as compared to 69% of the European American soldiers. Bassin and Skerlj (1937) did a study in Europe. They investigated eye defects and eye-color. In a group of more than a thousand children, they found that light-eyed children had more visual defects than dark-eyed children.

An environmental adaptation theory might explain the phenomenon of the high incidence of dark-eyed people. Consider the following:

> Most human beings around the world have dark eyes. Among northern Europeans and their descendants, however, light eyes are in the majority. The highest percentage of light eyes is found around the Baltic Sea. That area is characterized by frequency of heavy cloud cover. This aspect of the environment may have been an important factor in permitting the light-eye mutation to survive. Light eyes in humans have evolved together with lightly pigmented hair and skin. The three traits are correlated positively with each other but the correlations are far from perfect. (King 1979: 33)

As has been stated, the majority of the world's population has dark eyes and exhibits greater visual acuity when compared with light-eyed people. This finding coincides with the fact that the majority of the world's population are people of color who possess larger quantities of melanin compared to the noncolored or the minority population of the world.

Melanin's contribution to the physiological and psychological dimensions of sensorimotor development is exemplified when the importance of visual stimulation and movement are considered. Barrage (1976) pointed out that much of what is learned and experienced by the sighted infant is through visual stimulation. She asserted further that "sensori-motor development (may) proceed with greater rapidity when the reciprocal action between vision and movement is optimal" (25). Keeping this in mind, Blasley's study of visual acuity in African American and European American neonates is most interesting.

Blasley (1933) investigated the development of various oculomotor processes during the first few hours of life. Blasley was also interested in whether there were any significant individual differences exhibited during this early period. Tests of visual pursuit (which measures the infant's visual acuity and ability to coordinate muscles enabling the infant to visually pursue moving objects) were administered to 109 European American and 142 African American neonates. The neonates ranged in age from two and a half hours to twelve days old. Blasley noted that:

> From 1,111 tests in the Negro group, there were 213 instances (19% compared with 29% for the Whites) in which *no* pursuit was elicited, and 898 instances (81%, compared with 61% for the Whites) in which some type of pursuit was elicited. For all subjects at all age levels for all kinds of pursuit, then, the Negro infants excelled the Whites.
>
> The Negro infants exhibited a greater percentage of pursuit responses on the first day (Negro, 77%; White, 60%); both racial groups showed marked functional improvement as indicated by the increased percentage of Type A pursuit throughout the three age levels; the Negroes not only began at a higher level of excellence, but also showed a more rapid improvement as indicated by

> greater increases in the percentage of Type A pursuit (Negroes: 26%, 48%, 53%; Whites: 21%, 28%, 39%). These data favor the conclusion that functional development is more advanced in the Negroes at birth than in the Whites at least with respect to the responses under consideration. (Blasley 1933, 111, 119)

Melanin and Childhood Autism

A relationship between levels or states of melanin pigmentation and childhood autism was suggested by Happy and Collins (1972). These authors conducted an experiment which employed both psychological and neurological hypotheses. The psychological hypothesis stated that autistic children were at the extreme introverted end of the behavioral continuum. The neurological hypothesis stated that introversion was limited to the ascending reticular activating system (ARAS) with special regard to its dopamine and neuromelanin content as well as to the color of the skin, hair, and eyes through the implications of melanin.

> The biophysical evidence implicating melanin in a protective capacity in nerve cells (Mason et al., 1960) and the differential incidence of schizophrenia in hyperpigmented and hypopigmented patients (Moffson, 1954) could be taken to indicate that melanin has a function other than mere pigmentation (Wasserman, 1968). Furthermore, since there is evidence that the ARAS uses noradrenaline as a transmitter substance (Grossman, 1967) and that trosine is a precursor of both noradrenaline and melanin, it could be argued that a link exists between melanin, pigmentation and a postulated defect in the noradrenergic pathways in the ARAS. (Happy and Collins 1972, 1484)

Thus, it was expected that the autistic group of children would have an overrepresentation of blue-eyed children (blue eyes representing a lack of melanin deposits) and an underrepresentation of brown-eyed children in comparison to the normal population. Happy and Collins concluded that blue-eyed children would have less neuromelanin pigmentation in their ARAS and thus less neural protection provided by the melanin substance. These children would also be more introverted than their brown-eyed counterparts and, therefore, be more prone to autism.

Melanin depositions in the irises were found to be the most reliable index of the presence of melanin levels throughout the nervous system. An eleven-point scale was used, ranging from light blue (relative lack of melanin) to dark brown (heavy deposits of melanin pigmentation). Subjects with light, medium, and dark blue eyes were classified as hypopigmented, and subjects with light, medium, and dark brown eyes were considered as hyperpigmented. The experimental group consisted of thirty-five autistic children. The criterion for autism was as follows: referral to the children's admission center in New South Wales and an independent diagnostic agreement (according to the World Health Organization classification) by two psychiatrists. Sixty-nine normal Australian-born Caucasian children acted as the control group and were drawn from the medium and upper range of the socioeconomic strata.

The results indicated a statistically significant difference between the proportions of hypopigmentated and hyperpigmentated autistic and normal children. An expected overrepresentation of hypopigmentated and autistic children was found when compared with the normal or control group. The findings suggested that, in some cases of autism, the children may be suffering from a particular metabolic error which is reflective of their possible lack of an adequate supply of neuromelanin throughout the central nervous system as detected by iris pigmentation.

Melanin and Diseases of the Central Nervous System

A further relationship between melanin and the central nervous system can be seen in the hereditary diseases known as Phenylketonuria (PKU) and Parkinson's. PKU is a hereditary disease which is caused by the absence or defect in performance of the enzyme phenylalanine hydroxylase. This enzyme is needed to catalyze the amino acid phenylalanine to tyrosine which is one of the raw materials necessary to produce melanin. PKU is regarded as an inborn defect of metabolism. When phenylalanine metabolism is not possible, its presence increases in the blood. When the blood phenylalanine increases due to the body's inability to metabolize it over a long period of time, mental retardation and other bodily changes occur.

The intellectual impairment accompanying PKU becomes more marked with age and usually leads to severe or profound retardation (Menalascins and Egger 1978). Since the production of tyrosine is negatively affected in children with PKU, they generally have light hair, skin, and eyes and may suffer from retinal disorders. A secondary feature, which often results from the brain damage, is seizures. An estimated one out of every fifty persons of Caucasian stock is a carrier for PKU (Menalascins and Egger 1978). PKU is more common among noncolored populations (McGee 1976; Wasserman 1965).

Parkinson's disease (a hereditary disease of the central nervous system) is associated with the lack or the loss of melanin pigmentation by the cells of the Substantia Nigra. Like PKU, Parkinson's disease is largely confined to the noncolored population (Cosnett 1964; Cotzio, et al., 1964; McGee 1976; Reff, Black, and Lipschitz 1958; Van Wieringen and Wright 1972; Wasserman 1974). The rare occurrence of this CNS disease among African people suggests that they may have a more highly pigmentated Substantia Nigra area. This is particularly noteworthy since Parkinson's disease is almost always a result of destruction or depigmentation of the Substantia Nigra area and is largely confined to the noncolored populations.

Substantia Nigra is located in the midbrain near the cerebellum and forms part of the cerebral peduncles near the red nucleus. Lesions to the Substantia Nigra create a complex motor syndrome commonly seen in persons with Parkinson's disease. McGee stated that:

> Research has suggested the Substantia Nigra has a critical relationship with the reticular formation in the sense that it provides "starter" impulses which facilitate phasic muscular contractions. The muscular contractions are important for postural adjustment and the rapid and exact movement of specific muscle groups. (McGee 1976:219)

Parkinson's disease is characterized by rigidity of the musculature in either widespread or isolated areas of the body and the loss of involuntary and associated movements. The gamma-activating system used for exciting the muscle spindles becomes completely, or almost completely, inactive in persons with Parkinson's disease.

This happens because the Substantia Nigra is one of the major areas of the brain stem controlling such behaviors. The voluntary motor control system must be used to overcome stiffness of the musculature. Thus, a person with Parkinson's disease has a masklike face showing almost no automatic, emotional facial expressions (Beeson and McDermott 1971).

Reff, Black, and Lipschitz (1958) investigated 1,384 Bantu neurological cases at Baragwanathn Hospital, South Africa. In these 1,384 patients only seven cases of Parkinsonism were observed. Cosnett (1964) investigated the incidence of neurological disorders in Edendale Hospital (South Africa) where special services were provided to African and Asiatic populations. Approximately 90% of the patients were Zulu-speaking Bantu. Cosnett reported on 1,302 patients with neurological disorders, hospitalized between March 1959 and November 1962. Those disorders, listed as "unusually rare," included debilitating disorders of all types, including multiple sclerosis, primary tumors, cerebellar disturbances, and Parkinsonism. It was also noted that Wilson's and Huntington's Chorea did not occur. Wilson's disease is a genetic disorder of the CNS characterized by degeneration of the brain stem and liver structure. Huntington's Chorea is also a genetic disorder of the CNS which is characterized by a degeneration of the brain tissue.

McGee (1976) and Cress-Welsing (1974) have both concluded that *melanin refines the central nervous system which produces a highly sensitive sensory-motor network.* This conclusion has also been drawn by Happy and Collins (1972), Andrews (1974), Hearne (1975), and others. One could then conclude that persons possessing larger quantities of melanin may also possess a more sensitive or finely tuned sensory-motor network. This notion becomes even more viable when information on congenital malformation of the CNS is considered.

Congenital Malformations of the Central Nervous System

Anencephaly and spina bifida are the most common of the gross developmental defects of the CNS (Center for Disease Control 1975; Ford 1966; Menalascins and Egger 1978). A child born with anencephaly is characterized by the absence of the forebrain, midbrain, and major portions of the skull. A child born with spina bifida has a defect in neural tube development or spinal column defects. Several studies have noted distinct racial differences in the incidence of birth defects related to CNS abnormalities (Altemus and Ferguson 1965; Center for Disease Control 1975; Chung and Mysianthopoulous 1967; Erickson 1976; Ivy 1962; Lalovel, Jackson, and Morton 1979; Leck 1969; Murphy 1937; Penrose 1975; Simpkiss and Lowe 1961).

Murphy (1973) investigated the influence and importance of heredity and environmental conditions on the production of congenital defects. During his investigation, he found that European Americans in Philadelphia, Pennsylvania, between 1 January 1929 and 31 December 1933 produced twice as many congenital defects per 1,000 births as their African American counterparts. In an international survey of the incidence of anencephaly, Penrose (1975) noted that the incidence of anencephaly was greater in European populations than in Asian or African populations.

In an effort to investigate the incidence of congenital abnormalities in African people, Simpkiss and Lowe (1961) examined 2,068 African neonates between December 1956 and September 1957 at Mulago Hospital in Kampala, Uganda. There were 141 stillborn neonates and 101 of these were examined for cause of death; only two had a CNS defect (hydroencephaly). The authors also found that 112 of the 2,068 babies born had some type of congenital abnormality. They observed striking racial differences between African and European populations with regard to the incidence of major CNS abnormalities. There were very few severe abnormalities of the CNS found among the African population. Specifically, there were no cases of spina bifida or anencephaly found among the African population. It was also noted that the two cases of hydroencephaly found among the stillborn infants were not in any way related to spina bifida.

Chung and Myrianthopoulous (1967) conducted a comparative study of the incidence of birth defects in African American and European American children. Their data were based on information collected from fourteen institutions throughout the United States. The study included a total number of 35,680 malformed births (including both live births and fetal deaths). Included in these births, 1,549 were abortions, stillborn, and neonatal deaths. Central nervous system abnormalities such as spina bifida, encephalocele, and anencephaly were among those malformations found. The author combined meningomyelocele, meningocele (both forms of spina bifida), and encephalocele (inflammation of the brain substance) for analysis, owing to the small number of cases. There were no racial differences found in the pooled incidence of these particular CNS malformations, although it was noted that the small number of cases made conclusions difficult. Anencephaly was found three times as frequently among European American births when compared with births of African Americans (14.0 and 4.1 cases per 10,000 births). The authors concluded that European American infants were at a higher risk than African American infants to be born with anencephaly.

Leck (1969) conducted a study of the incidence of a selected group of congenital malformations among offspring of the main immigrant groups in Birmingham, London (West Indians, Pakistanis, and Irish), and the British-born population. Between 1960 and 1965, data regarding malformations, ethnic origins of both parents, and social class of the father or persons caring for the child were collected. Information was gathered from the records of the Birmingham Health Department and the Department of Social Medicine at Birmingham University. Of the 133,539 children born (including stillbirths) 1,201 had defects of the type focused on in the study. Leck found that offspring of the West Indian immigrants were distinctively different from the European population with respect to the incidence of neural tube defects.

> The most conclusive finding in these tables is that the children of West Indian immigrants to Birmingham are quite unlike the offspring of Europeans there in respect of the incidence of malformations, but they do not differ significantly from Negro populations elsewhere. The most striking aspect of the contrast between the two groups in Birmingham were the much lower figures for neural and oral defects in the West Indians. (169)

In children of European, Indian, or Pakistani parentage,

> anencephalus, spina bifida, and clefts of the lips and palate were much more common than in those of West Indian origin, among whom incidence was approximately the same as in published series of American and African Negroes. The children of migrants from Ireland and from India and Pakistan differed significantly from populations previously studied in their countries of origin and resembled more closely the rest of the Birmingham population in respect to the incidence of neural tube defects. (172)

He concluded that the variations in the incidence observed among European populations may be environmentally influenced, although he asserted that the marked contrast between children of European and African descent was "probably due mainly to genetic differences" (Leck 1969, 172).

After analysis of the 1964-1975 statistics on the common major congenital defects of the central nervous system (anencephaly and spina bifida), the Centers for Disease Control, in Atlanta, Georgia, reported the following results:

> The common major congenital defects of the central nervous system, anencephaly and spina bifida (ASB), are particularly interesting to epidemiologists for they exhibit features which are taken to be indicative of environmental causes. Marked differences in the incidence of these defects occur in different parts of the world; the highest rates are in Great Britain and Ireland, where as many as 1% of births may be affected. ASB incidence is characterized by rather substantial racial differences, as evidenced by our findings in Metropolitan Atlanta where the rate for whites has been about 2.4 per 1,000 births while that for blacks has been about 0.8. (Centers for Disease Control 1975:1)

It is this author's contention that the rarity of major central nervous system diseases (Parkinson's and PKU) and congenital defects (anencephaly and spina bifida) in African and African American people, when compared with European and European American populations, is strongly suggestive of a genetic explanation. I also contend that the genetic explanation may be related to levels of melanin present throughout the central nervous system.

The relationship between melanin, CNS diseases, and birth defects becomes more apparent when one considers the developmental origin of the CNS alone with one of melanin's important functions. It was previously mentioned that the CNS develops from the ectoderm layer of the developing embryo which contains the black pigment melanin. It was also noted that melanin functions in a protective capacity in all the major organs of the body. It was further revealed that melanin protects and refines the CNS, creating a finely tuned sensorimotor network. It is this author's contention that, since the CNS develops in the midst of this protective, refining substance (melanin), it follows logically that individuals or groups processing larger quantities of the substance would not be at high risk for CNS birth defects and diseases. Research in this area suggests support for this premise. It follows as well that sensorimotor development should be enhanced for individuals or groups that process larger quantities of melanin.

Melanin and Sensorimotor Development

Stewart (1980) also used iris pigmentation as an indicator of the level of neuromelanin present throughout the central nervous system. She conducted a pilot study which investigated the possible sociocultural and biological influences of early and advanced forms of sensorimotor development during infancy. The investigator was particularly interested in scores obtained on the Bayley Scales of Infant Development as they related to levels of neuromelanin (as measured by iris pigmentation present through the central nervous system), parents' formal education level, race, and sex.

Twelve African American (five males, seven females) and sixteen European American (nine males, seven females) infants with a mean age of eleven months were included in the study. The parents' educational status ranged from twelth grade only to one year or more of college. Infants were given the Bayley Scales of Infant Development at their respective day care facilities. Iris pigmentation was rated on a scale ranging from light blue (relatively small amount of melanin deposits) to black (heavy deposits of melanin). Infants scoring 1, 2, 3, or 4 on the iris pigmentation rating scale (1 = light blue and 4 = hazel/green) were classified as hypopigmented; while infants scoring 5, 6, or 7 on the iris pigmentation rating scale

(5 = light brown and 7 = black) were classified as hyperpigmented.

Analysis of the data revealed a significant relationship between levels of melanin (as measured by iris pigmentation) and performance on the Bayley Mental and Psychomotor Scales ($p=0.01$ and $p=0.002$, respectively). Hyperpigmented infants exhibited significantly better performance on the Bayley Mental and Psychomotor Scales when compared with the hypopigmentated infants. African American infants exhibited significantly better performance on both the mental and psychomotor scales ($p = 0.04$ and $p = 0.0004$, respectively) when compared with the European American sample. The data also revealed that hyperpigmentated European American infants performed significantly better on the Bayley Mental and Psychomotor Scales ($p = 0.01$ and $p = 0.001$, respectively) when compared with hypopigmentated European American infants. No significant relationship was found between children's sex or parents' formal educational status and sensorimotor development. Since the majority of the parent group had at least one year of college (ten Black parents and ten white parents), no real conclusion could be drawn regarding the relationship of parents' educational status and sensorimotor development. There was no significant sex difference which confirmed the Bayley (1965) report.

Results from this study led the investigator to assert that levels of melanin present throughout the central nervous system may partially explain the reported developmental differences of African and African American children when compared to European and European American infants. This notion was further reinforced when the comparative analysis of European American infants was considered. Hyperpigmentated European American infants exhibited significantly better performance on the Bayley Mental and Psychomotor Scales when compared with hypopigmentated European American infants. Thus, greater quantities of melanin as measured by iris pigmentation may be related to sensorimotor development among European American infants as well as African American infants.

SUMMARY

To summarize thus far, research has found that during their first two years of life, African and African American neonates exhibit sensorimotor development in advance of their European and European American counterparts. Findings have been suggestive of greater cognitive, neurological, and sensory maturation at birth. In addition, infants of color around the world have also been found to exhibit advanced forms of sensorimotor development when compared to their non-colored counterparts (European and European American). It has also been noted throughout the literature that African, African American, and other infants of color around the world do not generally experience the same type of nutritional and medical advantages as European and European American infants.

Cultural child-rearing practices have been viewed by the majority of researchers as the primary explanation for the developmental style exhibited by African and African American infants. Werner (1972) observed that infants of color around the world exhibit advanced psychomotor development relative to that observed in European and European American infants. She found that:

> In spite of a great deal of cultural and geographical diversity, all of the infants from pre-industrial communities shared certain common experiences during the first year: membership in an extended family system with many caretakers; breast feeding on demand, day and night; constant tactile stimulation by the body of the adult caretaker who carried the infant on her back or side, and slept with him; participation in all adult activities, with frequent sensorimotor stimulation. (130)

Nobles' (1977) study of the child-rearing practices of African American families noted that the family structure and belief system continues to be influenced by an African-oriented world view. Thus, similarities in cultural child-rearing practices of infants exhibiting advanced forms of development suggest that such practices may have a hand in influencing a particular style of development.

Freedman (1974) favored the genetic explanation for African infants' advanced development at birth. An interaction between child-rearing practices and genetic endowment has also been suggested as a possible hypothesis for developmental differences.

Brazelton, Koslowski, and Tronick (1971), for example, noted that the child-rearing practices embodied in the African culture create a highly energetic and stimulating environment which is in some way tuned in to the child's natural genetic ability.

The research evidences lead this author to favor the interaction hypothesis. The fact that African and African American infants have demonstrated a developmental style which is in advance of their European and European American counterparts *at birth* makes it impossible to ignore the influence of genetic endowment. This advanced development has been reported from birth to two years of age. The fact that other infants of color around the world also have been reported to exhibit a developmental style which is in advance of their noncolored counterparts led Stewart (1980) to further hypothesize that melanin and its influence on the development and quality of functioning held by the central nervous system may be the genetic factor influencing these apparent developmental differences.

The Melanin Hypothesis: Infant Development

Because of the profound role of melanin in the central nervous system and the associated implications for psychological and physiological functioning, as we have just seen, it follows that melanin hypotheses may be deducible in many areas of human functioning. For example, human consciousness (King 1978, 1982), African (Black) personality (Azibo [in press]; Azibo 1983; Baldwin 1981), European (white) personality (Welsing 1974), and athletic performance (Clegg 1980) are just a few diverse subjects where melanin hypotheses are prominent. Regarding infant development, Stewart (1980) hypothesized that different levels of melanin possessed by the central nervous system may be related to a genetic factor that contributes to early and advanced forms of sensorimotor development. This genetic factor may operate over and above or in addition to environmental and cultural factors.

Sensorimotor Development of African Children

There is a significant body of evidence indicating early and advanced forms of sensorimotor development among African children in the United States and in those residing on the continent of Africa (Ainsworth 1967; Bayley 1965; Brazelton, Koslowski, and Tronick 1971; Curti, Marshall, and Steggard 1935; Cump and Horton 1961; Evans 1970; Geber and Dean 1957, 1958; Goldsberg 1972; Grantham-McGregor and Beck 1973; Hayes and Percy 1975; Hindley 1960; Kilbride and Kilbride 1975; King and Seegmiller 1973; Knobloch and Pasamanick 1953; Leiderman et al. 1973; Lusk and Lewis 1972; Morgan 1976; North and McDonald 1977; Scott et al. 1955; Stedman 1953; Stewart 1980; Super 1973; Vincent and Hugo 1962; Walters 1967; Werner 1972, 1979). Surprisingly, the fact that African children exhibit advanced forms of sensorimotor development and intelligence and the possible biological, cultural, and educational implications of such development has been given little or no attention in the "scientific" community. It is interesting to note, however, that when Jensen (1969) hypothesized the genetic inferiority of the African race, his hypotheses were given much attention. The more liberal social scientists disagreed with Jensen's genetic-based explanation for the inferiority of African children. It was their belief that African children exhibited inferior cognitive abilities due to environmental influences. It should be noted that, although the two groups, conservative and liberal, disagreed as to why African children are inferior, they both agreed with the underlying assumption that these children are indeed defective. As Hilliard (1977) pointed out, investigators who have written about the genetically based intellectual deficits African American children are said to have, almost to the person, failed to deal with the data which indicate early and advanced forms of sensorimotor intelligence exhibited by these children when compared to European or European American children. Morgan (1976) stated that:

> Knowledge of early and advanced sensori-motor development among Black neonates has been with us for sometime. The notion has never generated a level of concern strong enough to withstand the onslaught of disbelievers or the backlash of those who believe that the reverse is true. (3)

Continental African Children

Geber (1958) was one of the first researchers to discover the differentiated development between European and African infants. While investigating the psychological changes that accompany kwashiorkor disease in Uganda, she observed that most of the healthy children under observation were precocious in the development. She also observed that the younger the child, the greater the precocity.

Geber proceeded to conduct a study comparing the growth and development of African infants with standards for the development of children. The Gesell was used with children over one month of age and the Andre Thomas technique was used to assess the development of neonates (infants under six weeks of age).

> The results of the test showed an all-round advance of development over European standards which was greater the younger the child. . . . Although most of the African children had never seen anything resembling the test material, they used it in the same way as European children and succeeded in the tests earlier than those children.
>
> The development was not entirely homogeneous in all the sections of the tests. Up to the fifth month, the motor precocity was remarkable, especially in regard to posture. Between the fifth and seventh months, adaptivity, language and person-social relations came to equal the motor development: the level was that of European children two or three months older. (Geber 1958:186)

Geber's (1958) findings were sharply criticized by Warren (1972). His major criticisms were based on the inadequacy of the measurement instruments used. Geber used the Gessell scales which Warren notes were standardized on a very small and nonrepresentative sample. He also felt that the neonatal assessment scale used in her study had been designed to diagnose pathologies of the central nervous system and may or may not have had adequately measured differences within the normal range of development.

Although the results obtained by Geber (1958) may have been affected by the instrumentation used in her study, similar findings have been reported when very good infant assessment instruments, such as the Brazelton Neonatal Behavioral Assessment Scale and the Bayley Scales of Infant Development, were used.

Brazelton, Koslowski, and Tronick (1971) compared sensorimotor development of infants born to urban Zambian mothers with that of infants born to an equal number of European American mothers. The Brazelton Neonatal Behavioral Assessment Scale was used as the instrument of evaluation. The Zambian mothers were described as having had multiple pregnancies, low protein diets, and related infections. As a result, their newborn infants were lower in weight and length than the European American babies and generally not as healthy. Despite their physical and environmental circumstances, within a short time (approximately ten days) the Zambian infants surpassed the white infants in cuddliness, reactivity to stimulation, alertness, social interest, and consolability. These researchers also noted that the Zambian mothers created an active and energetic environment for their infants. They provided what was described as a high contact, loving environment which it was suggested facilitated the rapid recovery of the infants. The European American mothers, in contrast to the Zambian mothers, handled their children less and used different feeding practices.

Goldsberg (1972) also conducted a study using a population of Zambian mothers and their infants. The major focus of this study was to observe the mother-infant relationship and the way in which this relationship structures the infant's world. Goldsberg noted the following:

> At the six month's visit, all but five subjects were capable of performing at the most advanced levels in the prehension scale while the remainder completed the scale by the nine month visit. At six months, performance on the object and space scales was slightly in advance of the American validation sample (Corman and Escolona 1969). While at 9 and 12 months, their performance was less *advanced.* We found more advanced performance on the space scale at every age level (6 months, p 0.02; 9 months, p 0.04; 12 months, p 0.001). (184)

Lusk and Lewis (1972) reported results that also confirmed African infant precocity. They focused on caretaker-infant interaction within the first year of life. A sample of ten Senegalese families was studied. It was noted that infant scores on the mental scale were representative of infants one and a half months older than their own age. On the psychomotor scale, infants scored on the average two months in advance of their ages. They also stated that, while infants exhibited precocious development in comparison to American infants on both the mental and psychomotor scales, there was no relationship between scores on the Bayley and any of the mother-infant interaction measures. Such a relationship had been inferred by other studies in their effort to explain as nongenetic the precocious development of African infants.

Leiderman et al. (1973) compared the Kikuyu (Kenya) infants performance on individual test items of the Bayley Mental and Psychomotor Scales against the United States norms. They noted that if Kikuyu infants were scored by United States standards, results would indicate performance superior to the expectations in the United States. Kikuyu infants scored significantly ($p<0.01$) better on both the mental and psychomotor scales than would be expected in a United States group. They were superior on thirty-eight of the mental test items and twenty of the psychomotor items. Their performance fell behind the sample from the United States on seven items on the mental test and two items on the psychomotor scale. The author found no apparent pattern in the type of items which differentiated the two groups, although it was noted that the items on which the Kikuyu infants lagged behind the United States norms were those which involved implements which were less common in their environment than in the United States.

The results led Leiderman et al. to conclude the following:

> A definitive explanation of why sub-Saharan African infants have precocious mental and motor development during the first year of life and why their test performance is apparently influenced by the economic level of their families and other social factors, cannot yet be given. . . .
>
> In agreement with others we recognize that the genetic factors account for a large proportion of the variability of mental and motor test performance in the infant's first year.

> The remaining variance, however, is not random but can be associated with identifiable social and demographic variable predictive of precocious psychological development. (294)

Freedman tested a group of Hausa neonates in northern Nigeria with the Cambridge Neonatal Examination between days one and ten of their hospital stay. Significant psychomotor precocity was reported. It was specifically noted that:

> The African infants were simply precocious in exhibiting fully integrated musculature at so early an age. For example, one Nigerian (Hausa) infant of 45 minutes of age had full head control in the pull to sit, exhibited a straight back with no Kyphasis, and was able to hold a sitting position and look around the chamber while held by his hand. Another, 24 hours old, exhibited the Wolfe-Landau responses, a full extension of the head and feet while rocking on the belly, a response not usually seen in Caucasians before the second or third month. (Freedman 1974, 167)

Freedman favored a genetic explanation for the developmental difference found between African and Caucasian neonates, primarily because the African neonates demonstrated the precocious forms of neuromuscular and sensory development even before they had any contact with their mothers (forty-five minutes to twenty-four hours old). He also acknowledged that, as a result of the apparent touchiness of a genetically based explanation of African infant precocity, logical discussion has suffered.

A 1956 study by Ainsworth (cited in Freedman 1974) was among the first to report psychomotor precocity *at birth* in an African sample, although she explained the continued precocity of these infants as a product of child-rearing practices. Freedman (1974) asserted that at no time did Ainsworth seriously consider genetic influences as a possible and logical explanation for precocity exhibited at birth. Similarly, he noted that Geber and Dean's (1957) study was also among the first to report precocity at birth in Ghanaian infants; and she too chose to emphasize child-rearing practices and nurturance as the primary explanation for African infants' precocious developmental style. Geber and Dean (1958) also emphasized, but presented no data, that middle-class African infants were less precocious than infants from lower-class status, thus implying that the differences were due to child-rearing practices. Freedman asserted that the Leiderman et al. (1973) study strongly and logically suggested that the opposite is true. Leiderman et al. reported that middle-class Kikuyu infants exhibited more advanced mental and psychomotor performance as measured by the Bayley scales than lower-class Kikuyu infants. Freedman cited the studies of Ainsworth (1967), Geber (1958), and Geber and Dean (1957, 1958) as examples of researchers' avoiding observations that might lead to possible genetic interpretations or explanations of phenomena. The importance of these studies is that they set a pattern for the interpretation style of future research in this area.

Freedman suggested that racism may have also played a major role in the type of interpretation employed when evaluating data regarding African infant precocity. He used Warren's (1972) literature review on African infant precocity as an example of such influence:

> Warren (1972) in a most helpful review of infant testing in sub-Saharan Africa, found evidence for African motor precocity in 10 out of 12 studies which were adequately conducted. (Two of the others were deemed inadequate.) Despite this apparently decisive ratio, Warren chose to favor the results of the two studies which yield no differences (both were conducted in South Africa). We can only assume that these apparently illogical positions have been taken because of the taboo on genetic explanation of ethnic differences seen in recent decades and the related problems of racism. (Freedman 1974:170)

This author is in partial agreement with Freedman regarding the "apparently illogical position which has been taken because of the taboo on genetic explanation of ethnic differences," although it is this author's contention that the apparent taboo has been directional, to say the least. That is, historically Europeans and European Americans have had very few problems generating genetically based explanations regarding the physiological and psychological inferiority of people of color when their behavioral and/or cognitive styles *allegedly* differed in a negative direction from the European or European American cultural pattern. This trend has survived even in the face of public controversy (Chase 1977; Guthrie 1976; Hilliard 1976, 1977; Jensen 1969; Kamin 1974; Ladner 1973; Thomas and Sillen 1972). However, taboo does seem to exist when it comes to generating an adequate genetic hypothesis to explain African excellence. This process is somewhat harder because the reported physiological and psychological excellence of an African people, when compared to European or European Americans under any circumstance, rubs roughly against the dogma of white supremacy (Chase 1977; Clegg 1980b; Guthrie 1976; Ladner 1973; Thomas and Sillen 1972; Welsing 1974). The notion of white supremacy had been ingrained into the very fabric of society as has the innate inferiority of people of color. Thus, it is not surprising that even in the face of extensive and consistent contradiction, response from "objective scientific investigators" are inappropriate and illogical.

African American Children

Advanced forms of sensorimotor development among African infants in the United States have been found repeatedly (Bayley 1965; Cump and Horton 1961; Grantham-McGregor and Beck 1973; King and Seegmiller 1973; Morgan 1976; Knobloch and Pasamanick 1953; Scott et al. 1955; Stewart 1980, In press; Walters 1967; Werner 1972, 1979). Knobloch and Pasamanick (1953) conducted an extensive study in New Haven comparing the growth and development of African American infants with three European American comparison groups. The first group of European Americans was composed of children living in foster homes, the second group was composed of infants from higher socioeconomic homes who were examined as candidates for a special nursery school, and the third group consisted of New Haven children on whom the Yale Development Schedule (Gesell and Amotruda 1962) had been standardized. Knobloch and Pasamanick noted that the high standard of living experienced by the European American groups made it impossible to equate their environmental variables with those of the African American group. They reported the following results:

> The general conclusion which can be drawn from the data which have been presented is that this group of Negro children have maintained a normal rate of development and continues to be somewhat more advanced than the group of New Haven White children from whom the Yale Developmental Schedules are derived. While gross motor development is undeniably markedly accelerated, there has been no failure to maintain normal developmental rates in the other fields of behavior. No deterioration in development has occurred with advancing age, and no depressing environmental factors appear to be operating up to the age of two and one-half years for the group as a whole. (Knobloch and Pasamanick 1953:151)

A comprehensive study of the growth and development of African American infants was conducted by Cump and Horton (1961). They also reported significantly advanced forms of psychomotor development in their infants as measured by the Gesell test.

Walters (1967) conducted a study comparing the development of African American and European American comparison groups on the Gesell Developmental Test. She hypothesized that when influencing variables were controlled there would be no significant differences between African American and European American infants. She controlled for gestation period, birth weight, prenatal care, delivery circumstances, infant's health, and socioeconomic background of the infants used in the study. The mean scores of the African American infants were higher than those for the European American infants for all test areas of development at twelve weeks of age. For the African American and European American groups, both of which were high SES, the following was reported:

> Sixteen Negro infants and 15 White babies comprised this sample. . . . It is evident that these two groups were fairly well matched on the factors affecting development. When the groups were compared significant differences were found, in favor of the Negro infants, in total development and in personal-social behavior at 12 weeks and in motor behavior at 24 weeks (.05 level of significance). (Walters 1967, 248)

Walters concluded that the overwhelming superiority of the high

SES African American infant group indicated that social circumstances may be responsible for these results. However, this conclusion seems to overlook the fact that both groups were high SES (and well matched on this variable). It is suggested, therefore, that some factor other than educational, socioeconomic status, or factors in conjunction with those variables may be responsible for the reported sensorimotor development.

In an extensive study of the mental and motoric abilities of 1,409 babies from one to fifteen months, Nancy Bayley (1965) found sensorimotor differences to exist between African American and European American infants. Of these infants, 55% were European American, 42% were African American, and 2.3% were of other races. The ratio of boys to girls was about equal for each age group. The sample was representative of the 1960 United States census population. Using the revised form of the Bayley Scales of Infant Development (Bayley 1969), she reported no significant group differences in mental test scores. However, African American babies scored significantly higher than the European American babies on the psychomotor scales. Not one of the sixty items favored the European American infants by as much as half a month. The African American infants did better by at least 0.7 months on eleven of the items. Bayley (1965) described this phenomenon by stating that:

> Negro babies tend to be more advanced than the Whites during the first 12 months. Although there is considerable overlap among Whites and Negroes of the same age; a genetic factor may be operating. This is, Negroes may be inherently more precocious than Whites in their motor coordinations.
>
> It would appear that the advantage the Negro babies have is a pervasive one which may be in a generally heightened muscle tone. (Bayley 1965, 408)

More recently, King and Seegmiller (1973) conducted a study observing the cognitive development of first-born African American males (ages fourteen to twenty-two months). The purpose of the study was to investigate the hypothesis that African

American male infants begin to show a drop in Bayley mental and psychomotor scores below standardization groups between the ages of eighteen and twenty-two months. The mean mental scores of the longitudinal sample were significantly higher than the means of Bayley's standardized sample at fourteen months and dropped to a level "closer to" the expectations based on the normative sample of eighteen and twenty-two months. On the psychomotor scale the mean scores were reported to be significantly higher than those of the standardization sample at fourteen months. Psychomotor scores showed as many decreases as increases over an eight month period although, by the twenty-second month, the infants' psychomotor scores were closer to, but still above, those of normative population. It was concluded that the scores of African American male infants did not drop below the standardization population scores on the mental or psychomotor scales between the ages of eighteen to twenty-two months of life.

The developmental abilities of African neonates are further exemplified when the United States perinatal mortality data are examined. In the North and McDonald summary of the perinatal data collected by the National Center for Health Statistics in 1972, the following was revealed:

> Perinatal mortality data from the United States indicate that low-birth weight Afro-American neonates are more likely to survive the neonatal period than are white infants of similar birth weight. . . . Differences in gestational age do not explain the higher survival rates of small black neonates; neonatal mortality rates for black infants are lower than those of white infants at each gestational age at all birth weights less than 3,000 gm. (North and McDonald 1977:809)

North and McDonald investigated whether the differences observed by the National Center for Health Statistics were due to characteristics associated with the lower socioeconomic status of African Americans. They compared the survival of low birthweight infants born at Magee Women's Hospital in Pittsburgh, Pennsylvania, between 1971 and 1974. They utilized "care by a private attending obstetrician" as an indicator of socioeconomic status when comparing the neonatal survival of African American and European American live-birth infants. The results indicated that:

> In almost every low-birth weight category black infants were more likely to survive than white infants of comparable birth weight, regardless of socio-economic status. In neither black nor white low-birth weight infants was lower socio-economic status associated with higher survival.
>
> These data provide no support whatsoever for our hypothesis that low-birth weight in lower socio-economic groups is caused by factors which are less noxious to neonatal survival. The alternative hypothesis that black babies are genetically endowed with greater capacity to survive at low birth weight than are white babies is given further credence. (North and McDonald 1977, 809)

Summary

In summary, numerous studies have documented advanced sensorimotor development among African and African American infants. Such results have been obtained through use of less sophisticated instruments, such as the Gesell (Gesell and Amotruda 1962) and Andre Thomas' technique, as well as the newer, more comprehensive and sensitive instruments such as the revised Bayley (1969) and the Brazelton and Brazelton (1973). The majority of studies infer a possible genetic explanation coupled with cultural child-rearing practices.

Emmy Werner (1972), after an extensive review of cross-cultural studies of psychomotor development around the world, drew the following conclusions:

1. There was a distinct acceleration of psychomotor development among samples of infants reared in traditional, preindustrial communities in Africa, Asia, and Latin America, with the African samples (from Uganda, Cameroon, Congo, Nigeria, Senegal, and South Africa) showing the greatest acceleration, followed closely by Latin American infants (from Jamaica, Mexico, and Guatemala)

and samples from different parts of the Indian subcontinent (Baroda, Myore, New Delhi, Bombay).

2. The acceleration was most pronounced at birth and during the first six months of life. Neonatal observations of samples of infants in Africa (Uganda, Congo) and in Latin America (Mexico, Guatemala) indicated a precocious sensori-motor development, equalling that of European and U.S. infants 3-4 weeks old. EEG examinations of newborn African babies were suggestive of greater maturity of the central nervous system, and even "premature" babies in African and Latin America, weighing less than 2,500 g., showed adequate motor development.

3. In spite of a great deal of cultural and geographical diversity, all of the infants drawn from pre-industrial communities shared certain common experiences during the first year; membership in an extended family system with many caretakers; breastfeeding on demand, day and night; constant tactile stimulation by the body of the adult caretaker who carried the infant on her back or side, and slept with him; participation in all adult activities, with frequent sensory-motor stimulation.

Of all the *ethnic* groups studied, the Negroid samples, both in Africa and in the U.S., showed the greatest early acceleration of psychomotor development, the Caucasian samples showed the least, with the Latin American Indian and Mestizo and the Asian samples occupying an intermediary position—even if they live in the same *ecological* setting (Africans, Gujarati Indians, and Caucasians in Uganda; Negro and Caucasian in the West Indies, and Mestizo and Caucasian in Latin America; Caucasian, Negro, and Indian samples in the U.S.). (130)

There are three major similarities among these different ethnic groups that may be related to their advanced form of sensorimotor development when they are compared with European and European American infants. *One such similarity is that of environmental conditions*. Many African mothers and infants observed in and out of the United States received inadequate prenatal care, housing, and diets, etc., when compared with European and European American infants. *A second similarity is likely found in cultural child-rearing practices and family structures* as documented by Werner (1972). It should be noted that similarities in child-rearing practices and style of infant development can be viewed in the African and African American populations (e.g., Nobles 1977). Thus, similarities in cultural child-rearing practices and the style of infant development exhibited by African and African American people suggested that such practices influence a particular style of development. Finally, Stewart (1980) suggested that *the third similarity is biological in nature.* That is, advanced forms of sensorimotor development have been reported to exist among African, African American, Asian, and Latin American infants. It also has been noted that the African and African American infants showed the greatest acceleration and the European and European American infants exhibited the least. It should be noted here that African and European people are, for the most part, at different poles on the physical color continuum with Africans possessing high levels of melanin pigmentation and Europeans possessing less. According to psychiatrist Richard King (see Clegg 1980c) Africans are said to possess stages 4 and 3 melanosomes (more 4 than 3) Europeans stages 1 and 2 melanosomes and, intermediately, Asians stages 3 and 4 melanosomes (more 3 than 4). Melanin is stored and made inside the melanocyte in a capsule that is called the melanosome. Stages 1 and 2 melanosomes are empty of melanin for the most part, and, in stage 1 the machinery to make melanin is absent. In stages 3 and 4 the machinery to make melanin is present. The stage 4 melanosome is completely filled with melanin whereas the stage 3 melanosome is only half filled with melanin (Richard King in Clegg 1980c).

The extensive amount of literature reviewed here appears to support Stewart's (1980; in press) melanin hypothesis for infant development: that there is a genetic factor related to levels of melanin that contributes to early and advanced forms of sensorimotor development, in addition to or beyond cultural and environmental factors. An immediate implication of the production of evidence that supports the melanin hypothesis for infant development is that there must be a rethinking of the approach to assessment of African infants.

IMPLICATIONS FOR THE ASSESSMENT OF AFRICAN CHILDREN

This final section shall address the general approach to conceptualizing normative infant development, which is in need of reversal, and specific concerns for physiological and psychological assessment. The literature compels this investigator to reanalyze the conclusions drawn regarding the early and advanced forms of sensorimotor development found to exist among African and other infants of color when compared with their more privileged noncolored counterparts. The production of color, and thus the possession of certain levels of melanin throughout the central nervous system and the body as a whole, is the norm in terms of the world's people. The literature has shown that people of color throughout the world exhibited similar developmental styles during infancy. Therefore, the question must be asked: "Do African and other infants of color really exhibit early and advanced forms of sensorimotor development? Or, can it be said that they are exhibiting normal growth patterns when compared with the majority, and not the minority, population of the world?"

It is this author's contention that evidence supporting the latter conclusion is overwhelming. The acceptance of this conclusion implies that cross-cultural researchers (who have been, predominantly, noncolored people) have had a limited and rather egocentric frame of reference in their attempt to conceptualize relationally the developmental progress of human infants. That is, it is this author's belief that the developmental progress exhibited by African and other infants of color around the world should not be viewed in general as early or advanced but rather as normal, or the norm, for human infants as a whole. This reasoning issues from the logic that, if the majority of the world's population exhibits a particular style of sensorimotor development, it is absurd to view such developmental progress as a unique phenomenon. Unfortunately, scientists interested in human development have failed, repeatedly, to draw such conclusions and the denial or ignorance of such logical deductions is a serious oversight.

Regarding both physiological and psychological concerns, children of color have been subjected to the physiological, psychological, and cultural norms of European and European American society. Systematic child abuse has occurred because of these practices. That is, pediatricians are trained to assess growth and development, general health status, nutritional needs, and prescribe medicine based on the biochemical and maturational realities of the "normal" child. The problem here is that the standards for what is viewed as normal growth and development, biochemical makeup and neurological maturation has been based historically on European and European American children. Children of color experience a somewhat different internal reality influenced by the presence of larger quantities of melanin throughout the body's system. Thus, a highly trained pediatric assessor may misassess the health needs and developmental status of these children (Hayes and Percy 1975; Moriarty 1972; Owen and Lubin 1973; Sandler, Ratner, and Van Campen 1970; Thomas 1979b). An example of such misassessment was observed by Hayes and Percy (1975) when they investigated the suitability of the Dubowitz in assessing maturation of full-term African American infants:

> One hundred full-term black AGA infants were examined according to the method of Dubowitz and Dubowitz to determine if this method for assessing gestational age is applicable in a non-white population. Up to 38 weeks test scores were similar to those reported by Dubowitz. Beyond 38 weeks, black infants tended to score lower on some neurologic test items. Paradoxically, black infants appeared to be more advanced in items testing passive on one, causing them to score falsely low. Failure to exhibit passive tone ordinarily seen in full-term white infants is scored as tone not yet developed in the Dubowitz. This suggestion of greater neurological maturation was supported by more advanced reflex development (loss of Moro, grasp, etc.) items not scored on the Dubowitz. Some external characteristics (e.g., black infants have darker skin, less hair and fewer plantar creases) scores either lower or higher but tend to cancel each other. It is suggested that in the assessment of gestational age, the neurological exam be modified to take these findings into account and a regression curve established for black infants. (Hayes and Percy 1975, 259)

An anthropometry of African American and European American preschool children was conducted by Owen and Lubin (1973). They observed striking differences between the two groups, which they felt had direct implications for assessing the nutritional needs of African American children. They found that:

> Both on an absolute basis and when examined with socioeconomic status held constant, black preschool children in comparison with white preschool children are taller, heavier and have less subcutaneous fat. The magnitude and direction mean differences are summarized for 621 children, 271 black and 350 of comparable socioeconomic status.
>
> These findings, based on a national probability sample, suggest the need for different standards when assessing nutritional status of childhood populations. (297)

To the best of this author's knowledge, the medical profession has not adopted the recommendations offered by Owen and Lubin (1973). Because of the importance of proper nutrition and its influence on the physiological and psychological well-being of a developing child, it is imperative that the medical profession develop appropriate physiological, health, and nutritional standards that take into account the particular needs children of color experience. The quality of existence experienced by these children may be dependent on such development.

Similarly, the *psychological assessment* instruments used to evaluate the developmental status of African American and other infants of color are viewed as extremely questionable because they measure what is viewed as normal for a European population that has been found to differ developmentally from their own. It is imperative that students of pediatrics, child psychology, and other child care professions be able to conceptualize what can be viewed as normal growth patterns for African and other children of color. Such knowledge would enable us to more readily identify children at high risk for developmental problems. At present, if an African American child performs in the "normal" range of infant development on a test that has been standardized on a European

American population, this author would not be confident in suggesting that there are no developmental problems. That is, if African American children are, as a rule, more neurologically prepared at birth than their European American counterparts, then scoring in the "normal" range on a scale designed to measure the expected performance of European American infants may suggest some type of delay in the African American infant. At present, such a delay would go unnoticed and unattended until it became more serious and possibly uncorrectable. Such practices can be physiologically, psychologically, and educationally abusive.

CONCLUSION

In conclusion, this author asserts that African and other children of color around the world do not exhibit advanced forms of sensorimotor development but rather normal growth patterns when compared with the majority and not the minority populations of the world. It is also my contention that the genetic factor of melanin and its influence on the quality of functioning exhibited by the central nervous system may explain the reported developmental differences which exist between the majority and minority populations. The lack of appropriate physiological and psychological instruments of assessment and concepts has put African and other children of color at high risk for *misassessment*, which has led to medical, psychological, educational, and political abuse in this society. The quality of life experienced by these children will depend on whether this state of affairs will continue to be ignored or will be corrected. Africans must take the lead in this regard.

REFERENCES

Ainsworth, M. D. S. *Infancy in Uganda: Infant care and the growth of love*. Baltimore: Johns Hopkins University Press, 1967.

Altemus, L. and A. Ferguson. Comparative incidence of birth defects in Negro and white children. *Pediatrics* 36 (1965):56-61.

Andrews M. *PsychoBlackology*. Berkeley, Calif.: Achebe Enterprises, 1974.

Azibo, D. A. *African (Black) personality theory, status characteristics theory, and perceived belief similarity: Which is predominant in dominance/reactance behavior?* Ph.D. diss., Washington

University, St. Louis, Missouri, 1983.

Azibo, D. A. Advances in Black/African personality theory. *Imhotep: An Afrocentric Review* 2, 1 (1990):22-47.

Baldwin, J. Notes on an Africentric theory of Black personality. *Western Journal of Black Studies* 5 (1981):172-79.

Barrage, N. C. *Visual handicaps and learning: A developmental approach*. Belmont: Woodsworth Publishing, 1976.

Bassin, R. and B. Skerlj. Augenfëhler und augenfarbe (Eye defects and eye color). *Klinische Monatsblatter Augenheilkinde* 98 (1937):314-24.

Bayley, N. Comparisons of mental and motor tests scores for ages 1-15 months by sex, birth order, race, geographical location, and education of parents. *Child Development* 36 (1965):379-411.

Bayley, N. *Bayley scales of infant development: Birth to two years*. New York: Psychological Corporation, 1969.

Beeson, P. and W. McDermott. *Textbook of medicine*. Philadelphia: W. B. Saunders, 1971.

Blasley, W. C. Visual pursuit of 109 white and 142 Negro newborn infants. *Child Development* 4 (1933):106-120.

Brazelton, B. and T. Brazelton. *Neonatal Assessment Scale*. Philadelphia: J. B. Lippincott, 1973.

Brazelton, T., B. Koslowski, and E. Tronick. Neonatal behavior among urban Zambians and Americans. *Journal of Child Psychiatry* 15 (1971):97-107.

Center for Disease Control. *Congenital Malformation Surveillance Report: July 1974-June 1975*. Atlanta:CDC, 1975.

Chase, A. *The legacy of Malthus: The social costs of the new scientific racism*. New York: Alfred Knopf, 1977.

Chung, C., and N. Mysianthopoulous. Racial and prenatal factors in major congenital malformations. *American Journal of Human Genetics* 20 (1967):44-60.

Clegg, L. Why Blacks run faster. *Sepia* (July 1980a): 18-22.

Clegg, L. The world's best-kept secret: Black genetic superiority, Part II: The black child. *Sepia* (May 1980b): 16.

Clegg, L. Melanin: Key to Black genetic superiority. *Sepia* (April 1980c): 21.

Copenhagen, W., M. Bunge, and R.Bunge. *Bailey's textbook of histology*. 16th ed. Baltimore: Williams & Wilkins, 1975.

Cosnett, J. E. Neurological disorders in the Zulu. *Neurology-Minneapolis* 14 (1964):443.

Cotzio, G. O., P. S. Papavasibou, A. Sakamoto, and M. H. Van Woert. Melanogenesis and extrapyramidal diseases. *Federation Proceedings* 23 (1964):713.

Cump, M. D., and C. Horton. Growth and development in Negro

infants and children. *Lancet* 81, 12 (1961):507-17.
Curti, M., F. B. Marshall, and M. Steggerd. The Gesell schedules applied to one, two, and three year old Negro children of Jamaica. *Journal of Comparative Psychology* 20 (1935):125-126.
Daniels, F. The physiological effects of sunlight. *Journal of Investigative Dermatology* 32 (1959):147.
Dirchon, J., T. Fitzpatrick, and M. Seiji. Melanin 1968: Some definitions and problems. In *1967-68 Yearbook of Dermatology*, 1. Chicago: Yearbook Medical Publishers, Inc, 1968.
Dixon, J. V. World views and research methodology. In *African philosophy: Assumptions and paradigms for research on Black persons*, ed. L. King, V. Dixon, and W. Nobles 51-102. Los Angeles, CA.: Fanon Center Publications, 1976.
Erickson, D. Racial variations in the incidence of congenital malformations. *American Human Genetics* 39 (1976):315-20.
Evans, J. *Children of Africa: A review of psychological research*. New York: Columbia University, Teachers College Press, 1970.
Ford, F. *Diseases of the nervous system in infancy, childhood, and adolescence*, 5th ed. Springfield, Mass.: Charles C. Thomas, 1966.
Freedman, A. G. *Human infancy*. Hillsdale, N. J.: Lawrence Erlbaum Associates, 1974.
Geber, M. The psycho-motor development of African children in the first year, and the influence of maternal behavior. *Journal of Social Psychology* 47 (1958):185-95.
Geber, M., and R. Dean. Gesell tests on African children. *Pediatrics* 20 (1957):4055.
Geber, M., and R. Dean. Psychomotor development in African children: The effects of social class and the need for improved tests. *Bulletin of the World Health Organization* 18 (1958):471-76.
Gesell, M., and C. S. Amotruda. *Developmental diagnosis*. New York: Paul B. Holber, 1962.
Goldsberg, S. Infant care and growth in urban Zambia. *Human Development* 15 (1972):17-89.
Grantham-McGregor, S., and E. Beck. Gross motor development in Jamaican infants. *Developmental Medicine and Child Neurology* 13 (1973):21-25.
Guthrie, R. V. *Even the rat was white*. New York: Harper and Row, 1976.
Happy, R., and J. K. Collins. Melanin in the ascending reticular activating system and its possible relationship to autism. *Medical Journal of Australia* 2 (1972):1484-86.
Hayes, A. and A. Percy. Suitability of the Dubowitz in assessing matu-

ration of full-term Black infants. *Pediatrics* 9, 4 (1975):259.

Hearne, A. Review of the dyskinesia-schizophrenia-melanin triad. Paper presented at the Conference of the Bay Area Association of Black Psychologists at Hyatt House, San Francisco, California, 1975.

Hilliard, A. *Alternative to IQ testing: An approach to the identification of gifted "minority" children. A Final Report of Project #75-175*. Sacremento: California State Department of Education, Special Education Support Unit, 1976.

Hilliard, A. Bias in the development of information about black children. Paper presented at the Conference on Black Life-Style, February, at the African American Studies Department, University of California, Berkeley, 1977.

Hindley, C. B. Social class influence on the development of ability in the first five years. In *Proceedings of the XIV International Congress of Applied Psychology*, ed. G. Nielson. Vol. 3. *Child and education*. London: University of London, 1960.

Isenberg, I. Free radicals in tissue. *Physiology Review* 44 (1964):487.

Ivy, R. The influence of race on the incidence of certain congenital abnormalities, notably cleft lip-cleft palate. *Plastic and Reconstructive Surgery* 30, 5 (1962):582-85.

Jensen, A. How much can we boost IQ and scholastic achievement? *Harvard Educational Review* 39 (1969):1-123.

Kambon, K. *The African personality in America: An African-centered framework*. Tallahassee, Fla.: Nubian Nations Publications, 1992.

Kamin, L. *The science and politics of IQ*. Hillsdale, N. J.: Lawrence Erlbaum Associates, 1974.

Karpinas, B. D. Racial differences in visual acuity. *Public Health Report* 75 (1960):1045-50.

Kilbride, J. E., and P. E. Kilbride. Sitting and smiling: Behavior of Baganda infants. The influence of culturally constituted experiences. *Journal of Cross-Cultural Psychology* 6, 1 (1975.):23-27.

King, R. From mental slavery to mastership, Part III. *Uraeus* 1, 3 (1978):22-35.

King, R. *Melanin selected annotated references*. Los Angeles: Fanon Research and Development Center, 1979.

King, R. Black Dot the Black seed: the archetype of humanity, Part II. *Uraeus* 2, 3 (1982):4-22.

King, W., and B. Seegmiller. Performance of 14 to 22 month-old black firstborn male infants on two tests of cognitive development. *Developmental Psychology* 8, 3 (1973):317-27.

Knobloch, H., and B. Pasamanick. Further observations on the behavioral development of Negro children. *Journal of Genetic*

Psychology 83 (1953):137-57.
Ladner, J. *The death of white sociology*. New York: Vintage Books, 1973.
Lalovel, J. M., J. Jackson, and N. E. Morton. Neural tube malformations: Amplex segregation analysis and calculation of recurrence risks. *Journal of Medical Genetics* 16 (1979):8-13.
Langman, J. *Medical embryology*. 2nd ed. Baltimore: Williams and Wilkins, 1969.
Leck, I. Ethnic differences in the incidence of malformations following migration. *British Journal of Prevention in Social Medicine* 23 (1969):166-73.
Leiderman, P. H., B. Babu, H. Kagia, C. Kroemer, and G. Leiderman. African infant precocity and some social influences during the first year. *Nature* May 23 (1973):242.
Lerner, A. Melanin pigmentation. *American Journal of Medicine* 19 (December 1955):902.
Lusk, D., and M. Lewis. Mother-infant interaction and infant development among the Wolof of Senegal. *Human Development* 15 (1972):58-69.
McGee, P. Melanin: The physiological basis of psychological openness. In *African philosophy: Assumption and paradigms for research on Black persons*, ed. L. King, V. Dixon, and W. Nobles Los Angeles: Fanon Center Publications, 1976:215-22.
Menalascins, F. J., and M. L. Egger. *The medical dimensions of mental retardation*. Lincoln, Nebraska: University of Nebraska Press, 1978.
Moore, K. *The developing human*. Philadelphia: W. B. Saunders, 1974.
Morgan, H. *Towards a theory of selected knowledge acquisition of patterns among Black children*. Syracuse, N. Y.: Syracuse University Press, 1976.
Moriarty, A. Review of the Denver developmental screening test. In *Seventh Mental Measurement Yearbook*, ed. K. Buros Vol. 2 Highland Park, Michigan: Gryphon Press, 1972.
Murphy, D. The etiology of congenital malformations in the light of biological statistics. *American Journal of Obstetrics and Gynecology* 34 (1973):890-97.
Nobles, W. *Changing child rearing orientations and Black child development*. San Francisco: Office of Child Development, Westside Community Mental Health Center, 1977.
North, A. F., and H. M. MacDonald Why are neonatal mortality rates lower in small black infants than in white infants of similar birth weights? *Journal of Pediatrics* 90, 5 (1977):809-19.
Okum, M. Pigment formation in mask cells in tissue culture. *Journal of Inventive Dermatology* 48 (1967):44.

Owen, G. M., and A. Lubin. Anthropometry of preschool children: Differences between black and white children. *Pediatrics* 7, 4 (1973):297.

Penrose, L. Genetics of anencephaly. *Journal of Mental Deficiency Research* 1, 1 (1975):4-15.

Reff, H., J. Black, and R. Lipschitz. Neurological disorders at Baragwanath Hospital: A survey. *Medical Proceedings* 4 (1958):292.

Sandler, L., G. Ratner, and J. Van Campen. Responses of urban preschool children to a developmental screening test. *The Journal of Pediatrics* 77 (1970):775.

Scott, R. D., F. Cutter, A. Ferguson, and M. Jenkins. Growth in development of Negro infants: V. Neuromuscular patterns of behavior during the first year of life. *Pediatrics* 16, 1 (1955):13-23.

Simpkiss, M., and A. Lowe. Congenital abnormalities in the African newborn. *Archives of Diseases in Childhood* 36 (1961):404-406.

Stedman, G. A. 1953. Current knowledge of melanin structure. In *Pigment Cell*, ed. S. Krager Basle Vol. 1 151.

Stewart, M. (now Neferkare Abena Stewart). *Melanin and sensorimotor development during infancy*. Master's thesis, George Peabody College, Vanderbilt University, Nashville, Tenn., 1980.

Stewart, N. *The gift of melanin and African infant development*. Oakland, Calif.: Re-Birth Images and Publications (P.O. Box 4651, Oakland, CA 94605) (in press).

Super, C. M. Infant care and motor development in rural Kenya: Some preliminary data on precocity and deficit. Paper presented at the regional meeting of the International Association for Cross-cultural Psychology, April, Ibadan, Nigeria, 1973.

Terman, L., and M. Merrill. *Stanford-Binet intelligence scale*. Boston: Houghton Mifflin, 1960.

Thomas, R. *Comparative study of gestation age between black and white fetuses by ultrasonography*. Paper presented at the Annual Convention of the National Medical Association, Detroit, Michigan, 1979a.

Thomas, R. White norms skew dating of black fetus. *Obstetrics-Gynecology News* 14, 19 (1979b):1.

Thomas, R., and S. Sillen. *Racism and psychiatry*. Secaucus, N. J.: Citadel Press, 1972.

Van Wieringen, H., and J. Wright. Observations on patients with Parkinson's disease treated with S-dopa I: Trial and evaluations of L-dopa therapy. *South African Medical Journal* 46 (1972):1262.

Vander Wende, C., and M. Spaerlein. Oxidation of dopamine to melanin by enzyme of right brain. *Life Sciences* 6 (1963):386-92.

Vincent, M., and J. Hugo. Lensufficance ponderale du premature African au point de vue de la sante publique. *Bulletin of the World Health Organization* 26 (1962):143-174.

Walters, E. Comparative development of Negro and white infants. *Journal of Genetic Psychology* 110 (1967):243-51.

Warren, N. African infant precocity. *Psychological Bulletin* 78, 5 (1972):353-67.

Wasserman, H. P. The circulation of melanin—its clinical and physiological significance. *South African Medical Journal* 28 (1965):711-16.

Wasserman, H. P. *Ethnic pigmentation.* Amsterdam: Excepta Medica, 1974.

Welsing, F. The Cress theory of color confrontation. *Black Scholar* (May 1974): 32-40.

Werner, E. E. Infants around the world: Cross-cultural studies of psychomotor development from birth to two years. *Journal of Cross-Cultural Psychology* 3, 2 (1972):111-34.

Chapter 8

Integration: Dead Horse For the Race?

Amani na Uwezo ya Ukombozi
(Michael McMillan)

The quest for integration of America's schools is an effort that was initiated by the NAACP in the early 1930s (Rabin 1976) and culminated in the celebrated 1954 *Brown v Board of Education* of Topeka, Kansas, decision. Social science statements played a prominent role in this decision, as indicated by this quotation from a finding in the Kansas case:

> Segregation of white and colored children in public schools has a detrimental effect upon the colored children. The impact is greater when it has the sanction of the law; for the policy of separating the races is usually interpreted as denoting the inferiority of the negro group. A sense of inferiority affects the motivation of a child to learn. Segregation with the sanction of law, therefore, has a tendency to retard the educational and mental development of negro children and to deprive them of some of the benefits they would receive in a racially integrated school system (394).

It also added that "whatever may have been the extent of psychological knowledge at the time of Plessy vs. Ferguson, this finding is amply supported by modern authority." (394).

Given the current debate on legislative and legal levels about this more than four decades issue and the advances in social science theory, research, and practices during this same period, it is felt that this issue merits reexamination. The thrust of this paper is the examination and critique of the social science research used to support the 1954 Supreme Court decision.

THEORETICAL IMPLICATIONS

In the *Brown v. Board of Education* of Topeka, Kansas, court opinion, several "authorities" were listed as references for the social science perspective (Brameld 1949; Chein 1949; Clark and Clark 1950; Deutscher and Chein 1948; Frazier 1949; Myrdal 1944). The rationales of these authorities merit individual inspection.

Brameld (1949) suggested that segregated facilities are more costly than integrated facilities because of duplication of services. He also referred to statistics which indicated that much more money is allocated for teacher salaries and educational facilities in Euro-American institutions. He additionally indicated that education in African American educational facilities was inferior and noted that they tended to be vocational in their educational thrust. He also alluded to the psychologically detrimental effects of "social neurosis" as a result of their being thwarted from goal-directed behavior (Brameld 1949:45).

Chein (1949) and Deutscher and Chein (1948) echo Brameld's opinions (although Brameld refers to Deutscher and Chein's survey). In both of the aforementioned sources a poll was used, consisting of

> eight hundred and forty-nine social scientists, including the entire membership of the American Ethnological Society . . . . and the Division of Personality and Social Psychology of the American Psychological Association, and all of the members of the American Sociological Society who listed race relations or social psychology as their major field of interest (Chein 1949:231).

It is interesting that this method was used, given that Chein stated:

> I have myself had occasion to argue in another connection that facts are not established scientifically by holding a poll among scientists concerning their preference (230).

Yet such a poll was used. Chein (1949:231) stated:

> For our present purposes, it is sufficient to note that 90% of the respondents indicate their opinion that enforced segregation has detrimental psychological effects on the members of the segregated groups even though equal facilities are provided.

Kenneth B. and Mamie P. Clark were cited in the proceedings of the Midcentury White House Conference on Children and Youth titled *Personality in the Making* (Witmer and Kotinsky 1952:142). Examination of the Clarks' work of this era reveals an assessment methodology based on African American children's responses to crayon drawings or their responses to evaluative questions regarding dolls with variances in skin color. The Clarks' research indicated that African American children tended to make pro-Euro-American and anti-African-American responses to the examiner's varying inquiries and concluded that these results were evident of the effects of racism and segregation. The implications of this particular research methodology has been critiqued (Baldwin 1979; Banks 1976; Brand, Padilla, and Ruiz 1974; Semaj 1980), and it has been generally concluded that, other than the evidence of outgroup orientation, the negative inferences concerning the personality or psychological structure of these children is unfounded.

Although the majority of the ill effects of segregation were posited toward African American children, there were effects that were considered as mutually harmful to African American and Euro-American children:

> Segregation imposes upon individuals a distorted sense of social reality.
>
> Segregation leads to a blockage in the communications and interactions between the two groups. Such blockages

> tend to increase mutual suspicion, distrust, and hostility. Segregation not only perpetuates rigid stereotypes and reinforces negative attitudes toward members of the other group, but also leads to the development of a social climate within which violent outbreaks of racial tension are likely to occur. (Minnesota Law Review 1953:432)

These conclusions were prefaced with a definition of segregation:

> segregation refers to that restriction of opportunities for different types of associations between the members of one racial, religious, national or geographic origin, or linguistic group and those of other groups, which results from or is supported by the action of any official body or agency representing some branch of government. (428)

Questions about the validity of the research presented in the Brown decision have already been mentioned. However, the valid points also merit mentioning. It is conceptually plausible that segregation (as previously defined) might lead to a blockage in communication and interaction, with a resultant increase in suspicion and hostility. It is also conceivable that segregation might perpetuate rigid stereotypes and reinforce negative attitudes resulting in the aforementioned social neurosis or frustration spoken of by Brameld (1949:45). Perpetuation of racist attitudes by the dominant Euro-American society would seem to be the root of this particular problem, given that Euro-Americans are the only parties guilty of socially sanctioned segregation and racism. They are also responsible for the self-negating socialization process experienced by many African Americans, part of which was the denial of education. This process was historically known as "seasoning" (Quarles 1964:26) and often resulted in "Mentacide" (Wright 1976), defined as the systematic destruction of the identity and culture of a group. Therefore, it is also plausible that African American children might suffer from out-group oriented conceptualizations of positive attributes or beauty. The previously mentioned inadequate allotment of funding and/or access to quality education was part and parcel of the same process.

Given that the segregation process did result in inadequate allotment of funds, as well as some psychosocial problems that affected

Euro-Americans and African Americans, it would seem logical to attempt to remedy these problems. Since the vast majority of these psychosocial problems can be attributed to racism, it would seem logical to deal with the elimination of this as a problem. Unfortunately, the vast majority of Euro-Americans have historically denied or sanctioned and supported racism. Euro-American social scientists themselves have often lent their support to the functional end of racism, as Thomas and Sillen (1972) have well documented. It would also seem logical to address the inadequate allocation of resources, but adequate redress in this area has been woefully lacking. It is a historical fact that African Americans have never received reparations for the ravages of the war commonly known as the slave trade, which was (is) the root of the psychosocial and economic problems of African Americans (Ukombozi 1978; Schucter 1970). Direct reparations might have more adequately addressed the goal-directed behavior of African American parents: access to the acquisition of knowledge and skills could reinforce the positive group identity and enable the recipient to contribute to the defense and development of the race. What has happened in actuality is far from adequate.

THEORY INTO PRACTICE

Based on the aforementioned theoretical premises, desegregation became law, with integration as the solution. Given that many of the theoretical premises upon which this law was based are of questionable validity, one might ask why this practice received the sanctioning from African Americans which it has. It would seem like a very insulting concept to accept, that is, that African American children cannot get a "quality" education in the absence of Euro-American children. The aforementioned process of mentacide gives an explanation for this. In 1981 syndicated columnist Tony Brown spoke to this issue:

> They remember when blacks were forbidden to be with whites; now they seem to be attempting to fulfill their need for self acceptance with the status condition of being with and liked by whites, i.e. integration and busing at any and all costs to black parents and children.

This type of mentality is in line with the concept of anticipatory socialization. Berkowitz (1975) explained the behavioral consequences of this phenomenon, in which a person adopts the values and belief system of another group:

> A person is in a very precarious position if he has low status in his group or isn't well accepted by the others, and he is afraid that he might be excluded altogether. Clinging to his precious foothold in the group, maybe even hoping he can better his position, he walks the straight and narrow, not daring to deviate openly from the group's standards. (331)

It is no accident that this type of leadership and mentality has dominated the social political arena of African Americans, as they have tended to be well financed by whites. It is a historical fact that the NAACP was formed based on a convening of Euro-Americans (Rabin 1976). Euro-American racists, who wish to control the commodity that was once chattel slaves without chains and whips, understand the critical function of mind control as well as rewards and punishments. This paternalistically racist attitude which mentacidal African Americans support has resulted in the NAACP's thrust to eliminate "segregated not substandard schools" (Straus and Schrager 1978).

The legal application of desegregation has also been questioned. Former NAACP attorney, Derrick Bell, Jr., (1976) has stated:

> Desegregation efforts aimed at lunchrooms, beaches, transportation, and other public facilities were designed merely to gain access to those facilities. Any actual mixing has been essentially fortuitous; it was hardly part of the rights protected (to eat, travel, or swim on a non-racial basis). (477)

Although the concern of African Americans had been access to quality educational facilities, the practice insured race mixing. This is also understandable, given the aforementioned mentality of African Americans in leadership positions as well as Euro-Americans' historic efforts to control. One of the potential benefits of integration cited in the Brown decision was fewer race riots in integrated neighborhoods (Minnesota Law Review 1953).

With these theoretical and legal considerations in mind, it becomes politic to examine whether integration has accomplished or rendered its intended benefits. One might ask, how can you assess the results of efforts based on less than sound theoretical premises? Unfortunately, the soundness of theory often has no bearing on the application. Assessment of the end results of this process have often been difficult, because the state of integration often fades. As Bell (1976) stated:

> the disinclination of white parents to send their children to black schools has not been lessened by charges made over a long period of time by civil rights groups that black schools are educationally bankrupt and unconstitutional per se. (479)

Consequently, predominantly African American schools would often return to their predominantly African student population due to European resistance. Interestingly enough, there has been more resistance to recent efforts in the North. This is similar to the phenomenon which occurred after the Civil War, when the North, supposedly for humanitarian reasons, backed the release of the slaves. The "humanitarianism" faded when the newly freed Africans competed for the jobs that whites held.

In those situations in which integration has been achieved, the results have been inconclusive. St. John (1975) indicated that the integration process sometimes resulted in raising of scores, but sometimes resulted in the lowering of scores. Her study also concluded that desegregation lowered the self-esteem and the educational and vocational aspirations of the African American children involved. Weinberg's (1977) review of the literature in this area also indicated inconclusive results, as Thomas and Brown's (1982) literature review further supports.

There have also been studies that refute the premise that a predominantly African American educational setting is inferior. In Chicago, Operation Higher Achievement involved parents, teachers, and students in a project that resulted in an improvement of reading scores on an average of 1.1 years per term (Free Choice Plan 1982). These same types of results have been documented in New York (Arthur v. Nyquist, 415 F. Supp. [W. D. N. Y. 1976]) and California (Bell 1973). Thus there is a substantial body of literature which supports the thesis which has been supported by a vocal minority of African Americans, that is, that African American children have, will, and can achieve in predominantly African American settings.

It seems, therefore, that there is a definite need to set priorities in the African American community. We have spent twenty-eight years trying to whip the proverbial dead horse to win the race. As indicated by a recent University of Michigan study, Europeans, while in settings which bring them in contact with African Americans, have tended to change their behavior but not their actual attitudes. So for those African Americans who felt that they could change Euro-Americans' racism by mere proximity, they have found themselves confronted with unwilling subjects. And for those who felt (feel) that their children would gain through osmosis by association with Euro-Americans, this had not proven to be valid. What is a reality is that the vast majority of African American children are still presented with Eurocentric, inadequate educational opportunity.

SOLUTIONS

There are some viable alternatives to this continued unproductive effort. There are already alternative independent African educational institutions in operation. These tend to be limited in funding, support, and focus, because the masses of African Americans have neither the will nor the ability to support them. A more viable solution is for African American social scientists to challenge this effort, to educate African American parents to the false claims of this effort, and to become actively involved in designing African American educational institutions that are truly Black. That is, these institutions must be Black in population and must place an emphasis on Afrocentric teaching methods and Afrocentric culture reinforcement. It is time that we stop treating ourselves as the children of Euro-Americans and demand what is rightfully ours. There have already been such efforts in Boston (Free Choice Plan 1982), New York (Guttentag 1972), and St. Louis (Parents File Motion Against Deseg Plan 1983). Only we will decide if we will stop beating the dead horse and get on a horse that has a chance of winning.

REFERENCES

Baldwin, J. A. Theory and research concerning the motion of Black self-hatred: A review and reinterpretation. *Journal of Black Psychology* 5, 2 (1979):51-77.

Banks, W. C. White preference in Blacks: A paradigm in search of a phenomenon. *Psychological Bulletin* 83, 6 (1976):1179-86.

Bell, D. A. *Race, racism, and American law.* Boston: Little, Brown, 1973.

Bell, D. A. Serving two masters: Integration ideals and client interests in school desegregation litigation. *The Yale Law Journal* 85, 4 (1976):470-516.

Berkowitz, L. *A survey of social psychology.* Hinsdale: Dryden Press, 1975.

Brameld, T. Educational Costs. In *Discrimination and rational welfare*, ed. R. McIver, New York: Harper & Brothers, 1949.

Brand, E., A. Padilla, and R. Ruiz. Ethnic identification and preference: A review. *Psychological Bulletin* 81 (1974):860-90.

Brown, R. NAACP is not Black America. *News World Forum*, 11 July, 1979.

Chein, I. What are the psychological effects of segregation under conditions of equal facilities. *International Journal of Opinion and Attitude Research* 3 (1949):229-34.

Clark, K. B., and M. Clark. Emotional factors in racial identification and preference in Negro children. *Journal of Negro Education* 19 (1950):341-50.

Deutscher, M., and I. Chein. The psychological effects of enforced segregation: A survey of social science opinion. *Journal of Psychology* 26 (1948):259-87.

Frazier, E. F. *The Negro in the United States.* New York: Macmillan, 1949.

Free choice plan for Boston schools. *Newsweek* 5 April 1982:13.

Green, R., J. Darden, J. Schweitzer, R. Griffore, M. Parsons, and J. Smith. *Metropolitan school desegregation in New Castle County Delaware: Final Report to the Rockefeller Foundation* 1982.

Guttentag, M. Children in Harlem's community controlled schools. *Journal of Social Issues* 28 (1972):6-16.

Minnesota Law Review. 37 (1953):427-39.

Myrdal, G. *An American dilemma; the Negro and modern democracy.* New York: Harper & Brothers, 1944.

Parents file motion against deseg plan. *St. Louis American*, 3 March, 1983.

Quarles, B. *The Negro in the making of America.* New York: Macmillan, 1964.

Rabin, R. L. Lawyers for social change: Perspectives on public interest law. *Stanford Law Review* 85, 4 (1976):207-61.

St. John, N. H. *School desegregation outcomes for children.* New York: John Wiley, 1975.

Schucter, A. *Reparations: the Black manifesto and its challenge to white America.* Philadelphia: Lippincott, 1970.

Semaj, L. T. Racial identification and preference in children: A cognitive developmental approach. Ph.D. diss., Cornell University, Ithaca, New York, 1978.

Straus, K. and S. Schrager. Pro-Detroit: a pragmatic approach to school desegregation. *Theory into Practice* 17, 1 (1978):86-90.

Thomas, A., and S. Sillen. *Racism and psychiatry.* Secaucus, N. J.: Citadel, 1972.

Thomas, G., and F. Brown. What does educational research tell us about school desegregation effects? *Journal of Black Studies* 13, 2 (1982):155-74.

Ukombozi, A. U. (aka Michael McMillan) *Forty acres, fifty dollars, and a mule: Has the African American been adequately compensated for the ravages of slavery?* Rockville, Maryland: Black Reparations Commission, 1978.

Weinberg, M. *Minority students: A research appraisal.* Washington, D.C.: U.S. Department of Health, Education, and Welfare, 1977.

Witmer, H., and R. Kotinsky, eds. *Personality in the making; the fact finding report of the mid-century White House conference on children and youth.* New York: Harper, 1952.

Wright, B. A psychological theory of educating the Black child. *Black Books Bulletin* 4 (1976):12-16.

CHAPTER 9

Community Psychology and Systems Intervention

Na'im Akbar
Rashad Saafir
Dorothy Granberry

This chapter is concerned with the conceptualization of human beings and communities and suggests ways of intervening in the lives of people and their communities. This process of conceptualization and decision making is an arduous and complex one and requires a systematic approach to analysis as well as to the development of strategies of intervention. It has long been realized that the problems of individual humans and society as a whole are integrally tied together and that an attempt to unravel the intricate relationships among the various social, political, educational, economic, religious, and familial influences on these problems requires a conceptual framework that permits us to see how these forces affect each other. Additionally, our model should suggest ways of influencing change in these problems at multiple levels in a number of situations.

Essentially, we assume that there are multiple causes for the mental health problems we face today. Consistent with this assumption is the concept of "systems." A system is a set of objects considered together with the relationship(s) between or among the objects themselves and between or among their attributes (Seiler 1967). In other words, in a system everything is so related in an interdependent fashion that a change in one object will bring about a change in the other objects. This idea of a system forms the basis for a more elaborate discussion of the problem at hand: to organize our thoughts about some very complex situations in such a way as to simplify matters to a level that is manageable for us (the thinker or analyzer) so that we bring order to confusion and can map out some ways of making an impact on the community. To get the maximum benefit from our discussion, it is first necessary to gain some basic knowledge about systems.

BASIC FACTS ABOUT SYSTEMS

SYSTEMS TERMINOLOGY

One encounters a monstrous complexity of terminology in any discussion of systems analysis. The basic term is that of "system," which is ordinarily used to refer to any set of interrelated elements which share a basic function or which have some purpose in common. The term "subsystem" is often used to denote the relationships of a system that is a part of a much larger system (e.g., the person is a subsystem of the family). The term "suprasystem" is often used to refer to structures which develop out of the combining of systems (e.g., society is a suprasystem in relation to the family system and the person subsystem, or the Department of Health and Human Services is a suprasystem which is made up of several systems relating to health, mental health, schools, social services, etc.).

One also encounters the use of the terms "micro," "mezzo," and "macro," used to refer either to the influence of a system or the level of analysis one is conducting in relation to the hierarchy of systems. That is, one may conceptualize systems as relating to each other in some order of influence or importance. The subsystem or microsystem is ordinarily thought to have the least influence, and the system or mezzosystem is thought to have the next higher level of influence, followed by the suprasystem or macrosystem which has the greatest level of influence.

HIERARCHY OF SYSTEMS

The level of analysis of the influence of systems may be conceptualized in a hierarchic fashion so as to simplify or clarify where one is working in relationship to the complexity of the total problem. A hierarchy of systems is presented in Figure 1.

Figure 1.

SYSTEMS HIERARCHY INDICATING LEVEL OF ANALYSIS OR PRIMARY INFLUENCE

Suprasystem or Macrosystem Level

(Government, Society, Executive Management in an Organization)

System or Mezzosystem Level

(Neighborhood, Community, Middle Management in an Organization)

Subsystem or Microsystem Level

(Social Group, Persons, Lower Level Stage in an Organization)

The idea of a hierarchy of systems allows one to focus on a single internal system at a time without being overwhelmed by infinite complexity (Seiler 1967). It also permits us to see the interrelatedness of all of the systems while concentrating on one level at a time. The influence of higher-order systems (i.e., macrosystems and/or mezzosystems) has an effect on other, lower-level systems. Also, the lower-level systems (i.e., microsystems and/or mezzosystems) have an influence on higher-order systems. However, the influence is thought to be greatest when it originates at the macro level and disseminates downward as reflected in Figure 1.

The importance of the systems hierarchy idea is that each level requires a different, if not a more sophisticated, scheme of knowledge and strategies that will begin influencing change. Obviously, if one hopes to intervene at the macro or mezzo level, then techniques which are thought to be effective at the micro level will probably not have very much effect. Because community mental health requires change at the mezzo (community) level, then we must acquire knowledge and skills that are influential at that level. More will be said about this in our discussion of strategies of intervention.

CHARACTERISTICS OF SYSTEMS

Here we must distinguish between closed and open systems. Basically, a closed system is one that is isolated from the environment, and an open system is one that is constantly exchanging information and/or energy with the environment (Bertalanffy 1968). An understanding of open systems is important for our discussion here. Openness is a characteristic of all social systems, in that they are in constant interplay with the surrounding environment (Rappaport 1977). Open systems have the capacity to receive "input" in the form of information and energy from the external environment, which is acted upon or transformed by the internal mechanism of the system to produce "output" back into the environment. This output is also recycled as input back into the system.

Open systems are also characterized by a tendency toward increasing complexity and developing a means of self-maintenance (Rappaport 1977). The best example of this is the increasing complexity and differentiation that occurs as a child grows. The more intellectual input there is, the more complex the cognitive system of the child becomes, and the more elaborate are the outputs. To witness this phenomenon, one need only observe the developing verbal and motor responses of a growing infant.

The next characteristic of open systems is that of "equilibrium." Open systems are said to be in a state of dynamic equilibrium: they are constantly making adjustments (Rappaport 1977). Social systems are also characterized by the same tendency to maintain an equilibrium around which change occurs. When the state of equilibrium is disrupted, the system becomes mobilized to engage in activity designed to bring it back to a state of balance. This is not to say that open systems are static; quite the contrary, they are in a constant state of change. This notion of dynamic equilibrium is similar to that of homeostasis, where the organism initiates many changes to maintain such things as body temperature. When the body reaches a certain temperature, perspiration is produced to lower the temperature to an acceptable level, and the organism remains comfortable.

Figure 2.

A Simple Feedback Scheme

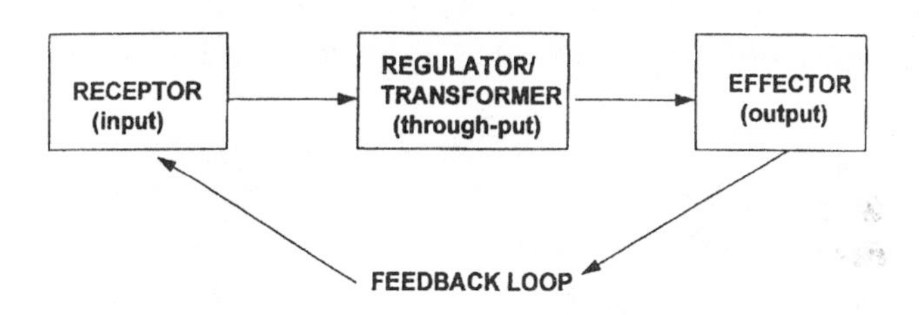

The system's ability to maintain equilibrium depends on its ability to regulate inputs and the availability of feedback. The term "regulate" is being used here to denote a situation in which the system simply allows information to be channeled through whatever mechanism it uses to handle information or one in which the system either alters the form of the information or converts the input into energy. In either case, systems usually become "differentiated," that is, they develop specialized ways (i.e., channels) of handling various kinds of inputs. Most organizations are good examples of this, with specialized departments which are designed to fulfill specific functions.

The last characteristic on our list is "feedback." Whenever the system performs any function that generates output, and information is produced which can be directed back to the system (input), this is termed feedback. When this information is received the second time, it may serve to keep the system going the way it was or change its present functioning. Whether or not change occurs depends upon the type of feedback. Negative feedback (a wrong or unacceptable response) will—if the system is functioning properly—cause the system to make corrections; positive feedback indicates that the proper response has been made, and no corrective action is required. Most systems have what are called feedback loops that insure the availability of feedback. However, the mere existence of such a mechanism does not guarantee the efficient and/or effective use of feedback. Figure 2 shows the way in which information and/or other inputs flow through open systems.

It is important to keep in mind that a system operates in and is an integral part of the whole environment. In looking at any system, whether biological or social, it is important to view the system in relation to other systems and how they fit into the environment. This notion of "environmental fit" introduces the concept of ecology or ecosystem.

ECOLOGY AND THE CONCEPT OF ECOSYSTEMS

The concepts of ecology and of ecosystem are important because they provide a kind of gestalt view of the interrelatedness and interdependence of all systems. We assume that everything in the universe is interconnected and that a change in one system will influence change in all other systems. Also, it is essential that all systems function in such a way as to maintain an equilibrium, not only with each system but throughout the universe.

Ecology has emerged as an integrated study of populations, communities, and ecosystems (Boughey 1971). Populations are regarded as groups of organisms having a common origin, form, and function. Communities are associations of populations linked by some interdependent function. Ecosystems are conceptual systems formed by relating a community or communities with the totality of prevailing environmental factors. These basic ideas have contributed to the thinking of biologists, anthropologists, ecologists, and community psychologists about the role of environmental factors on various forms of life and human behavior. The discipline of ecology has more recently evolved into the study of living systems in relation to one another and to their environment. This is shown in Figure 3. (All of the systems that exist are not

Figure 3.
The Interconnectedness and Interdependence of a Sample of Systems and How They Exist in the Environment of the Ecosystem

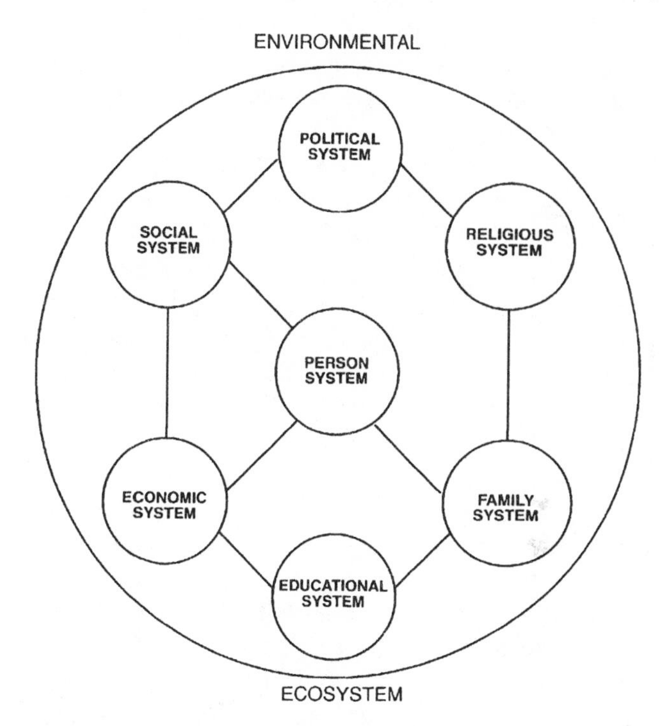

represented here, only a sample of those that have relevance for our present discussion.)

The systems approach emphasizes an essentially holistic view, which has been incorporated in the ecosystem concept (Boughey 1971). Ecology as it is now understood is the study of populations and communities as a whole in relation to one another and to their total environment (Odum 1959). Regardless of where one chooses to intervene, one should proceed with an expectation that whatever influence one manages to have will affect systems beyond the immediate situation. The notion of multiple cause for behavior along with a view of systems, hierarchy of systems, and ecosystems should serve to reduce the infinite complexity of the mental health problems we are currently concerned with and suggest some strategies for dealing with these problems.

HUMANS AS SOCIAL PRODUCTS

The use we make of the ideas discussed in the preceding paragraphs depends in part on our conceptualization of the person; in other words, how we answer the question, "What is a human being?" The nature of this answer determines whether a psychologist's analysis of a behavioral event focuses on the individual person and his/her characteristics, the social group and its organization and functioning, or some combination of these elements. It also dictates whether values and value conflicts are recognized as legitimate aspects of human interaction regardless of their nature or the contexts in which they occur. Finally, and perhaps most important, the character of this conceptualization defines the ultimate goals of all interventions.

A human being is neither a blank sheet on which experience etches its characters nor an entity which emerges complete with all ingredients for further development and growth. A human is a unique configuration of elements whose exact dimensions and characteristics are a joint product of the interaction of these elements and the person's physical, social, and psychological environments. Furthermore, the person has intrinsic value which the environment either enhances or curtails. This intrinsic worth or value is what makes human beings, themselves, values.

This notion of humans as values is the cornerstone of our conceptualization of a person. It is a view of humanity which holds that people have a basic inherent worth which must be nourished and respected. This basic worth results from the capability of each to master his or her being as well as his or her environment. We all have the potential for greater personal effectiveness and for the creation of surroundings supportive of this functioning. Thus, every individual person is of value, even though his/her actions may be valueless for the group and even highly undesirable—for example, the actions of a drug addict or an alcoholic. One implication of this position for intervention is that intervention must focus on the development and cultivation of psychological, social, economic, political, and moral environments capable of enhancing and sustaining this humanness.

People exist in a complex, symbiotic relationship with their surrounding environments. In fact, we are active elements whose behaviors produce environmental changes and modifications. Yet, at the same time, we are shaped and molded by these forces. A simple physical illustration of this relationship is the case of a group of persons in a room in which the temperature is a chilly fifty degrees. Because of the temperature, the people are naturally cold. Being fairly wise, they move about and stay close together, generating heat which in turn raises the temperature in the frigid room. This symbiotic relationship produces harmonious human activity which is both self- and group-enhancing. An analogous relationship holds for all human environments including those which have very few physical properties, such as our ideological, political, economic, and social surroundings.

It is the interplay of these abstract environments and their relationship to physical environments with which we are mainly concerned because much, if not most, of what we think of as the quintessential characteristics of humans is of a psychological nature. Our psychological worlds, including our attitudes, values, beliefs, and perceptual styles constitute a large part of what we see as being the human person. Hence, to more fully grasp the essence of the idea of humans as both products and creators of their environments let us examine these concepts more closely.

Our psychological worlds are profoundly influenced by the socio-cultural matrices in which we are embedded. When a person is born, a unique arrangement of elements like the person's physical makeup—including sex, race, body structure, neurological temperament, and immunological systems—begins an interaction with a multiplicity of belief systems and their resulting customs and organizational patterns and, as such, exert pressures which influence the psychological beings we become. For example, when a Black, female child is born her parents give her a name consistent with their beliefs about what a black, female child should be named and one which will bespeak their expectations for her. (These parental expectations, by the way, are themselves partially products of their social group's customs and values.) The baby girl's psychological world is steered in a particular direction as a consequence of this act of naming, for a name or label directs others to the ways to behave toward that person or object, and, hence, it tells something about the character or quality of the person or object. To get a feel for the impact of the naming act on our conceptualization of ourselves, try to imagine yourself with a name inconsistent with your idea of yourself. Of course, the pressures outlined are not the only determining factors, any more than the weight of a hammer is the sole factor determining the depth of an indentation in a piece of steel because other factors, such as the force behind the blow and the angle at which the blow was delivered, must also be considered. Environmental pressures shape the person primarily though three channels. First of all, they define the realm of possibilities for the person. This is accomplished through the reactions and expectations that others exhibit toward us as well as through our access to information about what is possible and for whom it is possible.

Second, environmental pressures shape our perceptions and knowledge. In other words, they influence what we see and the conclusions we draw when we look out on the world. For example, when you meet a Black person it is these forces which determine whether you see a new world negro whose beginnings are in Western slavery or the representative of a long and glorious African history that has nearly triumphed over an episode of Western slavery and oppression. This point, in particular, is highly relevant for intervention in mental health from two perspectives. First, from the angle of the intervener, it is these forces which make it mandatory that mental health workers examine their definitions of a situation before attempting an intervention. This holds for Blacks working with the Black community as well as mental health workers from other ethnic groups. We must remember that the view taken of a situation determines what actions to take in the matter. The implied action to be taken for a half-filled glass is different from that for a half-empty glass. Secondly, from the point of intervention itself, this effect of the environment on our knowledge and perceptions suggests that this area itself (the environment) is a possible point of intervention.

The third channel through which environmental pressures shape the person is the values he/she holds. Values are the degree of emphasis or importance we attach to objects or ideas. They are our preferential ratings of the various elements which surround us.

These include conceptual entities, such as honesty, integrity, respect, etc. as well as objects possessing physical properties, such as money, cars, houses, etc. One measure of the value of any entity is the extent to which we strive for it. The characteristics of the systems in which we exist and our locations within them help to mold the values we come to hold. This molding process is accomplished through a number of means, both direct and indirect. Parental exhortation to be honest is an example of a direct means of value acquisition; whereas exposure to value orientations embedded in mythology, movies, television shows, folklore, the "top ten," and other forms of popular culture is an example of acquisition through indirect means.

The values we develop constitute a primary channel through which we make an impact on our socio-cultural surroundings For they are, in part, the determiners of the relative emphases placed on the various elements in our surroundings, thereby indirectly influencing how we perceive events. Values are seldom, if ever, constant. They rise and they fall. They push other values aside and are in turn pushed aside. They are not constant across social groups. Different groups may emphasize different sets of values. For example, a dominant Western culture emphasis is on contemporary machines, and the emphasis on the development and enhancement of human and social relations is significantly more dormant. The ascent or descent of any value is a function of environmental contingencies (for example, the relative controlling power of a particular group of people or the survival demands in a situation).

It is the ascendancy of certain values that has led to the contemporary perception of people as servants to the machine rather than to views which promote the enhancement of humans. In order to fully grasp the means through which any values come to predominate, it is important to understand their current material or economic basis as well as the history of their ascendancy. Unfortunately, most existing training models in mental health and human services do not emphasize this point. Consequently, mental health personnel are often ill-equipped for intervention based on such an analysis.

If we take a close look at modern psychology we can see that, for the most part, its perspective emphasizes making people fit into existing molds. The value of the human is a function of his/her fit. Intervention strategies are geared toward the control of misfitting behaviors. Little emphasis is directed towards behavior enhancement and possible resulting environmental changes. Furthermore, the existing molds constitute a narrow sampling of the possibilities which exist in a pluralistic society. Often these alternative possibilities are not pursued because of ignorance, ethnic bias, and fears of possible social reorganization. Before discussing the implications of the above for training procedures and intervention strategies, let us examine the idea of community which is the context in which our interventions must occur in order to have maximal effects.

WHAT IS COMMUNITY?

Since the rise of interest in the "community" approach to mental health, which began in the mid 1960s, there have been many attempts to define "community psychology." Most efforts have proven inadequate in capturing the subtlety of this rather amorphous approach. The major difficulty seems to lie in accurately identifying what is, in fact, "community psychology." "Community" has proven to be an elusive concept, and the experts have generally opted for oversimplification in their efforts to adhere to something concrete. Such oversimplification has worked against the effective application of the potentially powerful concepts of community psychology.

In most general terms, community is a network of interconnecting processes which form the physical, mental, and spiritual environments for effective human development. These processes constitute the various shared definitions which interconnect human beings into a web of experience. Community, on the one hand, is a definition of who the person is, what his allegiances are, and what her responsibilities are. In this sense it is an important source of one's self-concept which is nourished by one's identifications from the various planes of community.

On the other hand, community is a set of resources or environments in which the various components of the self receive nourishment for growth. In this sense, community is an ecology or atmosphere which both confines and unites diverse expressions into a unified matrix of survival.

Physical Community

The most basic (and most usual) definition of community is the "physical" definition, which defines the relationship between people as based on the sharing of some particular, definite geographical area or space. The physical boundaries can be small, such as a particular neighborhood, housing project, or even a building, or as broad as the geographical borders of a nation. Either level of this geographical boundary definition still constitutes community to the extent that it leads to people adopting a shared self-definition on the basis of those geographical boundaries. It is not unusual for people to identify themselves as belonging to the "Oaklawn area" or some similar neighborhood as a significant definition of self. Particularly if that neighborhood is readily associated with some particular attributes of wealth, prestige, status, cohesion, ethnicity, etc., one's self-concept may be heavily influenced by that definition.

The common element is that the people who occupy some particular plot of land come to define themselves on the basis of that plot in very significant ways. That shared location becomes the foundation of one's orientation as a community or interacting unit. Usually, the shared geography also encompasses the intense affective ties. Not only are primary relations most usually found in closest physical proximity, but people tend to be more intimately attached to those who occupy proximal turf. The extent to which such affectionate ties do not exist among the physically proximal could be the basis for community instability and consequent human stress.

The physical community provides crucial elements for human development. In addition to the obvious attributes of shelter and other services for human maintenance, there are indirect factors which stem from the physical aspects of community. The active relationships among people who make up physical communities require systems for distributing power, goods, and services. Government, politics, economics, etc., all arise as systems for the maintenance of ecological balance in the physical community system. These processes are dynamics of community which facilitate the constructive growth of human life within. Therefore, the effective measure of adequate community systems is the quality of human life which emerges from it. Too often the human being is assessed as inadequate when, in fact, improper attention has been given to the atmosphere or community which has produced that life. This takes us to the heart of the conceptualization of community psychology which addresses the community system that surrounds and affects the person. The recognition that physical community is the womb of human life, in a real sense, is the essence of the meaning of a community psychology. It then becomes impossible to conceive of a human being without considering the environment out of which he is produced.

Contrary to many thinkers, we do not conceive of governmental, political, and economic systems as entities of themselves. In a "humanocentric" conceptualization, these are merely vehicles for the facilitation of human growth. They are actually subsystems of the physical community system. Therefore, their utility must be assessed by their adequacy in maintaining the community system. If all subsets of members of the physical community do not have adequate participation in government regulation, economic resources, political power, and dispensation of justice, then the community system is dysfunctional. If human beings fail to develop those characteristic sensitivities and values which typify fully functioning human life, then the physical community is dysfunctional. Mental disorder from this perspective becomes a symptom of community dysfunction rather than personal dysfunction. This captures the real essence of the assumptions of community psychology.

What are some of the characteristics of an effectively functioning physical community? As we have pointed out above, communities are environments for successful human growth. Therefore, the conditions of an adequate community should facilitate that growth. Communities should provide protection for both the physical and human quality of life. In other words, communities should be reasonably secure from the danger of enemies or other destructive intruders. An effective security system provides the people in the community with a sense of safety which is necessary for limiting stress. The human quality of life is protected by preventing those influences in the community which destroy the dignity, self-respect, and general well-being of people in the community. Inhuman treatment and subhuman behaviors, such as brutality and uncontrolled impulsiveness, are conditions which reduce the quality of human life.

Communities are able to accomplish those mutually necessary physical functions only if contact is maintained among those within the network of community. Thus, communication is vital for an effectively functioning physical community. Because of the widely shared functions and services among people in physical communities, there must be ways of communicating mutual responsibility for those functions and services. Without such communication of shared responsibility, communities become dysfunctional. Decisions regarding community operation must be reached by mutual consent. The extent to which members of a community are absent from decision making affecting the community is the degree to which they do not feel bound by those decisions. When decisions are imposed externally or decided by a minority, the physical community functions begin to fall apart.

There are many other specific features which characterize effectively functioning physical communities. There are critical resources which must be provided, such as opportunities to acquire products for survival, facilities for recreation, etc. The current discussion does not allow for greater detail in this regard. The essential point of these brief illustrations is to demonstrate specifically some of the characteristics of the effective physical community. As indicated above, the criterion for a sound community is the degree to which it facilitates and nourishes the growth of human life. Any community characteristic can ultimately be judged by this criterion.

MENTAL COMMUNITY

There is a higher definition of community that transcends geography. This is the mental or intellectual community. "Mental community" refers to the interrelationship among people on the basis of shared ideas, concepts, ideology, and systems of organizing knowledge. People who share such ideas may or may not occupy related turf, but are nonetheless tied together by an invisible bond which unites them in their orientation to the world. They thus form a mental community.

People who share mental communities define themselves in accord with their ideas, ideologies, or systems of knowledge. A psychologist shares a mental community with other psychologists in China, Nigeria, anywhere; those who accept the idea of democracy are bound together with other people who share that idea. Often these ties of mental community are more powerful than those of physical community. Physical communities are more easily identifiable, but they are also deceptive by their appearance. Many behaviors which are incompatible with effective physical community life can be understood in terms of the stronger influence of mental community.

The mental community as an ecology for human growth is seen primarily in its contribution to problem-solving. People utilize the resources of their mental community as a means of solving problems. Moreover, the organization and the conceptualization of experiences receive a structure that is based on identification with one mental community. The lawyer looks at a lawbreaker from the perspective of his legal knowledge; a psychologist views the same person from the standpoint of her intrapsychic functioning; the warden views him as a custodial case, and so on. The same event or problem is viewed differently depending on one's mental community. The amount of time and energy devoted to technological development, scientific pursuits, philosophical debate, or recreation is directly connected with one's mental community. Choices and priorities are to a great extent determined by the mental community.

Obviously, the mental community is greatly determined by the learning experiences that people have. These experiences may be obtained in formal educational settings such as schools, or more informally, in families, through the media, or through other cultural experiences. Though one's mental community is intangible and transcends physical perimeters, its source is fairly tangible and identifiable. Since the mental community affects one's self-concept in that it lays a foundation for one's priorities and one's problem-solving orientations, it is worthy of consideration in understanding people's choices. When working to bring about change in the self-concept and community activity, it is particularly important to scrutinize closely the educational settings to determine with what mental community students are being encouraged to identify.

Observation has shown that such encouragement can be no more than the system of thinking that is presented in the educational settings. One of the arguments from the proponents of the community school concept is that such schools foster a symmetry between physical and mental community. To the extent that such communities are conducive to effective human growth and do not foster elitism, separatism, or other forms of bias which retard balanced human growth, such a concept is commendable. It certainly reduces much potential stress that may emanate from the disharmony between the physical and mental communities. In areas where careful scrutiny of the educational setting is not possible, assurance that the building of the mental community is occurring within the physical community can be a safeguard. It is important to recognize that much physical community discord and personal individual stress can be attributed to disharmony in mental community membership. Much of the personal stress suffered within the confines of a particular physical community originates in the person's alienation by virtue of his membership in some other mental community.

The criterion for assessing adequate mental communities is the degree to which the community's ideas, concepts, and ideologies foster effective human growth and expansion. If those ideas restrict the human intellect or clog the mind with unrealistic biases and superstitions, then that mental community is inadequate. If the mental community offers problem-solving means which are ineffective for mastering and facilitating a person's functioning in the physical community, then careful attention must be paid to the mental community. If the mental community fosters alienation from oneself and one's primary relations, then that mental community should be carefully evaluated.

The mental community should give a person greater expression, growth effectiveness, and contact than does the physical community. It should begin to release the person from the limitations of his physical community and bring him into contact with an even larger human community. In combination with one's physical community, one's mental community should nourish him/her physically and stimulate his/her intellectual growth.

MORAL-SPIRITUAL COMMUNITY

The shared geography of the physical community finds expansion in the shared ideas of the mental community and reaches infinite horizons in the shared ideals of the spiritual community. We define spiritual community as those shared values and ideals which unify people in terms of their human aspirations. We use the word "spiritual" advisedly, knowing the plethora of superstitious ideas surrounding such a concept. We feel that the ideals and values of the moral life are the real substance of the spiritual life. As the mental life is a more exalted though less tangible form of the physical life, so is the spiritual an even higher order of human experience. This, too, forms a community in the sense of our definition of those interconnecting processes which form the environment for effective human development.

The moral ideals which structure the spiritual community are capable of overriding the influence of either the physical or mental communities. People's concept of the human essence and the values stemming from that concept fosters far-reaching control over their choices. A person's affiliation with a spiritual community can have the most powerful influence on self-concept. The ideals of the spiritual community define the nature and destiny of the human, and organize at a higher plane the experiences of the physical and mental communities. Membership in a particular spiritual community can either nullify or validate the processes of the less powerful communities. If the boundaries of the physical community are set by some geographical border and boundaries of the mental community are defined by a certain knowledge or set of ideas, then the boundaries of the spiritual community are as broad as can be conceived. They are usually expressed in the infinite image of God.

Adjustment in people's physical communities and mental communities is often regulated by spiritual community membership. The degree to which people adequately shoulder the responsibility of physical and mental community membership is often determined by the degree to which those goals and objectives are in accord with the spiritual community. As social scientists, we often miss critical information regarding community functioning and human adjustment because of the tendency to ignore this least tangible but most influential aspect of the communities we study.

The spiritual community, ultimately, should tie the person with the broadest possible contacts. As the mental community transcends physical boundaries, the spiritual community should help the person transcend boundaries of ideas and concepts. It should open the person to the highest expression of him/herself; it should be the basis for reconciling any discord that may occur in either of the other two communities.

Figure 4.
Possible Intersections of Community Experience

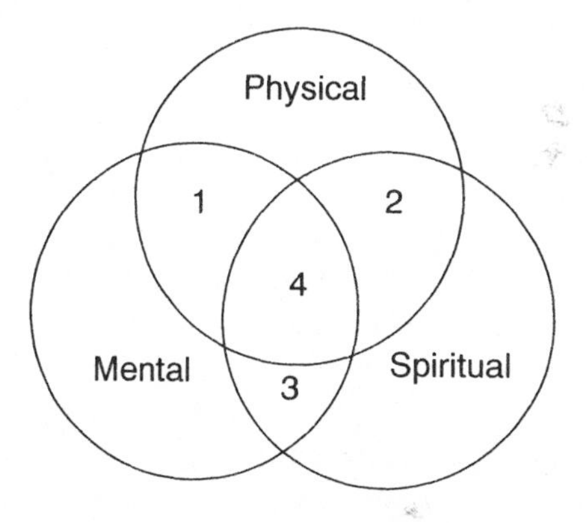

THE INTERRELATIONSHIP BETWEEN COMMUNITIES

All human life occurs in communities. Every human being with enough rational faculty to still be called human finds him/herself constantly participating in these three communities. The community experience for any individual can take on various combinations of these three planes of community, and much can be understood about the person by understanding his/her relationship with each plane. The possible intersections of community experience are depicted in Figure 4.

Intersect 1: This is the area in which interconnections of the physical community interface with interconnections from the mental community. An example occurs when people who share the same ideas or occupations occupy the same physical area, e.g., capitalists living in America. *Intersect 2:* This represents the overlap between the physical and the spiritual communities. An example is the situation in which people with the same values and ideals share the same terrain, e.g., Jews in Israel. *Intersect 3:* The interconnection between the spiritual and mental communities is shown here. An example is the situation in which people who share the same spiritual ideals and values also share the same knowledge, e.g., doctors who are Roman Catholic. *Intersect 4:* This is the shared intersection among all three communities. This is the situation in which a portion of the person's total community contacts all intersect with each other. An example would be, an Orthodox Jewish physician living in a medical complex in Brooklyn. In such a setting all of his communities are likely to intersect though not fuse, because he would undoubtedly share each of these communities with groups which do not overlap.

Philosophically, one might postulate that the human objective is to increase the overlap in the fourth area of intersection of Figure 4 and to reduce the disconnected portions of one's experience. Where there is no overlap there is individual stress and potential community discord. The degree to which "Physical" does not overlap "Mental" represents a separation between the activity of the two communities. The same is true for all disconnected areas. To the extent that each community provides an aspect of the person's self-definition, ideally all should completely overlap for the self to be united.

Area "4," the shared intersection among all the communities, is the area of maximum activity and stability. It represents the union of one's activities, relationships, and self. It is the area of greatest harmony. The other spheres of community activity are areas of potential disharmony and conflict. The symmetry within this area should not be accomplished by increased restriction on one's other communities, however.

In the Western world, there has been a destructive tendency to attain symmetry in one's various communities by greater and greater restriction of those communities. People have attempted to define their physical communities as smaller and smaller areas with great restrictions for membership; they have adopted excessively rigid and conservative ideas and concepts which have narrowed their intellectual contacts and mental community, and they have viewed the universal in ever-narrowing terms with ideals of limited applicability which has restricted the spiritual community. In so doing, they have attained a deceptive overlap in area "4" giving the appearance of a harmonious and stable community which necessitates constantly policing its borders to exclude the unfamiliar.

Figure 5.
THE IDEAL MODEL:
THE PHYSICAL, MENTAL, AND SPIRITUAL COMMUNITIES AS COMPLETELY OVERLAPPED

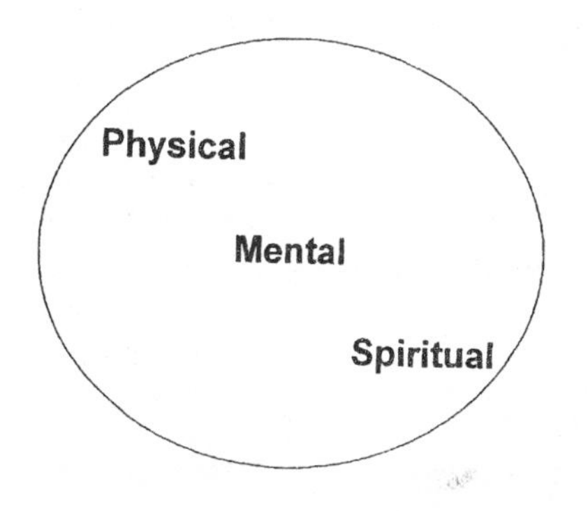

Not only do these communities represent the separate spheres of community activity for people, they also represent the stages of any single community's evolution and development. Be it the entrance of a new human being into the world or the clustering of a new group of people, the initial basis for contact is that of physical community. An infant finds itself in the same geographical area as its parents, and this forms the first community. Later the community grows from simply shared geography to shared ideas, concepts, and knowledge. This makes for a more substantial community than one simply tied together by geography. The child is soon tied to his family by mutual knowledge both of each other and of the environment. Ultimately, the community grows to become a spiritual community in which the inhabitants come to share the same values and ideals of human destiny. A thoroughly united community is one that has evolved through these three stages and comes to share one common sphere of activity.

Returning briefly to the philosophical notion, an ideal model would have all three communities united as in Figure 5. In such a model one's physical, mental, and spiritual communities would all merge into one community. If the definition of physical community could in fact become a world community, then, the Earth as a whole would be the limits of this community. If truth rather than partisan interest guided ideology and knowledge, then the mental community would become one as well. Finally, if the spiritual destiny and ideals of humanity were focused on a unified image of God, then the spiritual community would become as one. However idealistic, it is imperative, given the current state of affairs in the world, that we conceptualize models toward which to work. In so doing, we can have some absolute standard by which to assess human development and community functioning.

The human and community problems which we observe are a result of the incompatibilities among the person's various communities. Those incompatibilities result from the faulty or inadequate self-definitions issuing from any one or more of the three communities. The other source of discord is the degree to which any of the communities does not provide the kind of adequate ecology for constructive growth.

ASCENDING *VS.* DESCENDING SYSTEMS HIERARCHIES

The concepts of ascending and descending systems hierarchies are important for determining where to intervene in a system and what to expect from our interventions. Along these same lines, it is important to understand the distribution and control of power as they relate to the maintenance of a system. All systems, from the basic cell to the most complex social systems, are characterized by an interplay of elements or forces which serve to provide movement in the system. Anyone who intends to intervene in a system must learn where the control is located and how power is distributed throughout the system. As discussed earlier, one way of organizing our thinking about systems is to conceptualize in terms of a hierarchy. There are essentially two kinds of hierarchies, ascending and descending.

The ascending hierarchy is one in which the source of power or control is localized within the microsystem and flows upward through the mezzosystem and macrosystem levels. If the microsystem were removed then the source of power or energy for the system would cease to exist and the system's functioning would be seriously affected if not discontinued altogether. The cardiovascular system provides a good example of what we mean. The heart may be considered a subsystem of the human body (a system) and is integrally related to all of the body's functions. Though the heart may be influenced by other subsystems and by what we may choose to call a macrosystem of the body (i.e., the brain), the source of power for the body is directly related to the functioning of the heart. Should the heart stop, then the body would cease to function and the macrosystem of the body (the brain) would be directly influenced.

The descending hierarchy is one in which the source of power or energy originates with a macrosystem and flows downward through the mezzosystem and microsystem levels. The funding policies of federal agencies are a good example of what we mean here. The Department of Health and Human Services (HHS) may be considered as a macrosystem of which the Community Mental Health Center (CMHC) is a subsystem (mezzosystem level). The Department of Consultation-Education (C&E) of the Community Mental Health Center is a subsystem (microsystem level) of the mezzosystem. If the macrosystem (HHS) decides that funding will be provided to Community Mental Health Agencies specifically for C&E activities, then the end result will probably be improved C&E services to the community. The source of influence originates at the macrosystem level and descends to the mezzosystem and microsystem levels. If the systems interventionist is concerned with influencing C&E services, then she must not only address herself to the microsystem and mezzosystem levels and directly make an impact on the C&E department and the Mental Health

Agency, but she must also attempt to influence the macrosystem level (HHS) at which the policy decisions are being made (see Figure 6).

Figure 6
A DESCENDING SYSTEM HIERARCHY WITH THE SOURCE OF POWER ORIGINATING AT THE MACROSYSTEM LEVEL

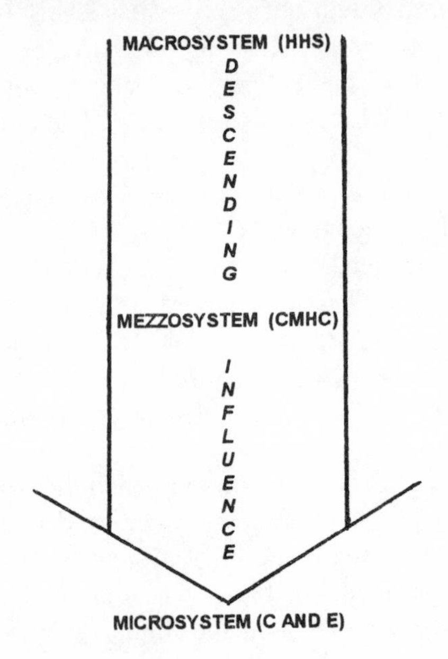

While Figure 6 shows a descending order, by reversing the direction of the arrow we can indicate an ascending order. The reader should keep in mind that the designation of an agency at any level of analysis is somewhat arbitrary and by no means indicates that the relationships being described at the moment are the only ones relevant to the problem. Clearly, within the HHS there are several subsystems which could be designated at the mezzo- or microsystems level. However, because our concern is with the relationship between the broad macrosystem (HHS), the Community Mental Health Center, and the C&E department, it is not necessary to complicate matters with the inclusion of the various subsystems of HHS. On the other hand, if we were concerned with how decisions are made and flow within HHS, then we would analyze that system in terms of its hierarchical structure. This level of analysis may be necessary for the systems interventionist to have the greatest impact on the HEW system and to influence the delivery of C&E services.

Thus, it is important to study systems and how they function and how they relate to other systems. It is also important to study where and by whom the power is controlled. This control may rest within a macrosystem, which is the case with most social problems, or it may rest in some microsystem, such as a powerful individual member of a system. Problems of maladjustment may also originate within individuals, or they may begin within the interrelations of many people. Where we intervene will depend upon where we judge the problem to be primarily controlled. The traditional models of psychiatry assume that the individual is the source of his problems and that the conflict is localized within the human microsystem. As a consequence of this type of reasoning, there has been a proliferation of therapeutic techniques directed toward internal intrapsychic conflict to the exclusion of external variables which may have some bearing on the problems. More contemporary modes (e.g., social learning theory, general systems theory, and social ecology) assume there are external forces operating on the individual's ability to make social adjustments and that these forces must be understood and manipulated to maximize the effects of therapeutic interventions. Clearly, once we move beyond the individual and consider the complex relationships that exist among a number of seemingly different forces as they relate to a problem, then we must adopt models of conceptualization that serve to organize our thinking around more complex issues and suggest where to begin working to improve the situation. Systems theory and the concepts of ascending vs. descending systems hierarchies provides such a vitally needed framework.

The decision where to intervene rests with the intervener. Those who are competent in dealing with the socio-political forces may choose to work at the macrosystem or mezzosystem levels, and those who are competent in persuading individuals on a one-to-one basis may choose to work in smaller microsystem circles. Though one should keep in mind that the interrelatedness of all the systems is in question, where we choose to invest our energy is to a great extent a matter of personal preference.

INTERVENTION

VALUES AND TENSIONS ASSOCIATED WITH INTERVENTION

Intervention in systems—whether families, communities, or larger societal networks—is not value-free. Values play a significant role in most decisions made concerning the intervention process. To clearly understand the role of values, let us look at three decisions which must be made in any intervention.

First, an intervener must make a decision regarding *when to intervene*. Is intervention warranted if only one person is detrimentally affected? Or must a group effect be present before intervention is justifiable? If a person is functioning successfully although adversely affecting the immediate social group, for example, the case of a drug pusher or a person who can cope as long as he/she wears a scarf over the face, should intervention be initiated? Associated with these questions is the question of "What is a detrimental effect?" Or, in other words, "When is behavior undesirable?"

Second, the intervener must make decisions concerning *where to intervene*. At what point in the system should intervention occur? Should it be at the immediate source of the disruptive behavior or at a more distal point? For example, in the case of a problem student in a classroom, should the student be the intervention point? Or should the organization of the classroom, or the teacher, or the organization of the school, or the student's family network be the intervention point?

Third, decisions must be made about the *nature of the intervention*. What should be done? Should re-education of elements within the system be attempted? Should systemic reorganization be attempted? What are the limits on the techniques which the intervener can use?

All of these questions are certainly answerable. However, the answers are in part based on values. In most cases, the values are some combination of the intervener's personal set of standards, those of the profession, and those of the broad social order. In some instances, the values from the various sources may all be the same; in others, conflict may exist. In such instances, the intervener's own values appear to take precedence.

Although the various value systems outlined above affect decisions regarding the intervention process, there does exist a standard by which interveners can assess the decisions they make. Throughout this paper, enhancement of human effectiveness has been emphasized. This forms the basic criteria against which intervention decisions must be made. Actions and techniques are warranted to the extent that they facilitate the effective support of human life.

Of course, this standard itself is a value, and in terms of translation into practical terms raises a number of questions, since the standard of facilitation of effective functioning does not remain constant, but, rather, is a dynamic entity whose shape changes as the cellular boundaries of the one-celled amoeba change.

Related to this is the effect of the value orientation of the system in which intervention is to occur. The success of any such venture is a function of the nature of this orientation, as actions and techniques at odds with it are likely to encounter only opposition, either actively or passively. For example, intervention emphasizing personal enhancement is unlikely to be enthusiastically received by a system for which this is not a priority value, without some attempt on the part of the intervener to relate this value to the system's existing values.

Once intervention is undertaken—even successful intervention—it does not solve all problems; in fact, it often creates new problems. We shall refer to this phenomenon as the tension-producing character of change. Generally, we define a system as being in need of intervention when tensions or negative forces exist. Intervention, regardless of its nature, is designed to alleviate these tensions. However, to the frequent dismay of many interveners, these efforts themselves often produce unforseen tensions. The reason for this is that within systems changes in one area have repercussions in connecting areas. For example, the desegregation of the public school system in the South resulted in a decrease in the number of teaching positions and a subsequent loss of both positions and status for Black teachers and principals. While the intervener can never anticipate all possible systemic effects of a change, one can anticipate some and be alert to the likelihood of the occurrence of others. This awareness of the possibility of the unforseen effects and their resultant tensions is extremely important as it can prevent disillusionment on the part of the intervener.

MODALITIES OF INTERVENTION

How then do we bring about change? The question of effective intervention for the purpose of bringing about change in the lives of human beings is the ultimate question of the mental health practitioner. Our discussion, which has defined the human being as an interactive entity with a socio-cultural matrix, certainly suggests real limitations with any form of individual intervention. The systems approach rather vividly describes the interaction between processes. So, with an understanding both of those forces which bring about change in systems and of systems' responses to change, we can now look at the community as a system and discuss intervention at the level of community.

The effectiveness of the community system can be assessed on the basis of its success in nourishing human life. A community which fails to produce effective, productive, developing human beings is a dysfunctional community. The purpose for intervention is to correct or reduce those processes that inhibit proper human development and to improve those processes that facilitate this function. We can systematically look at means and areas of intervention by returning to the levels of community. The degree to which the physical, mental, and spiritual communities function as mediums in which human life develops is a description of how to improve human life in those dimensions.

INTERVENTION IN THE PHYSICAL COMMUNITY

The level at which intervention is most observable and most manageable with traditional resources is in the physical community. A baseline condition for effective human functioning and development is the provision of a physical environment conducive to human growth. Conditions such as cleanliness, security, proper health care, and the availability of nourishing food and protective shelter and clothing are essential "basics." Abraham Maslow, in his hierarchy of needs, has described the necessity of such resources for the initiation and maintenance of human development.

As apparent as these necessities for physical maintenance are, mental health workers frequently fail to assess the adequacy of such resources before assessing the intrapsychic individual conditions. Certainly, one would not expect to find an "adequately" functioning human being under conditions that were inadequate for human life. Realistically, the starved, dirty, physically ill, unprotected human being can only respond in humanly disordered ways. Physical environments which deprive human beings of such survival necessities are environments that are destructive to human life.

The first level at which we must intervene in the physical community is to ensure that minimal conditions for human physical needs are met by that environment. Filthy, unhealthy, unsafe communities must be made reasonably clean, healthy, and safe; shelter and clothing that protect against the elements and meet minimal standards of human dignity, modesty, and cultural appropriateness must be available at the level of the physical community. If some in the physical community "have" and others do not "have," then the community is dysfunctional. This is particularly true when there are systematic barriers which prevent the "have nots" from having. We are not suggesting any kind of unrealistic utopia whereby there is a thoroughly equitable distribution of resources throughout the community. We are suggesting that a functional community must provide for the minimal necessities of its inhabitants and that those with excess should not be permitted to monopolize the vital resources.

Whatever may be the processes by which these basic resources may be obtained is the level at which community intervention must occur. If the hindrance is in governmental bureaucracy, then "city hall" must be confronted. If the barrier is with inadequate employment, then industry, merchants, and other potential employers must be confronted. If the barrier is with general human apathy and neglect, then the people must be generally confronted and motivated to correct their own physical community.

Another aspect of the physical community at which intervention may frequently be necessary is in terms of affective human relationships. Other people with whom we interact are the carriers of belief systems, customs, and organizational patterns. So, an essential part of what comes from the physical community is transmitted through other human beings. The tie which binds human beings together is generally an affective or emotional tie. How one receives messages from other people is to a great extent determined by the nature and quality of the affective ties.

There are various ways to improve the affective ties among people. Many of the traditional group and family therapy methods are effective for this purpose. The basic idea is to recognize that one's emotional reaction to family members and other significant people in the physical community will determine one's ability to gain from the physical community. Therefore, it often becomes necessary to facilitate contact, communication, and positive reactions to those in the physical environment. The degree to which people share a physical environment and operate either distantly or with hostility is the degree to which people are unable to receive proper benefits from the physical environment. Proper growth and development is not possible in an environment with negative effect. Community awareness groups, basic encounter groups, block clubs, and other activities foster positive ties. As we mentioned earlier, the ancient adage "love thy neighbor" could be a basic principle of community facility. In fact, the very universality of this proverbial statement is suggestive of its indispensability for community life.

Related to the need for good affective ties within the physical community is the necessity for justice. The only way that people can develop a sense of predictability and, consequently, trust in their environments, is when there is a system of reliable justice. When justice does not reign equally, life in the physical community becomes characterized by suspicion and distrust. The necessary respect and cooperation among members of the community begins to disappear. The result is that members in the community begin to display reactions which are likely to be characterized as disordered. Therefore, the mental health worker has a responsibility to remain in contact with the system of justice. It is necessary that occasionally there must be intervention at this level in order to encourage a functional system of justice. A part of the mental health worker's role is that of an advocate for people in the physical community to ensure that their environment is regulated in a balanced system.

Community systems must remain open, or at least semi-open, to effectively interact with people and other system levels. The vehicle by which this exchange takes place is communication. As a general rule, there must be an open system of communication within the physical community that effectively informs people. The communication system has the vital responsibility of providing feedback to those within the physical community. Feedback is essential for bringing about constructive changes in systems. Therefore, the mental health worker must occasionally intervene in, or at least monitor, the system of communication, since this system is so critical as a shaper of people. Even the direct service role to a client or system within a community is one of providing critical communication. The mental health worker must, therefore, understand the processes and be aware of the particular content of communications entering that physical community. The shared root word "commune" for both communication and community is indicative of the inseparable connection between the two processes.

In general, the physical community is a womb for human growth. It must be carefully watched and corrected when it fails to offer those things critical for the development of life within it. Intervention at the physical-community level goes far beyond "patient" or individual contact in the same way that an obstetrician cannot examine a fetus without examining its mother. Intervention must effectively be accomplished through the vessel that feeds the developing life within.

INTERVENTION IN THE MENTAL COMMUNITY

As with the physical community, the mental level of community provides an environment by which people define themselves and through which their developing lives are nourished. Therefore, the assessment of the mental community must be viewed in light of its effectiveness in cultivating human potential. There are some basic questions that should be asked about the quality of the knowledge, ideas, and concepts that are disseminated in the mental community. The degree to which educational institutions are the source of such ideas is the degree to which mental health intervention must make an impact on these institutions. Other components of the society, such as the media, are powerful purveyors of ideas which form the mental community and should also be viewed in this light. The questions that should be asked are related to the adequacy of the concepts and ideas for the stimulation of mental growth and human survival.

One basic question that must be addressed to the mental community is whether the concepts and ideas that characterize that community facilitate the solution of personal and community problems. If a body of knowledge and concepts are being disseminated for the purpose of improving human life, then the real test of those concepts is whether or not they equip people to bring about such change or improvement. For example, we should assess the quality of the social scientist's concepts by his effectiveness in solving social problems. We should be able to assess the caliber of an ideology by the quality of human life that is produced.

Another question that must be asked in assessing the mental community is whether or not people's choices based on these ideologies facilitate group and personal development. If an African American scholar has internalized concepts suggesting that the most effective learning is that which occurs in a predominantly Caucasian educational environment, then he is likely to contribute his skills to the development of those institutions. By making such a choice, he deprives the African American institution of his potentially valuable skills, and, if continued systematically, these institutions will die because of such neglectful choices. With such destructive choices being made, one would need to question the quality of the mental community and, perhaps, plan to make some systematic alterations in the knowledge that is being disseminated.

Another question that must be asked of the mental community is "Does the knowledge of mental community foster self-knowledge and a positive self-concept?" Do the attitudes, ideas, and beliefs that are acquired from the mental community facilitate a positive view of oneself? Does the cultural, historical, and general information acquired expand the person's knowledge of herself and of her historical antecedents? This is a critical question because, as the vast self-esteem literature on African Americans has demonstrated, the absence of a positive self-esteem can seriously retard human development. The absence of accurate and meaningful knowledge about one's origins, development, and functioning can seriously retard one's self-esteem, self-concept, and effectiveness in the community. Many of the identified mental health problems are actually rooted in low self-esteem, general ignorance, or misinformation about oneself and one's potentials.

Intervention at the mental community level can be one of the most important points of impact. It is also the most likely to be neglected because of the level or caliber of activity which must be performed to make an impact at this level. The nature of the opposition to new ideas, concepts, and undeveloped knowledge is likely to be vehement and intense; the tendency to maintain an existing system of knowledge is rigorously defended. Therefore, the workers who see fit to intervene at this level must be prepared to endure considerable opposition.

In addition, the worker must be committed to high quality research, scholarship, and criticism, and he must exemplify creative thought as well as a good mastery of the foundation of the existing mental community. This, of course, involves intervention at the highest ranks of the mental community. At less advanced levels, the community intervener should simply be aware of the needs of the person from his mental community and be capable of helping that community facilitate a more serviceable dispensation of knowledge. It may involve meeting with teachers and providing them with information about African American or Hispanic contributions to world civilization. It may simply involve sensitizing teachers to the realities of cultural variation and effects it has on people, both in their perception, expectations, and behaviors. It may involve meeting with school boards or college administrators about making changes in their curricula that will better accommodate the needs of certain students. It may involve contacting libraries or local educational TV stations about making changes in their offerings to provide better, more effective knowledge for the public that they serve. All of these are ways to intervene in the mental community to create effective environments in which human beings can grow.

INTERVENTION IN THE SPIRITUAL COMMUNITY

As intangible and difficult as the mental community is to identify, the spiritual community is even more nebulous. By its true nature, direct intervention in the spiritual community is probably out of the range of possibility for most mental health workers. The spiritual community brings us into the realm of the potential, the sphere of the ideals, and the unrealized areas of human possibility The ideas and concepts of the mental community are tangible enough for one to describe observable patterns and behaviors. Concepts are reflected in certain organizational forms and rational structures. You can test the logic of such organizational forms with certain objective rules of reasoning and internal consistency.

In the spiritual community, however, many ideals are not necessarily rational, simply because they reflect what is potentially real rather than what is already real. The spiritual community ultimately represents a goal which, in its highest form, is not realizable in this life. It offers merely a direction for attaining a higher form. Despite the intangible quality of the spiritual community, it is still a vital and influential determinant of human growth and functioning. Though we cannot directly intervene in the spiritual community, we can assess its adequacy. Despite its futuristic form, it must offer some observable impact on the present life of the developing human being. Therefore, there are questions that can be asked which can tell us about the adequacy of the spiritual community, at least as it offers meaningful direction for the human being.

The first question is: "Does the spiritual community stimulate human aspiration or human decay?" In other words, do the ideals of the spiritual community encourage human beings to be more humane, i.e., more in control of their lives and more effective as masters of their environments? If the ideals invite the person to a kind of hedonism and loss of personal control, then one must raise questions about the adequacy of that community. If the ideals encourage a surrender to animalistic impulses and behaviors, we must view those ideals as detrimental to the higher human form. We view as adequate those spiritual communities that encourage human beings to develop their rational and moral processes. These represent the unique powers of the human being, the development of which the spiritual community should foster.

If the person's vistas are limited by his spiritual community, and she finds herself incapable of growth, improvement, perfectibility, then the community is deficient. Or, if the spiritual community fosters an unrealistic self inflation whereby the person does not deal with her human limitations, then the ideals are destructive. If the ideals of this community encourage a kind of egomania that breeds disrespect for higher causes, purposes, and processes, then the ideals render the person self-destructively vulnerable to the greater power of those forces.

The next question that can be asked in assessing the spiritual community is: "Does this community facilitate a harmonious relationship at other levels of community experience?" For example, does the spiritual community offer direction for living more effectively with other people in the physical community, or does it encourage a kind of elitism which makes compatible relationships with other people difficult? Does it offer direction for obtaining a stable and harmonious life from the resources of the physical community? Do the spiritual ideals consistently foster conflict with rational and sense experiences? Are people encouraged to reject sense information in order to aspire for spiritual ideals? Such reactions result in an unnecessary alienation from the mental community. As we described earlier, the ideal relationship is for the various communities to increasingly overlap; this can be facilitated by the nature of the ideals in the spiritual community.

As a related perspective in assessing the adequacy of the spiritual community, it is important to ascertain the appropriateness of the ideals to the solution of contemporary problems. Occasionally, the spiritual community can project such a futuristic perspective that people become alienated from the "here-and-now." They become incapable of dealing with current physical and mental community realities because they are suspended in a "pie-in-the-sky" state. Such an orientation becomes maladaptive for effective human development. If the spiritual community sits apart and separate from the person's other community experiences, then it encourages a fragmentation in the human being. Such fragmentation prohibits effective value formation, self-mastery, and general functioning.

CLOSING REMARKS

Intervention at the various community levels is the key to resolving human problems. The degree to which the person is a by-product of the impressions made by these communities places the onus of human failure on the community. Defect in the human material becomes another topic of consideration and is probably only a minor determinant of the vast number of mental disorders which plague our society. Certainly, the overwhelming emphasis over the last one hundred years has been on the defects in the human material. Until the growth in the community mental health movement of modern times, inadequate attention had been given to the detrimental effects of community on human functioning. This chapter represents a further contribution to uncovering the vital importance of community. Hopefully, it is now apparent, (even if unstated to this point) that, throughout, this chapter has been informed by, fuelled by, and infused with the African worldview assumptions of the inextricability of the person from the community concept and the higher natures (mental and spiritual) characteristic of the human being.

REFERENCES

Bertalanffy, L. V. *General system theory*. New York: George Braziller, 1968.

Boughey, A. S. *Fundamental ecology*. New York: International Textbook Company, 1971.

Myers, E. R. *The Community psychology concept: Integrating theory, education and practice in psychology, social work and public administration*. Washington, D.C.: University Press of America, 1977.

Odum, E. P. *Fundamentals of ecology*. 2nd ed. Philadelphia: W. B. Saunders, 1959.

Rappaport, J. *Community psychology: Values, research and action*. New York: Holt, Rinehart and Winston, 1977.

Seiler, J. A. *Systems analysis in organizational behavior*. Homewood, Illinois: Richard D. Irwin, 1967.

CHAPTER 10

Science and Oppression

Jacob H. Carruthers

> The only question which concerns us here is whether these educated persons are actually equipped to face the ordeal before them or unconsciously contribute to their own undoing by perpetuating the regime of the oppressor . . . . The so-called modern education, with all its defects, however, does others so much more good than it does the Negro, because it has been worked out in conformity to the needs of those who have enslaved and oppressed weaker peoples. For example, the philosophy and ethics resulting from our educational system have justified slavery, peonage, segregation and lynching.
>
> Carter G. Woodson, *Miseducation of the Negro*

The following observations are not original. They grow from our collective wisdom and have been said quite forcefully and well by our elders such as Carter G. Woodson and young warriors such as "Rap" Brown. There is, however, a need to reemphasize and restate this wisdom as it relates to the idea of science or scientific knowledge and methods of inquiry. The scientific community and its admirers arrogantly assert that science is itself objective and neutral, i.e., that it can be used for good or bad; *but our wisdom instructs us otherwise*.

Whenever one is engaged in the discovery and/or collation and/or dissemination of knowledge, he is, consciously or not, legitimizing a particular theory of knowledge and knowing. That is, he is saying real knowledge is thus-and-so, or the way to know about something is to perform these approved operations. Modern science tends to merge the theory of knowledge and the theory of knowing into a single methodological solution. In short, the theory states that valid knowledge is that which can be verified by any qualified observer using the same methods, all other things being equal. Thus, if I say that the fusion of oxygen and hydrogen in certain proportions and under certain conditions will produce water and if another observer (or many others), after duplicating the process, reaches the same conclusion, one can then say that the conclusion is knowledge, or, "this we know."

The methodology is generally known as the experimental method and is ideally the model for all modern scientific disciplines, modified only by practical considerations. Physics is thus generally considered the most scientific discipline and the social science disciplines the least scientific. Mathematics and logic are analytical tools or methods which help clarify the relationships studied by the sciences, but are not in themselves sciences.

When one analyzes the experimental method, he soon sees that this particular methodology is itself considered science. When experimentation is impossible, inconvenient, or impractical, the process most resembling experimentation is resorted to—usually called systematic observation. Astronomy and anthropology are examples of the latter. Physics and sociology are considered quite experimental, although some argue that sociological data is not so amenable to the scientific method. Nevertheless, the experimental persuasion determined the standards of validity, however imperfectly the particular science is developed, and all of this is legitimized by way of widespread and longstanding agreements among members of the scientific community.

Time and space are in this methodology either minimized by elimination of qualitative distinctions, or qualitative distinctions are converted into quantitative distinctions. This latter feature poses special problems for the social sciences, but "fortunately" a theory of "social progress" (cultural Darwinism, philosophy of history, dialectics) is kept in reserve to explain qualitative differences in time. Thus modified, the methodology lends itself to the exploration of most significant mysteries and problems.

The first question we must ask is whether and in what way this methodology is useful to us. Obviously this is the methodology that increasingly legitimizes the opinions that determine policies in social, economic, and educational areas. The opinions now influencing public policy, especially in the field of education, are widely criticized and to some extent challenged by studies using the same scientific methodology (from the vantage point of different biases or assumptions). Thus, one possible use for this methodology is to buffer against undesirable conclusions generated by the "abuse" of the methodology. This in itself is a valid reason if its limits are properly understood. One problem this poses for us is the usual powerlessness of the challengers and the unwillingness of the controllers of institutions to change or to put down established experts for rebel upstart experts. Another problem is the possible use of the challengers' opinions to accomplish objectives not intended. For example, the report may be received, shelved, and pulled out ten years later to respond to a different problem and an unintended end.

Another possible use of the methodology is that it is an effective resource to generate the necessary knowledge for liberation, because it is the only methodology designed to deal with the ills of this system. This use is analogous to modern Western medicine, but, since Africans today suffer from European diseases, it must be used for survival. But this use in itself does not change the system and may make the oppression more perfect.

Another possible use gets closer to the problem. It seems necessary that those who represent the interests of the powerless know the tools used to accomplish the oppression. In this regard social science knowledge and natural science knowledge are being used as instruments of oppression (e.g., birth control). Some of the oppressed must know how this knowledge is generated for us to nullify and/or prepare for its implementation. Consequently, one may contemplate the ultimate dismantling of the science itself because of its oppressiveness.

The dismantling of the scientific methodology would leave a void that must be filled or justified; so, at least, conventional Western wisdom informs us. First, we must understand more precisely why scientific methodology has such a limited usefulness for oppressed people. The answer, in short, is that it is the Master's science, not only in the sense that he uses it to control his subjects but also in the sense that it was established through and for oppression. That is, the original assumptions *are* oppression, suppression, and repression. Thus, the science or methodology is not neutral or objective; it is the science of control through intervention and/or the unnatural alteration (if possible) of all objects. When intervention and modification are successful, then the hypothesis is proved; if not, then impurity in the application of the methodology is alleged (either because of limited primary knowledge or bias). Thus, the conquest of Africa is not basically different from the conquest of uranium. Both started with a theory about harnessing certain forces and subduing certain oppositions to the desired change. Both required laboratory experiments (cyclotrons for uranium and the West Indies slave system for Africans). Both resulted in the unnatural re-ordering of the behavior of the objects. Lest the analogy be depreciated, we must realize that social science or philosophy occupies almost the same position *vis-à-vis* governance or social policy as does pure science *vis-à-vis* applied sciences or technology.

The assumptions are based on the so-called self-evident notion that nature is uneven in supplying the needs of man; thus, the maximization of individual survival can be achieved by modification of natural supply, e.g., cultivation and animal husbandry. While this fact may be universally shared wisdom (though not necessarily ultimate truth), Western science assumes that any desirable modification of nature is dictated by the same wisdom. Thus, not only is it right to modify nature to supply needs, but it is also right to conform nature to all other tastes, in keeping with the doctrine of enlightened self-interest.

Additionally, modern methodology is based upon ordinal classifications. The various phenomena are ranked according to imagined or imposed objective values such as magnitude or complexity or "natural" arrangements derived from so-called systematic comparisons. An offensive example is the classification of African societies as simplistic and primitive, and European societies as complex and advanced. A more subtle example is the assertion that amoeba are simplistic and apes are complex. The point is, that all the evaluative criteria for reaching such conclusions are tautological. Since modern science is based on superordinated-subordinated arrangements, the use of it by oppressed people will result at best in rearrangement or reordering which alone is not sufficient to solve the problem.

A final point is necessary for true insight into the modern scientific methodology. The experimental method does not necessarily discover more primary knowledge or raw data than any other possible methodology (at least per unit of effort expended), but "its" superiority lies in the fact that it assumes an obligation to impose reorder on every possible object whether of immediate relevance or not. This is often mistaken as pure science or the search for knowledge for knowledge's sake. Therefore, implicit in the scientific methodology is the command that no mountain will be unscaled, no fact will remain unexplained.

If the learning of the scientific method has such limited, albeit indispensable, usefulness, then what should take its place as it is dismantled? The solution is difficult to formulate, partly because we so often confuse the familiar with the necessary. The answer is, in short, the systematic gathering and studying of the collective wisdom of the oppressed people and then using the wisdom to determine such things as priorities and validity. The "methods" of research will be determined by the wisdom, which is in itself based upon the reality of the Black experience. Thus, liberation of documents may be more relevant as a research technique than many of the more orthodox ones. Similarly, a standard of validity may be the deception of some potential readers and at the same time the enlightenment of others.

What has stood in the way of using collective wisdom in the past is the influence of outside allies and foreign ideas which has been more directive than informative—a condition that must be radically altered. More often than not, the foreign influences have refuted our collective wisdom, all to our disadvantage. Needless to say, this absurdity was primarily the responsibility of the educated component of our people who accepted the outsiders' knowledge too uncritically. Woodson informed:

> The Negro thus educated is a hopeless liability of the race. . . . When a Negro has finished his education in our schools, then, he has been equipped to begin the life of an Americanized or Europeanized white man, but before he steps from the threshold of his alma mater he is told by his teachers that he must go back to his own people from whom he has been estranged by a vision of ideals which in his disillusionment he will realize that he cannot attain. . . . Even if Negroes do successfully imitate the whites, nothing new had thereby been accomplished. You simply have a larger number of persons doing what others have been doing. The unusual gifts of the race have not thereby been developed, and an unwilling world therefore continues to wonder what the Negro is good for.

The reason for giving our undivided attention to this matter is implied in the quotations from Brother Woodson's *Miseducation of the Negro*. Our students are caught between the philosophy of liberation and the methodology of oppression. Let us resolve the contradiction and put our program together.

Now Poem For Us

Don't let them die out
All of these old-Black-people
Don't let them cop out
With their memories of slavery-survival
It is our heritage U know. Part-African.
Part-Negro.
Part-slave.
Sit down with em brothas and sisthus.
Talk to em. Listen to their
Tales of victories - woes - sorrows.
Listen to their Blk-
MYTHS.
Record them talken their ago talk

For our tomorrows.
Ask them bout the songs of
Births.
The herbs that cured their aches
The crazy - niggers blowen some crackers cool.
The laughter.
Comen out of tears
Let them tel us their juju years
So ours will be that much stronger.

Sonia Sanchez

Chapter II

Towards a Cultural Science

Leachim Tufani Semaj

> It comes to the individual, the race, the nation, once in a life time to decide upon the course to be pursued as a career. The hour has now struck for the individual Negro as well as the entire race to decide the course that will be pursued in the interest of our own liberty.
>
> Marcus Garvey, *Philosophy and Opinions*

The debate between Mack Jones (1976, 1977) and Rutledge Dennis (1977)—"scientific practitioner or impassioned advocate?"—illustrates the ongoing concerns regarding the role of the Black scholar in the liberation struggle. The debate still continues, and, while it does, the "cause of the oppressed" is the greatest casualty. It is agreed that both roles are necessary, but Jones invests a great deal of confidence in the scientific method. He suggests that this method will "facilitate the maximization of certainty." Therefore, it is "after (with the help of science) we have presented the truth we should then become advocates and activists in the direction which that truth leads" (1976, 10). I share Dennis' concern regarding Jones' faith in science as it is known and practiced. Before we decide how much of the scientific method we adopt and what other methods should be excluded from consideration, we need to ask more questions.

WHAT IS SCIENCE?

For Carl Spight (1974), it is not possible historically to separate science as it has been formulated in Western society from Western culture itself. He therefore sees science as "the attempt of a people to achieve an ordered articulation of reality." Science is seen to have the following three aspects:

1. It is a body of knowledge, a set of ordered verifacts, an artifact of culture, an object defined by its constancy.
2. It is a methodology, a process, a dynamic phenomenon, an object defined by its historality.
3. It is a social activity, a human expression, an object defined by its subjectivity.

Wade Nobles (1978) elaborates on these points. He states that Western science and particularly social science are, like the economic and political institutions, instruments designed to reflect the culture of the oppressor and allow for more efficient domination. Like Spight, Nobles also sees that since science is a human activity, despite artificial divisions between hard and soft, it is therefore a social activity. Consequently, all science can be considered social science.

Drawing on Spight's (1974) work, Adams (1979) summarizes six standard myths of science:

1. Science is fundamentally culturally independent and universal.
2. The only reliable and completely objective language is scientific knowledge.
3. Science is dispassionate, unemotional and anti-religious.
4. Logic is the fundamental tool of science.
5. The scientific method leads systematically and progressively towards truth.
6. Technological progress is dependent on scientific progress.

To these myths we can add the role of science as articulated by Nobles (1978). He sees that there has been a change from the traditional role of enhancing technical and industrial power. Today in Western societies science is primarily concerned with "the creation and use of ideas and theories designed to control the use of power" (and oppressed people). "Where power before was defined by the use of physical energy, power, today, is defined by the creation of ideas and the ability to have people respond to one's ideas as if these ideas represented the respondents reality". This is similar to the concept of cultural imperialism:

> The oppressor defining reality . . . and having the oppressed respond to that definition of reality as if it were their own. This is usually achieved without even raising a finger because it involves the world of theories, concepts, and ideas—metaphysics, epistemology, ethics and even esthetics (Semaj 1981, 412).

Nobles therefore warns that any attempt on the part of the oppressed to build a science of liberation using the ideas and beliefs that construct the science of the oppressor can only further enhance the oppression.

Despite these observations, Marvin Harris (1979) and many others believe that science is a superior way of knowing and thus should be distinguished and elevated above all other methods (6). This position is strongly rejected by Paul Feyerabend (1975):

> . . . we arrive at the result that the separation of science and non-science is not only artificial but also detrimental to the advancement of knowledge . . . we must use all ideas, all methods and not just a small section of them. The assertion, however, that there is no knowledge outside science—extra scientism nulla salus—is nothing but a . . . fairytale. (173)

This therefore means that a science of liberation must go beyond science as we now know it and have been trained to practice it.

It is now necessary for us to examine specifically "social" science and decide if it can be saved or if we need a new superstructure within which to build a science of liberation. This is because most of us who desire to build a science of liberation were trained by whites as social scientists. Bernal (1971) provides an enlightening survey of bourgeois social sciences. A critique based on his work will be provided in three areas: the purpose of the social sciences, experimentation, and applications.

THE PURPOSE OF SOCIAL SCIENCE

In contrast to the natural sciences, which are primarily concerned with the productive forces of society, "the social sciences deal with productive relations and the ideological superstructure built to maintain and justify them." The knowledge one gains from studying society can never be passive; "it is always active, either in preserving or in destroying a social system." Therefore all through history it has been dangerous to look too closely at the workings of one's society because of the ruling class' desire to maintain the illusion that the order of society which secured them their privileges has been divinely ordained for all times or dictated by such doctrines as Social Darwinism. The result is that we have backward social sciences. Instead of being in the vanguard of social progress, "in practice social sciences under present day capitalism are apparently doomed to lag years or decades behind the situations they have to analyse." The reason for this backwardness is due not merely to the complexity of the subject matter but to strong social pressure from established ruling groups to prevent serious discussion of the foundations of society. When prevention fails, efforts are directed at distortion. The forces of imperialism and capitalism will permit social science to go but so far and do but so much under the watchful eyes of their gatekeepers in the universities, funding agencies, and publishers. Often the gatekeepers have insisted that social science should be pure and objective and divorced from direct concern with the changes in society. What this does is remove social science from the only means of solid advance, direct involvement with real issues. The result is that today social science is largely an accumulation of trivial studies occasionally invoked "to justify the existing order, either directly by pointing out the essential harmonies of the system or indirectly by pointing to the impossibility of any suggestion of changing it" (Bernal 1971:1025).

EXPERIMENTATION AND APPLICATION

Experimentation is the method most accepted by even bourgeois scientists for producing valid and reliable information. However, under capitalism, experimentation, practice, and application are severely curtailed by the restriction imposed by private property, vested interest, and profit. Despite the thousands of degrees granted in the social sciences every year, the problems of society remain largely unchanged. The inequities and injustices are still with us. It is obvious that these thousands of scholars have not been neutral in their study of society but instead have actively maintained the status quo or passively supported it. Bernal sums up his review of the social sciences by stating that its backwardness and emptiness are primarily due to the fact that societies stratified by class (and race) are inevitably corrupt. No real science of society can exist that does not begin with the recognition of this fact.

With regards to the Black community, Cross (1973) concludes that "social scientists have traditionally been content with a statistical, categorical, static descriptive analysis . . . with minimal time and effort spent on prescriptive analysis for rectifying the Black condition" (281). Clark (1972) raises similar questions by contrasting "Black Studies" and the "Study of Black People." As he sees it, "The task for Black Studies . . . is to describe the nature and limitations of `classical' social science and . . . develop a framework within which a `modern' social science can develop and hopefully flourish" (5). The purpose of this new science should be nothing more, or less, than the liberation of the Black mind (Clark 1972). Walters (1973) also presents similar arguments, from his perspective as a political scientist, for the need "to make the social sciences more meaningful and practical to the Black condition." He provides an analysis of the contribution of various Black scholars toward developing a "Black Social Science." In this "new" social science the scholar should also be an activist. The methodology and ideology of "Black Social Science" should be grounded in the uniqueness of Black life. The emphasis should not be on neutrality but on the development and utilization of theories of social change. Walters cautions that serious attention must also be paid to what kind of research is funded, who does the funding, who carries out the research, what are the findings, how they will be disseminated, and how the results will be used. Also, the Black scholar should not stand passive while the "destruction and dehumanization of our communities (continue) through white social science research" (206), but be prepared to intervene at any stage of this process. Finally, we are reminded that the tools of social science cannot reveal the whole truth, that the rest comes from the "moral and ethical implications of what (your) keen senses tell you to be true." Therefore, we who desire to build a science of liberation need to be more than just "good" social scientists.

CULTURAL SCIENCE

My culture is getting stronger,
I know I'll never surrender.
— *Black Uhuru*

It has therefore become apparent that the building of a science of liberation is contingent on the articulation of an alternate set of guidelines. This will allow us to make explicit some of the ideas which have so far only been implicit in the works of the few scholars who are presently attempting proactive solutions (for example, Maulana Karenga and Haki Madhubuti). Irvin Brown has suggested the name "Cultural Science," defined as the total study of a people. This term is useful because "culture" is a wider construct than "social" issues, which are limited to the interpersonal domain. The concept of culture is an optimistic one. Many of the life scientists, social scientists, and humanists who speak about the future are exceedingly gloomy because they do not think in cultural terms (Downs 1973:329). But man is more than biological, more than social: man is cultural. As Africans, four hundred years has provided concrete examples that culture made possible our survival, strengthened our resistance, and will make possible our liberation. We can completely redefine our reality, because of our cultural potential. We are products of our culture but, at the same time, have the ability to consciously reconstruct our culture. This means, therefore, that we are not dependent on any single line of explanation. We are free to go wherever truth leads, because boundaries become challenges.

The following are the minimum principles of a Cultural Science:

1. *The primacy of self-knowledge*: This means that research will be in response to the ancient African admonition "Know Thyself."

Drawing from the African ontology, we see that the "self" is represented by expanding concentric rings going from individual, to family, to clan, to tribe, to nation, to people, and finally to world. The extension of this principle will be knowledge of the forces working to oppress one's people and strategies for liberation.

2. *The absence of artificial divisions via discipline*: This will subvert the "divide and conquer" strategies and bring a diversity of perspectives for solutions. Scholars will also be encouraged to understand each other's orientation, thus enabling more collective efforts.

3. *No restriction on issues and methodologies*: This will naturally result from the second principle. More novel solutions should be possible since scholars would not be restricted by the dictates of disciplines and so should feel free to venture outside the confines imposed by social science.

4. *No scientific colonization*: This principle is discussed by Nobles (1976, 1978) and is almost always violated by white social scientists and many Blacks who have learned no other way. Scientific colonization is the process by which information (raw data) is extracted from the community for the benefit of the scientist and others located outside of the community. The scholar should be a servant of the people. Thus, *research conducted to serve the interest of the people takes primacy* over research which is conducted mainly to advance the scientist's career or satisfy some idiosyncratic curiosity.

5. *The scientist should be concerned with the possible interpretation and application of the data* and take necessary action to prevent distortion and ensure appropriate application.

6. *The publication and distribution of your work* cannot be entrusted to any individual or institution that does not share your commitment to the liberation of your people.

7. *Practice what you preach*: A scholar whose lifestyle is inconsistent with the implication of his work and the collective achievement of our people cannot be taken seriously.

With these principles it will be possible for the Black scholar to meet "the challenge . . . if not the obligation . . . to study, amplify, and develop those processes which (will) create conditions of Black liberation, even if these conditions are not to be legitimized in the sacred halls of Western scholarship" (Cross 1973:284). The Black scholar will also be able to resolve the dilemma aired by Mack Jones (1976). As a Cultural Scientist, the Sister or Brother will try to integrate knowledge gained by the interplay of reason and experimentation with knowledge gained by experience, inspiration, and revelation. This will provide a necessary movement towards a synthesis of the empirical and intuitive modes which characterized early African sciences (Adams, 1979). All this is designed for one primary purpose, the liberation of our people.

REFERENCES

Adams, H. H. III. African observers of the universe: The sirius question. *Journal of African Civilizations* 1, 2 (1979):1-20.

Bernal, J. D. *Science in history: The social sciences*. Vol. 4. Cambridge, Mass.: MIT Press, 1971.

Clark, C. Black studies or the study of Black people? In *Black psychology*, ed. R. Jones New York: Harper & Row, 1972.

Cross, W. E. The Negro-to-Black conversation experience. In *The death of white sociology*, ed. J. Ladner New York: Vintage Books, 1973.

Dennis, R. Science, knowledge, and values: A response to Mack Jones. *The Review of Black Political Economy* 7, 4 (1977):424-32.

Downs, J. *Human nature: An introduction to cultural anthropology*. New York: Glencoe Press, 1973.

Feyerabend, P. Science: The myth and its role in society. *Inquiry* 18 (Summer 1975): 167-81.

Harris, M. Research strategies and the structure of science. In *Cultural materialism: The struggle for a science of culture*. New York: Random House, 1979.

Jones, M. Scientific method, value judgments, and the Black predicament in the USA. *Review of Black Political Economy* 7, 1 (1976):7-21.

Jones, M. In defense of the scientific method: A reply to Rutledge M. Dennis. *Review of Black Political Economy* 7, 4 (1977):433-40.

Nobles, W. Extended self: Rethinking the Negro self-concept. *Journal of Black Psychology*, 2 (1976) 15-24.

Nobles, W. African consciousness and liberation struggles: Implications for the development and construction of scientific paradigms. Paper presented to the Fanon Research Development Conference, The Theory and Practice of the Social Scientist in the Context of Human Development: Developing People and

Institutions for Creative Struggle, February, Port of Spain, Trinidad.

Semaj, L. 1981. Race and identity and children of the African Diaspora: Contributions of Rastafari. *Studia Africana* 1, 4 (1978):412-19.

Spight, C. Towards a Black science and technology. *Black Books Bulletin* 56, 3 (1974):6-11, 49.

Chapter 12

Personality, Clinical, and Social Psychological Research on Blacks: Appropriate and Inappropriate Research Frameworks*

Daudi Ajani ya Azibo

Introduction

The purpose of this paper is to provide the structural framework for an *emic* (within-cultural) *research approach* for certain fields of psychology to be applied to U.S. African-Americans. When appropriately adjusted, the approach may be applicable for all persons of African descent irrespective of ethnicity or geopolitical status. This "emic" approach is termed *the theory-derived steady-state approach.* (It will be contrasted, below, with two more established approaches: the comparative and the cross-cultural.)

The lack of an extant, articulated approach to research on Black persons is a hindrance to quality—from the standpoint of significance in meaning—psychological research, particularly for students and the conceptually incarcerated professionals. The quality of psychological studies will be enhanced when the role of the Black personality (i.e., psychological Blackness) is made a central concern in the research. The theory-derived steady state approach requires the inclusion of the Black or African personality construct in one's research. The position is taken that in any personality, clinical, or social psychological research on African-Americans nontrivial variance can be accounted for by the Black personality. Firstly, then, we must try to surmount some of the "confusion and misrepresentation regarding black personality" (Akbar, 1979, p. 79) prior to discussing the research approaches.

THE BLACK PERSONALITY

The Black or African personality is a theoretical construct which attempts to explain the psychological functioning of persons with African origins (e.g., Azibo, 1982, 1984; Baldwin, 1981a, 1981b; Semaj, 1981; Williams, 1981). The African origins are fundamental to the Black personality rather than a mere happenstance: biogenetic factors like the essential melanic system (Nobles, 1976a), a melanated pineal gland and the Black Dot or locus coeruleus (King, 1978, 1982), spiritualistic energy, rhythm and others (Azibo, 1983a) so profoundly affect the Black personality that they are regarded as *structural constructs* in the Black personality theory advanced by personologist scholars of the Radical (Karenga, 1982, ch. 8) or Inventive (Jackson, 1979) Schools of Black psychology. These constructs play major roles in the Black person's extended and personal self-maintenance/self-preservative orientation. Therefore, the Black personality is a race-specific or biogenetically grounded construct which (1) is fundamental to individual and Race maintenance and (2) is manifested in behavior via the conscious, psychological operations of the individual. The usage of the term "psychological Blackness" as a synonym for the Black personality's manifest conscious state derives from these two points. This construct, while perhaps new to academia, is as old as African-American culture itself which has always maintained the distinction between genetic Blacks who were psychologically Black and those who were psychologically white (colloquially, Oreos, Toms, and Negroes).

One point to be taken is that there is inherent to *all* Black persons personality psychodynamics rooted in genetic Blackness (hence the nomenclature "the Black or African personality" and "the Black part of the personality") which function at a conscious, psychological level. And, it is here at the level of consciousness that individual differences in the Black personality are observable. Upon the assessment of this psychological (conscious-level) Blackness, considerable variation is found and hence we can empirically distinguish internalized *versus* noninternalized Blacks, Afro-Saxons *versus* Blacks, Afrocentric *versus* Anglocentric Blacks, Negroes versus Blacks, strong *versus* weak Black personalities, and so on. Irrespective of the descriptive terminology used by various writers, the underlying concept is practically the same.

FUTURE BLACK PERSONALITY RESEARCH

Since it generally holds true that people "proceed as they perceive," the demonstration that persons with strong versus weak Black personalities may have dissimilar inference processes (Azibo 1983b) underscores the potential of the Black personality construct for research. It is plausible that other psychological phenomena may be likely moderated (functional differences in strong versus weak Black personalities) and that the construct may have several meaningful psychological correlates as demonstrated by the author (Azibo 1983a, 1983c, 1984, 1991).

Future research must continue to bear empirical witness if this view is to be supported. The emphasis is on future studies because, to date, research involving the Black personality—that is, psychological Blackness and not Eurocentric personality constructs applied to genetically Black persons—is almost nil, except for the aforementioned research programs of the present author and Dr. Kobi Kambon and his colleagues and their students at Florida A & M University (e.g., Baldwin 1987; Kambon 1992). Of the research which has been done by others, most is process oriented: i.e., attempts to delineate how psychological Blackness develops (see Cross 1978; Semaj 1981) which has been misnomered

Nigrescence. Nigrescenality, on the other hand, has been defined as the state or level of psychological Blackness (Williams 1981). The nomenclature *psychological Africanity-development* and *Africanity* will be used hereafter in place of Nigrescence and Nigrescenality, respectively.[1]

This author takes the position that research must attend to the *product* of psychological Blackness as well as the process. Product-oriented Black personality research addresses the effects of psychological Blackness on Black behavior (overt and covert): it is of a functional nature. It can answer questions like: Of what benefit is Africanity to Blacks? How does psychological Blackness enhance the psychological functioning of African-Americans? In effect, product-oriented Black personality research attempts to elucidate the role of Africanity in the psychological functioning of Blacks (cf., Africanity-development).

The theory-derived steady-state approach is presented below to facilitate product-oriented Black personality research. At the same time, it can accommodate process-oriented studies by using a process theory and/or by being developmentally oriented (i.e., a longitudinal or cross-sectional study). The remainder of this article will (a) present the theory-derived steady state approach to research with Blacks, (b) delineate its psychological lineage, and (c) point out the implications of this approach for researchers. In so doing, the comparative and the cross-cultural approaches will necessarily be discussed, evaluated, and contrasted with each other and the theory-derived steady state approach in terms of their proper usage and merit for research into the psyche of Blacks. First, however, we must distinguish between research design and research approach.

DESIGN VERSUS APPROACH

It is the role of research/experimental design *per se* to determine how subjects are assigned to conditions, how the data are collected, analyzed, and so forth. Contradistinctively, a research approach provides the *conceptual framework* in which to, first of all, formulate research or theoretical hypotheses and then after this to conceive and execute a research/experimental design *per se*. Thus, applying the accepted principles of research/experimental design per se is a secondary consideration to the initial thinking which takes place in the context of a research approach.

THE THEORY-DERIVED STEADY STATE APPROACH

When Black persons constitute all or a substantial part of the subjects in a study, the theory-derived steady state research approach is the appropriate conceptual framework to be employed for them. This approach posits that the Black personality plays a significant role in virtually all aspects of Black social and psychological functioning. Therefore, psychological Blackness should be assessed and incorporated as a major or moderator variable in the research. It is imperative that the point be well taken that we are dealing at the level of a research approach here and not a design.

The approach is straightforward, true to its name with three steps: (1) constructs used in researching the Black personality are selected only from theoretical positions about psychological Blackness; (2) instruments conceptually derived from the constructs are used to assess the Africanity (i.e., state or level of Blackness) in the sample; and (3) data collection is completed and hypotheses are tested, etc. This approach puts the (Black) person in (Black) personality research (Carlson, 1971). The important points to be made here concern mainly the first two steps, as the reader may be familiar with collecting data or can get this information elsewhere.

STEP 1

In step 1 is where the "theory-derived" notion originates. Here the approach simply makes the arbitrary dictum that whatever construct of Black personality is utilized be derived from a well-articulated theory. Step 1 precludes any investigation into Black personality by arbitrarily selecting a hodgepodge of variables and instruments to see what, if anything, happens. It also precludes the accumulation of (anymore) resultant data which, in the main, researchers have been hard put to meaningfully interpret (a point returned to below). *Step 1 puts the theory-derived steady state approach in tune with the quintessence of scientific method and function: the advancement of knowledge by the collection of theoretically supportive or nonsupportive data.* Royce (1979) has eloquently stated the issue in the general sense:

> The mere inventorying of invariant factors *cannot* generate advanced forms of science because explanatory theory requires viable conceptual frameworks on which to hang empirical observables. (1929; italics original)

Moreover, a further constraint in step 1 is the dictum that the theories from which constructs and instruments are selected must, at best, come out of the Black perspective or, at least, not be incongruous with it. This constraint means that only theories "derived from a sense of black culture . . . and which embraces the social and political realities involved in existing symbiotically with the larger culture" (Jackson, 1977, p. 231) can fully sufficiently explain the psychological functioning of African-Americans. Prerequisite for theories to share the Black perspective is possession of knowledge of Black cultural identity and ideology on behalf of the theorist. Additionally, this perspective "demands a frame of mind that consciously and consistently affirms the truth of Afrikan-Americans' history and culture" (Smith, 1975, p. 43).

A most important point to be taken here is that requisite for the researcher to operate out of the Black perspective as just defined, his or her conceptual system must be Africentric (Azibo, 1992, and Semmes, 1981, define Africentricity). Only then can the researcher consciously and consistently affirm the truth of African-Americans' history and culture and psychological functioning too. Otherwise, without the Africentric conceptual system the Black researcher can fall prey to the conceptually arresting psychology of oppression inherent under Eurocentric conceptual dominance (see Baldwin, 1980b, 1985; Semmes, 1982). That is, without the Africentric conceptual system the Black researcher's ideation, beliefs, and concepts would probably be constrained to Eurocentric.

Step 1's intuitively appealing requirement for the inclusion of theoretically sound constructs of the Black personality in research on Blacks has hardly been evident in the literature (Black and nonBlack). The argument (excuse) by detractors of the Black perspective that there are not enough models of Black psychological functioning is untrue and unacceptable. Azibo (1982, 1983a, 1984,

1990, in press) has discussed ten theories of Black personality (e.g., Baldwin, 1981a, 1981b; Semaj, 1981; Williams, 1981) and models of psychological Africanity-development (e.g., Cross, 1978; Toldson & Pasteur, 1975) which meet the criteria of step 1.

Regarding theoretical constructs which are not of the Black perspective, researchers must be mindful that the white theorist's ethical, conceptual, and methodological orientations have been inadequate overall (T. Gordon, 1973). Further, many Black researchers were trained by white theorists and have functioned like them. But still, research combining constructs from Black perspective theories and other non-Black perspective theoretical constructs which are not incongruous with the Black perspective can be useful (the researcher is obliged to thoroughly elucidate congruity, however). Tounsel and Jones (1980) have shown how under certain conditions the skillful usage of Eurocentric concepts can be adjunctive in the praxis of the Black perspective in psychological work with Blacks. Two representative works which are incongruous with the Black perspective are discussed further below as are three works (Azibo 1983a, 1983b, 1983c) which will illustrate the implementation, utility, and viability of the theory-derived steady state approach.

STEP 2

In step 2 Africanity is assessed; not its developmental process, Africanity-development. The researcher simply measures the psychological characteristics of the Black personality with instruments developed to reflect the construct. These instruments will therefore have to be culturally specific in order to assess this biogenetically grounded psychological Blackness.[2]

As discussed earlier the author construes psychological Blackness as synonymous with the Black personality. This is so because one's Blackness is manifested in behavior via the level of consciousness (Baldwin 1980, 1981a, 1981b) or in conscious struggle (Williams 1981), i.e., psychologically. Hence, it is the psychological components of Blackness which are assessed in step 2. While fundamental, the biogenetic and unconscious aspects of the Black personality (Azibo 1983a, 1984; Baldwin 1980, 1981a, 1981b; Cedric X, McGhee, Nobles, Luther X, 1975; Nobles,

1976a) are not considered here. However, the approach does not rule out their inclusion.

The brevity with which step 2 has been treated should not be interpreted as reflecting its unimportance. Rather, it reflects the simplicity and fundamentality of the notion of incorporating psychological Africanity as a variable in research with Blacks. Amazingly, this notion is infrequently realized in the literature. Thus it warrants the explicit platform given as step 2 of the theory-derived steady state approach.

STEP 3

This step needs little elaboration. It is essentially the execution of research/experimental design in which data collection and data analysis are completed. It is the combination of steps 2 and 3 which affords a look at the functioning of psychological Blackness (Africanity) in its steady state (cf. Africanity-development): the behavioral (overt and covert) product of Blackness is revealed. That is, statistical relationships of psychological Blackness which are found in the data give insight into how the Black personality functions. It must be pointed out that the term "steady state" as used in this approach refers to the ongoing, day-to-day role of the Black personality in the psychological functioning of Black persons. No other connotations such as equilibrium, homeostasis, or static are intended. As used here, the term "steady state" refers only to the psychological effects or correlates of Africanity *versus* the developmental process by which Blackness is achieved (Africanity-development). Cross (1978, p. 29) alluded to this distinction and pointed out the lack of steady state data.

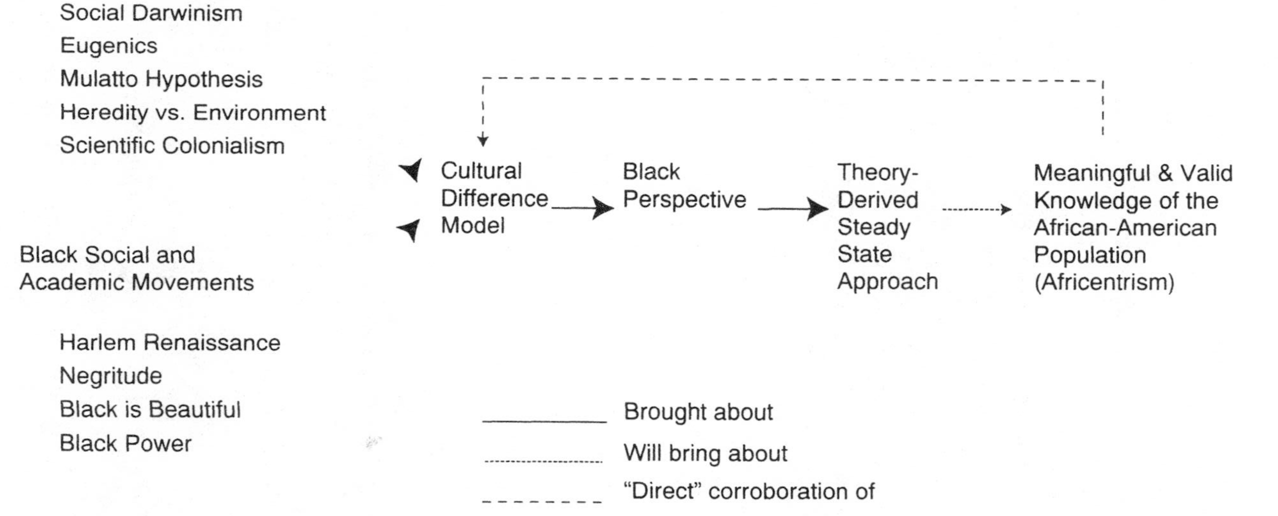

Figure 1. HISTORICAL LINEAGE OF THE THEORY-DERIVED STEADY STATE APPROACH

HISTORICAL LINEAGE

Restricting the applicability of the theory-derived steady-state approach to Black perspective theories clearly presumes the cultural distinctness of African-Americans. This brings us to the second purpose. Historically, the proactive theory-derived steady state approach was necessarily preceded by the advancement of the cultural difference model (see Simpkins, Gunnings, & Williams 1971; Williams 1971), a reaction "that emerged from the civil rights throes of the 1960s which exposed many of the shibboleths of the profession psychology" (Jackson 1977:231), which begot the Black perspective. Figure 1 presents a historical sketch: the applied and academic works of the Eurocentric disciplines along with Black social and academic movements eventuated in the difference model. It, in turn, begot the Black perspective which is a cornerstone of the theory-derived steady state approach to Black personality research.

The cultural difference model takes the position that "the differences noted by psychologists in . . . studies of the Black community are not the result of pathology, faulty learning, or genetic inferiority. These differences are manifestations of a viable and well-delineated culture of the Black American" (Simpkins et al. 1971:537).

Valentine (1971), representative of many white psychologists' viewpoint, reacted negatively to the commonsensical assertion of Black cultural distinctness. He argued that the difference model is lacking in explanatory validity and is possibly harmful. This is refuted with research evidence in a later section of this chapter, where both the explanatory validity and the psychodynamic insight which is afforded by the theory-derived steady-state approach (and, by extension, the cultural difference model) is discussed. This evidence bolsters the existing arguments pointing out the appropriateness and viability of the differences model (e.g., Baldwin 1979; Nobles 1972; White 1970, 1972).

IMPLICATIONS

The implications of the theory-derived steady state approach may be far reaching. Extremely noteworthy is that there now exists an extant, formally articulated research approach for the study of Black psychological functioning (at least for personality, clinical and social psychological studies) which stands on the cultural difference model and thereby protects and projects the integrity of Africentric culture. From the late sixties and throughout the seventies, Black psychologists have sought the establishment of a research approach which demonstrates the authenticity of Blackness.[3] The theory-derived steady state approach appears most capable in this regard! The advancement of this proactive approach is especially warranted because "to be [exclusively] reactive is to be nonproductive" (Goodman 1976:154).

Second, it was shown above in the delineation of Step 1 that Africentric conceptualizing is part and parcel to this approach. Thus Africentric thought has become a cornerstone in an epistemological treatise of scientific research inquiry in the Black psychology discipline. As Asante (1980) boldly predicted, Africentricity as a fundamental conceptual guidepost is sustaining itself and growing in influence.

Third, psychological Blackness (or African self-consciousness in Baldwin's [1981b] terminology) is posited here as the most important construct in Black psychology. This is plausible since Black psychology is first and foremost concerned with Black people and the most fundamental aspect of Black people is the Black personality (see Azibo 1983a; Baldwin 1981b; Williams 1981). The differences in mental health (Goldenberg, cited in Jackson 1979), general personality (Hilliard 1972), inference making (Azibo 1983b), race maintenance and preference (Azibo 1983a, 1991), and association with motivational strengths (Azibo 1983c)—all favoring those high in psychological Blackness—provide inklings of the profound role of the Black personality in Black psychological functioning. Therefore, the appropriate utilization of the theory-derived steady state approach can be seen as an initial step in enhancing the quality of personality, clinical, and social psychological research on Blacks. Further, if the trend of the association of positive psychological functioning and higher levels of psychological Blackness continues, Black social scientists will be armed with empirical evidence to take to the Black community in order that African-Americans *en masse* may be persuaded to be more consciously Africentric.

Considering the conceptual simplicity of this approach the reader may wonder why its formal articulation has been such a long time coming. Psychological Blackness as a construct is not new; its operationalization is. Valid measurement of the Black personality (and other psychological aspects of African-Americans, such as intelligence) on the one hand and meaningfully interpretable results on the other require *culturally specific* instruments. There are a few which are consistent with this author's product-oriented view of Black personality that also enjoy some good repute like Robert L. Williams' Black Personality Questionnaire (Azibo 1987; Wright & Isenstein 1978) and the African Self-Consciousness Scale (Baldwin 1987; Kambon 1992; Myers & Thompson 1994). Cross (1978, 1979) has reported other process-oriented scales. Additionally, Dr. Reginald Jones (in press) is publishing a collection of all types of U.S. African culturally specific instruments and Burlew and Smith (1991) have advanced a promising conceptual schema for various measures of racial identity. Unless culturally specific instruments such as these are used and continually developed, implementing the theory-derived steady state approach will be hindered. The resulting vacuum will be readily filled by non-culturally-specific tests and constructs.

COMPARING THE RESEARCH FRAMEWORKS— THE COMPARATIVE APPROACH

Using non-culturally-specific tests to operationalize aspects of Blacks' psychological functioning immediately invites a racially comparative analysis. Williams (1981) argues that little is learned from comparative studies. Simpkins et al. (1971) stated that:

> Two pieces of fruit, e.g., an apple and an orange, may be equal in weight, in quality of goodness, and marketability, but they are not the same. An apple cannot become an orange, and vice versa. Each must express its respective characteristics of "appleness" and "orangeness," yet both are fruit. (538)

To attempt to derive meaningful interpretations of the orange in terms of its (non)appleness is truly fruitless. Williams and Kirkland (1971) addressed this issue:

> Comparative research should be prohibited as it has no scientific rationale anyway. . . . It is already clear that Black and white cultures are different. . . . Would it not be more profitable to consider the processes by which each group attains uniqueness rather than to seize on differences? (116)

The theory-derived steady-state approach obviates such comparative proclivities of researchers.

This is a significant point because there is no shortage of shortcomings inherent to the comparative frame. For instance, it is virtually impossible to obtain racially equivalent samples upon which to base comparative inferences. Second, comparative researchers implicitly or explicitly adopt a posture of *cultural monism* which assumes equivalence of behaviors across race. This is clearly an inaccurate assumption which produces the next shortcoming. Third, meaningful and valid (see Banks, McQuater, & Ross, 1979) interpretations of observed differences have not been possible; the result, rather, has been the advancement of transubstantive errors, which are mistakes of meaning (African Psychology Training Module Handbook 1982). Fourth, differences obtained by comparison which actually (indirectly) may testify to cultural pluralism are (mis)used to halt and reverse social gains of African-Americans (e.g., Coleman 1966; Jencks 1972; Jensen 1969; Moynihan 1970). Further, these differences occur on primarily white-culturally-specific instruments: instruments developed by whites, on whites, and in some cases for whites. Fifth, the harm done to the Black community (Williams 1974) also produces mistrust toward psychologists, thereby alienating this subject population. Sixth, the comparative frame is the parent of the deficit and deviance models under which social scientists have studied African-Americans.

A PERSONALITY/CLINICAL EXAMPLE

These shortcomings are evident in existing works. E. Jones (1978) has provided an example, Black-White Personality Differences: Another Look, for illustration of the first three shortcomings. Racial comparisons were made on the MMPI, Embedded Figures

Test, and the California Psychological Inventory. Concerning sample equivalence, Jones acknowledged the difficulty:

> In this study, as in most comparative racial investigations, control of subjects' socioeconomic background proved to be a knotty problem. (245)

After matching his racial samples using an established socioeconomic measure, Jones continued:

> There was no guarantee that Black subjects were of the same SES as White subjects since both income and job conditions differed for members of the two races. Furthermore, Black subjects tended to fall in lower SES brackets. . . . It is clear that careful indices of socioeconomic status devised on White populations do not transfer readily to Black populations. (245-246)

This problem was partially dealt with by deleting certain Blacks from the sample. External validity suffers when this tactic is used. Moreover, Jones alludes to the questionable internal validity afforded by employing traditional measures to equate racial samples. Socioeconomic status, for example, is not isomorphic across race: Blacks and whites with identical job titles often have dissimilar paychecks; perceived "status" and its meaning depends, in part, on the race of both observers and targets and differences in the observer's cognitive structure (see Azibo 1983b; Linville & Jones 1980). The personality variable objectivity-subjectivity (Blass, Alperstein, & Block 1974) could also be important here.

I contend that implicit in the comparative frame is the assumption of cultural monism. This is evident in Jones' study even though he is aware of African-American and European-American cultural differences. In discussing the MMPI, he stated:

> What is needed is a comparison of Blacks and Whites on instruments oriented toward normal behavior, allowing race differences to be interpreted more objectively. (244)

As one ameliorative stratagem, Jones decided on an "item level analysis" instead of white-normed scale scores "for better understanding of the *meaning* of Black-White personality differences" (245; italics original). Clearly, to compare and meaningfully interpret race differences using comparative methodology and to simultaneously satisfy scientific dogma required (presumed) the races to be culturally homogeneous. Otherwise, it is difficult to surmise about racial differences, let alone to understand their meaning.

It must be pointed out that the comparative frame is not cross-cultural. In reality, the comparative frame is antithetical to the cross-cultural. The latter yields meaningfully interpretable differences, the former is devoid of them. Not one firm conclusion about the *meaning* of the observed racial differences was provided by Jones although that was his purpose (the factor analytic derivation of new conceptual categories notwithstanding). Operating out of the comparative frame only allowed Jones to caution about the meaning of differences, but not to meaningfully interpret them: for example, "It is possible the personality implications of field dependence may vary for Blacks and Whites" (250). The cross-cultural and comparative distinction will be revisited below.

To close out this discussion of Jones' study, note that the data were gathered on instruments which for Blacks were non-culturally-specific. To overcome the problem of not having "measures conceptually equivalent" (244) for the races, he chose an item level analysis of several measures derived from the Eurocentric tradition. Racial comparisons yielded differences which were meaningful at a superficial level at best. The points to be taken are that the theory-derived steady-state approach is far superior to the comparative frame—which is infected with shortcomings rendering it inept—and to any ameliorative strategies taking the comparative methodology as its base.

Research emerging from the theory-derived steady-state approach (Azibo 1983a, 1983b, 1983c) suffers none of these impediments to valid knowledge accumulation. Through the use of culturally specific instruments, the psychological Blackness or its state is assessed. This obviates the usage of the comparative framework and, more importantly, provides important *intra-African-American* sources of variance which yield meaningful interpretations in terms of the Black personality construct. Unless the researcher has culturally isomorphic groups, straightforward interpretations of differences lose their meaning: It is not proper to go beyond the simple description of the observed differences anyway, under this condition! Within-culture differences, however, can be important. This is why the moderating[4] capacity of psychological Blackness is of signal importance and must not be ignored in order to make generalizations about all genetic Blacks *per se* or for the sake of racial comparisons.

A SOCIAL PSYCHOLOGICAL EXAMPLE

The comparative framework has been extensively used in social psychology studies too (both sociological and psychological social psychology). Studies comparing Blacks and whites and examining responses to racial stimuli use a variety of preferential, judgmental, and evaluative tasks. The typically obtained differences are misinterpreted and overgeneralized. Misinterpretations stem from reliance upon the comparative frame and overgeneralizations arise from the noninclusion of pertinent moderator variables, which also is a consequence of the comparative approach.

For example, McCullers and Staat's (1974) tasks were to draw good-looking and ugly persons. Results showed larger and broader features were drawn on ugly faces by both whites and Blacks. These authors shamelessly posited that black is beautiful when it has (what they presumed to be) white features, small lips, noses, etc. There are several shortcomings and questionable assumptions in this piece of research which actually precipitated injurious, incorrect conclusions like the one just cited. This is compelled by the comparative research framework, which is racist in origin (Guthrie 1976). In addition to what may well be faulty interpretations and their faulty underlying assumptions, a point to be taken concerns the noninclusion of pertinent moderator variables issue. Disregarding assumptions and interpretations, McCullers and Staat may have overgeneralized. Perhaps the data would have been different for Blacks with different states of psychological Blackness. The theory-derived steady-state approach would have addressed this concern (as well as precluded some of the conceptual shortcomings).

THEORY-DERIVED STEADY-STATE EXAMPLES

Brief outlines of three studies conceived and conducted in the theory-derived steady-state approach will provide concrete examples for the reader. It will be pointed out how problems are attacked with this approach and how it better explains psychological functioning than do the comparative and cross-cultural approaches.

As noted above, step 2 of the approach requires the assessment of psychological Blackness with instruments conceptually derived from the construct. In the studies to be discussed, Williams' Black Personality Questionnaire (Azibo 1987; Wright & Isenstein 1978) was used for this purpose.

This author (Azibo 1982, 1984, 1990) has reviewed several theories of Black personality and models of psychological Africanity-development. I was struck by the fact that theories which took the Black perspective posited pro-Black behavioral syndromes in African-Americans with high psychological Blackness. The general hypothesis derived from these Black perspective models was that the Black personality must have some corresponding intrinsic motivational energy if there indeed are behaviors associated with Blackness. Specifically operating from Williams' theory (1981; Wright & Isenstein, 1978), a positive correlation between overall psychological Blackness and intrinsic motivational energy was predicted along with several other hypotheses pertaining to subcategories of the Black psyche described in his theory and their relationships with motivation.

Since none of these models contained an explicit formulation of motivation, a motivation construct not incongruous with the Black perspective, viz., personal causation (deCharms 1968), was selected. The results supported the hypotheses (Azibo 1983c). Prior to employing the personal causation construct, however, its congruity with the Black perspective was painstakingly established in (a) the value orientation of the construct; (b) its distinction from locus of control which is an incongruous construct (see Ogletree 1976); (c) its nonincorporation of the deficit model; and (d) its relationship to collective Black behavior. (It should be noted that points required to elucidate congruity may vary with the particular nonBlack perspective construct employed in the research. Also, it is recommended that congruity be reported, either in the text of the article or in a detailed footnote.)

In a perception experiment (Azibo 1983b) it was noted that theorists maintained that Black persons with high levels of psychological Blackness have a Black or Afrotypic worldview (Cross 1978; Williams 1981). From this, hypotheses pertaining to the perceptual judgments and, hence, cognitive structures, of persons with "strong" *versus* "weak" Black personalities were derived: specifically, Black female stimuli would be seen as more attractive than white female stimuli by strong Black personality Blacks (higher Black personality scores); vice versa for weak Black personality Blacks (lower Black personality scores). The results supported the hypotheses.

Putting the most fundamental tenets of Black personality theory to an experimental test, the author (Azibo 1983c, 1991) hypothesized that persons with higher psychological Blackness would engage in behaviors that reflected own-race maintenance and own-race preference more than persons with lower psychological Blackness. In addition, the experiment was designed such that the Black personality theory hypotheses competed with hypotheses from status characteristics theory, a major Eurocentric social psychological variable (Berger, Rosenholtz, & Zelditch 1980). The results supported the hypotheses derived from Black personality theory, which also was shown to better explain Blacks' behavior than status characteristics theory.

For present purposes the reader is asked to accept on faith that design requirements were met in these studies. There are eight points to be taken regarding the theory-derived steady state research approach.

(1) It demands considerable thinking and draws upon the theoretical skills of the researcher prior to conducting the research. This lessens the probability of poorly thought-out, meaningless, and otherwise obscure studies. By being yoked to the Black perspective, the approach compels the theorist to engage in Black psychology as opposed to Eurocentric psychological studies on Blacks. Further, the needed construction of Africentric Black theory and build-up of empirical data bases can be readily accomplished.

(2) It is implemented with ease. First, one makes theoretically-derived hypotheses. Second, the congruousness of nonBlack perspective constructs (if any) with the Black perspective is shown. Then steps 2 (measurement of psychological Africanity) and 3 (research design execution) are executed.

(3) It enables the researcher to document the steady-state product(s) of Blackness and point out any associated implications. For example, the three studies just outlined showed that persons higher in psychological Blackness have greater intrinsic motivational energies than those lower; such persons also perceive a Black stimulus more favorably than a white one and engage in own-race maintenance and own-race preference behaviors more than persons lower in psychological Blackness. It is important information to know that greater intrinsic motivation and race-sustaining behavior are associated with enhanced Black identity or African self-consciousness. An important implication here is that Blacks with depleted motivation and/or pejorative extended self-concepts (we, us as opposed to I, me) should receive therapeutically-directed Africanity-development in individual and community-level psychological intervention (Azibo, 1982, 1983c). An implication for future research is that the Black personality is an important moderator variable for African-Americans.

(4) It has great heuristic potential as a result of points (1) through (3).

(5) It obviates the use of the comparative research approach. First of all, the comparative frame is opposed to the Black perspective to which the theory-derived steady-state approach is yoked. The comparative frame is predicated upon the melting-pot thesis that Blacks and whites are a homogeneous group. This approach only recognizes the "American" perspective. Secondly, since the theory-derived steady state approach necessitates the inclusion of the Black personality as a moderator or independent variable in the research, a Black group *versus* other group significance test is precluded (psychological Blackness by conceptual definition is biogenetically grounded, as already pointed out, and hence nonexistent in nonBlacks).

(6) It is superior to the comparative approach, fundamentally because it is based on the sound assumption of cultural distinctness of African-Americans *vis-à-vis* other American groups rather than the assumption of cultural monism. The practical superiority of the theory-derived steady-state approach over the comparative stems from the meaningfully interpretative results yielded by the former, as seen in points (1), (3), and (5) above. If, for example, whites were included in the perception experiment and a race dif-

ference obtained, the results could not have been interpreted in terms of the Black personality. (I leave it to the reader to discern how this hypothetical Black-white difference could be meaningfully interpreted beyond the level of description!)

(7) The theory-derived steady-state approach is advanced because the articulation of a proper approach wherewith to undertake research on Black persons is way past due. Students, particularly Black ones, are being *forced* to do comparative studies and many white and Black professionals are undertaking comparative research by choice. To the extent that this embarrassing state of affairs is due to the lack of a visible alternative research framework, the theory-derived steady-state approach should be ameliorative. For students desiring to do Black personality research and who are subject to contrary mentoring faculty, the theory-derived steady-state approach might still be employed. One adds Step 1a to Step 1, which is to find a construct or variable satisfactory to the (tor)mentor—most likely a Eurocentric one—and devises the research such that there are competing hypotheses between it and the Black personality theory. Thesis proposals of this sort might satisfy all parties: the student can do Black personality research and contribute to Black psychology, while faculty are assured of a rigorous research effort which incorporates a variable or construct of interest and/or propriety to them (e.g., Azibo 1983a, 1991).

(8) Let me explicitly point out that it is not in the conceptual underpinnings of the theory-derived steady state approach, nor is it the author's position, that studies on or including nonBlacks should not be undertaken. The cross-cultural approach is appropriate when the interest lies in both Blacks and nonBlacks (or any culturally distinct groups). The focus of cross-cultural research is not a statistical difference between distinct cultural groups, rather it is the similarity in the data of the different groups. This requires the translation and abstraction of culturally specific constructs into comparable pan-cultural constructs. For example, the perception experiment could probably be used in cross-cultural research: The differences in perception, and presumably cognitive structure, of Blacks with high versus those with low psychological Blackness at the pan-cultural level of abstraction may refer to racial cognitive complexity or cognitive schema. Assuming that this is the case,

the racial cognitive complexity or cognitive schema of a sample of whites, for example, could be assessed and judgments of the Black and white female photos collected. If the data patterns of the white and Black samples are similar, then support for a cross-cultural hypothesis pertaining to racial cognitive complexity would be supported.

It is important to note here that (a) no racial or cultural group difference is tested, (b) data and constructs used in the translation/formation of the cross-cultural hypothesis are initially culturally specific (hopefully, derived from the theory-derived steady-state approach for Blacks), and (c) the pan-cultural interpretation is most meaningful at this abstract level. It loses significance (for Blacks in this specific example) at the culturally specific level: so what if Blacks with greater racial cognitive complexity or cognitive schema construe Black females as more attractive? The interpretive meaning of the results are more rich and profound when construed in terms of the Black personality—i.e., when the results (effects of racial cognitive complexity) are seen to be based upon the Black personality.

CONCEPTUAL CLARITY

For clarity, the distinction between the cross-cultural and comparative frames must be sharpened. Cross-cultural comparisons recognize explicitly the nature of such enterprises. Ford (1967), an anthropologist, stated:

> The classification and organization of information about a people, their environment, and their ways of life is not a simple matter. . . . Yet it is a crucial step. . . . The ways in which a people classify and conceptually organize their environment is of utmost importance to the understanding of their behavior. (10-11)

From this perspective, Triandis and colleagues have, for the most part, done well (1972, 1976). A balance is struck between the view that cultures can best be understood in their own terms with the desirability of establishing universal laws of behavior. Awareness of the appropriate utilization of both emic (within-cultural) and etic (cross-cultural) approaches has enabled them to avoid the pseudoetic error: using an emic approach of a particular group (e.g., white American theories, instruments, conceptual paradigms, etc.) on another cultural group (e.g., African-Americans). The pseudoetic approach rarely yields useful results (Triandis 1972, ch. 3).

Parenthetically, it must be pointed out that even though the methodological framework used by Triandis and colleagues is appropriate, several assumptions, interpretations, and conclusions concerning Blacks in their 1976 work are at considerable variance with the Black perspective. It appears that, irrespective of good or bad methodology, accurately researching and interpreting the Black psyche may be a Sisyphean task for white social scientists. When the investigation calls for African-American participants, nonBlack researchers are advised to: (a) follow guidelines given in Williams (1974), and (b) consult with or incorporate as a principle investigator, author, or editor a Black social scientist who shares the Black perspective as articulated above.

Unfortunately, the exemplary *methodological framework* employed by Triandis and colleagues is an exception. The comparative frame prevalent in Eurocentric psychology and sociology denies the cultural distinctness and integrity of African-Americans.[5] That is, psychological aspects of Black Americans are defined and interpreted *in light of*[6] Euro-Americans when this approach is employed. The pseudoetic error is plainly evidenced here. As a consequence, voluminous reports full of invalid interpretations of low Black self-concept (see Gordon 1977; Nobles 1973), scarred personality (see Azibo 1982; Karon 1975), damaged family structure (e.g., Moynihan 1965), self-hatred theses (see Baldwin 1979; Baldwin et al. [in press]) and white preference broadly conceived[7] (J. Williams & Morland 1979) have accrued. This accrual has taken place initially due to the racist origins of the comparative frame (Guthrie 1976) and Euro-American ethnocentrism. It continues despite contemporary delineations of Africanity in African-Americans (e.g., Dixon 1976; King 1976; Nobles 1972, 1976b).

J. Williams and Morland (1979) argue for the comparative frame:

> There is, of course, a more general rationale for making these comparisons by race. It is the desire to *increase*

> *understanding* of the development of racial preference and identity or any topic by seeing if they are significantly related to the race of the respondent. (29; italics added)

These authors are confused. The cross-cultural perspective can increase the conceptual understanding of the development of racial preference and identification panculturally; the comparative frame only muddles whatever phenomena which may be present (see "A personality/clinical example," above). Even if the comparative frame could provide meaningful interpretations of racial differences, "the null hypothesis pertaining to an empirical phenomenon fails consistently to be rejected" (Banks et al. 1979:35). The product-oriented theory-derived steady state approach and its process allies can best explicate the development and functional utility of racial preference and identity within the African-American culture. This is in line with Williams and Kirkland's (1971) argument cited above.

BY WAY OF CONCLUSION

Voluminous additional examples of comparisons not unlike the ones presented above (and worse) can be found in personality, clinical, and social psychological studies. The comparative frame is deeply ingrained in white cultures and, hence, Eurocentric psychology. But Khatib and Nobles have pointed out "that whites or Europeans are no longer the standard by which the psychology of people is judged" (1977:97-98) or compared against.

To be sure, the focus of some investigations may require various racial groups, but to adopt a comparative design (e.g., Adams 1980) is not warranted. It is imperative that venturesome comparative interpretations be avoided. An alternative when using Blacks and whites (or any combination of racial groups) and the same data has been obtained on both groups, would be to report two studies, one with white subjects and one with Blacks (e.g., Ugwuegbu 1979). However, these circumstances will not arise when the theory-derived steady state and/or cross-cultural approaches are employed.

The strong case against the comparative frame has been argued (e.g., Azibo 1988; Simpkins et al. 1971; Williams 1981; Williams

& Kirkland 1971), confirmed by numerous reviews (e.g., Baldwin 1979; Baldwin et al. [in press]; Banks 1976; Banks et al., 1979; Nobles 1973), and further substantiated by contrast with the cross-cultural and theory-derived steady state approaches here. It seems to the writer that any future psycho-social comparisons must be of the cross-cultural type. The pseudoetic error and concomitant transubstantive errors (African Psychology Training Module Handbook 1982) and category mistakes (Ryle 1949) can thereby be avoided.

Further, it must be pointed out that operating from the theory-derived steady-state approach can alleviate some of the problems peculiar to the *Black researcher's paradox*: being part of the Black community and being trained in theory and research approaches which simply do not jibe with the reality of life for African persons. The major, negative consequence of this paradox is summed up in Nobles' statement that "as long as Black researchers ask the same questions and theorize the same theory as their White counterparts, Black researchers will continue to be part and parcel to a system which perpetuates the misunderstanding of Black reality and consequently contributes to our degradation" (1976a:173). Here, too, under the fundamental heading of research paradigm, the comparative frame is inadequate. Insofar as the way a research question is addressed will influence the answer obtained, the theory-derived steady state approach will generate answers which more accurately represent the psychological functioning of Blacks.

That the comparative frame must be abandoned in favor of the theory-derived steady state approach if the accumulation of valid psychological knowledge of African-Americans and positive applications of this knowledge are to be realized is the major implication which presses on the discipline of psychology (Africentric and Eurocentric) and related areas. Knowledge generated out of the emic theory-derived steady state approach can, of course, be used for etic investigations (e.g., see Davidson et al. 1976; see Triandis 1972, ch. 3 for methodological concerns).

While philosophers of science debate several issues, there is general agreement that science is most fruitful when paradigm shifts form and take root (e.g., Kuhn 1970; Feyerabend 1978). The theory-derived steady-state approach is part and parcel of the current paradigmatic revolution in the area of race and identity (see Semaj 1980). Early works (Azibo 1983a, 1983b, 1983c, 1984; Baldwin 1987) have been very promising. So, it is hoped that with the advancement of a newer, more appropriate paradigm and research approach, an anachronism will be made of Fanon's insightful analysis:

> The Negro is comparison. There is the first truth . . . . Whenever he comes into contact with someone else, the question of value, of merit, arises. (1967:211)

The meaningful comparisons for Black social and psychological functioning are, for the most part, intra-race, addressing the role of the Black personality.

Notes

*A slightly different version of this paper was first presented at the 14th Annual Convention of the Association of Black Psychologists in Denver, Colorado, in August, 1981. I wish to express my appreciation to Dr. Kobi Kambon, Barbara Barnes, Dr. Robert Johnson, Stacy Morgan, and Dr. Arthur Shulman for their valuable commentary on an earlier draft and to Ms. Nadia Kravchenko for her diligent typing.

1. It is proposed that other writers, especially those who still use the terms Nigrescence and Nigrescenality, adopt this terminology because: (a) the displaced terms are derivatives of "Negro" which is, to say the least, anachronistic; (b) the displacing terms are more correct psycho-politically in that they link the psychological development of all Blacks with their roots; and (c) doing so will lend uniformity to the literature. These thoughts were stimulated by some comments by Dr. Kobi Kambon. Also, note that often the terms Africanity and Blackness (a) are used interchangeably and (b) are used with the adjective psychological implied rather than explicit.
2. Many instruments which assess psychological Blackness/Africanity are available: Joseph Baldwin's African Self-Consciousness Scale (Psychology Dept., Florida A & M University, Tallahassee, FL 32307); Robert Williams' Black Personality Questionnaire-Form B (6374 Delmar Blvd., St. Louis, MO 63130); William Cross, Jr. (1979); Jake Milliones'

Developmental Inventory of Black Consciousness. Some of these scales are multidimensional and/or developmentally oriented, but all can be used to assess psychological Blackness on a unidimensional continuum from low to high. Other instruments may have been inadvertently overlooked and the author would appreciate having the reader bring this to his attention. We must overcome the obscurity of our own instruments.

3. The convention theme of the 14th Annual Association of Black Psychologists meeting held 8/81 was "Creating and Actualizing Black Psychological Models."
4. In much race-related research, the term "moderating" has had different uses—sometimes actually calling for racial comparisons. It is specifically used at this point in the text to denote within-African-American sources of differences. More generally, "moderating" will be used to refer to intra-cultural sources of differences unless otherwise stated.
5. Because comparative research has been a major factor in perpetuating racism in all segments of society, the call for its *prohibition* by Williams and Kirkland (1971) is much more appropriate than saying it should be strongly discouraged. Many responses to their call for prohibition have been negative because, some say, Williams and Kirkland's is a political statement—not a scientific one. Even though Williams and Kirkland's position is scientifically sound, from our side of the tracks, Black social scientists see the political and scientific as so intertwined (at least on this issue) that where the one begins and the other ends is indistinguishable.
6. It should be clear to the reader that the principal weakness of the comparative frame is in its (generally) giving meaning to cultural, psychological, and behavioral events manifested by persons of one culture based on the perspective of some other cultural group. This amounts to what Williams (1981) called scientific and cultural racism when racial groups are involved. Some issues which are not of the personality, clinical, and social psychology type can be addressed adequately by comparative research (e.g., income, illness, mortality rates, etc.). Regarding social science constructs generally, only when racial/cultural differences are inherent to the construct itself is the comparative framework appropriate (still, the construct must be of or congruous with the Black perspective). Comparisons are justifiable so long as attempts to account for the differences found do not take cultural/psychological "norms" of one group and apply them in establishing the meaning and assessment of the cultural/psychological functioning of another, distinct cultural group. Clearly,

then, the defensible use and meaningfulness of comparisons in psychological and sociological investigations is much more restricted than many previously thought.

7. A notable point often overlooked by Black and white researchers in this area is that Blacks' preferences for "redbone" or "high yellow" (i.e., lightskin) others, when obtained, may be *less* valid indicants of white preference in Blacks than are whites' suntanning (at the risk of skin cancer no less!) and copying of African/African-American lifestyles (e.g., wearing dashikis, Afros, and African braid hairstyles) indications of *Black preference* (self-hatred?) *in whites* which, perhaps, is compensatory behavior for the inability to produce and utilize sufficient quantities of melanin (McGee 1976; Welsing 1974).

REFERENCES

Adams, K. A. Who has the final word? Sex, race, and dominance behavior. *Journal of Personality and Social Psychology* 38 (1980):1-8.

African psychology training module handbook. Atlanta: African Psychology Institute, 1982.

Akbar, N. African roots of Black personality. In W. Smith, K. Burlew, M. Mosley, & W. Whitney (Eds.), *Reflections on Black Psychology*. Washington, D.C.: University Press of America, 1982.

Asante, M. *Afrocentricity: The Theory of Social Change*. Buffalo: Amulefi Publishing Co, 1980.

Azibo, D. A. *Advances in Black Personality Theory and Implications for Psychology*. Unpublished monograph, 1982.

Azibo, D. A. *African (Black) Personality Theory, and Perceived Belief Similarity: Which is Predominant in Dominance/ Reactance Behavior*? Washington University, Unpublished doctoral dissertation, 1983a.

Azibo, D. A. Perceived Attractiveness and the Black Personality. *The Western Journal of Black Studies*, 7, 4, (1983b):229-238.

Azibo, D. A. Some psychological concomitants and consequences of the Black personality: Mental health implications. *Journal of Non-White Concerns* (1983c):59-66.

Azibo, D. A. *The Black Personality: Selected Papers of Dr Daudi Ajani ya Azibo*. Unpublished manuscript, 1984.

Azibo, D. A. *The Black Personality Questionnaire*. Manuscript accepted for publication, 1987. (cf. R. Jones' forthcoming *Handbook of tests and measurements for Black populations*.)

Azibo, D. A. Understanding the proper and improper usage of the comparative research framework. *Journal of Black Psychology*, 15, 1 (1988):81-91.

Azibo, D. A. Advances in Black/African personality theory. *Imhotep: An Afrocentric Review*, 2, 1 (1990):22-47.

Azibo, D. A. An empirical test of the fundamental postulates of an African personality metatheory. *Western Journal of Black Studies*, 15, 3 (1991):183-195.

Azibo, D. A. Articulating the distinction between Black Studies and the study of Blacks: The fundamental role of culture and the African-centered worldview. *The Afrocentric Scholar*, 1, 1 (1992):64-97.

Azibo, D. A. *Liberation psychology: An introduction to the African personality construct.* Trenton, NJ: Africa World Press [in press].

Baldwin, J. A. Theory and research concerning the notion of Black self-hatred: A review and reinterpretation. *Journal of Black Psychology* 5 (1979):51-77.

Baldwin, J. A. An Africentric model of Black personality. *Proceedings of the Thirteenth Annual Convention of the Association of Black Psychologists* (1980a):23-25 (Summary).

Baldwin, J. A. The psychology of oppression. In M. Asante and A. Vandi (Eds.), *Contemporary Black Thought.* Beverly Hills: Sage Publications, 1980b.

Baldwin, J. A. *Afrikan (Black) personality: From an Africentric framework.* Unpublished manuscript, 1981a.

Baldwin, J. A. Notes on an Africentric theory of Black personality. *Western Journal of Black Studies*, 5 (1981b):172-179.

Baldwin, J. A. Psychological aspects of European cosmology in American society: African and European cultures. *Western Journal of Black Studies*, 9, 4 (1985):216-223.

Baldwin, J. A. African psychology and Black personality testing. *The Negro Educational Review* 38, 2-3 (1987):56-66.

Baldwin, J., Brown, R., & Hopkins, R. Black self-hatred paradigm revisited: An Africentric analysis. In Jones, R., ed., *Black Psychology*, 3rd ed. (in press).

Banks, W. C. White preference in Blacks: A paradigm in search of a phenomenon. *Psychological Bulletin*, 83 (1976):1179-1186.

Banks, W. C., McQuater, G. V., & Ross, J. A. On the importance of white preference and the comparative difference of Blacks and othres: Reply to Williams and Morland. *Psychological Bulletin* 86 (1979):33-36.

Berger, J., Rosenholtz, S., & Zelditch, M. Status organizing processes. *Annual Review of Sociology* 6 (1980):479-508.

Blass, T., Alperstein, L., & Block, S. H. Effects of communicator's race and beauty and of receiver's objectivity-subjectivity on attitude change. *Personality and Social Psychology Bulletin* 1 (1974.):132-134.

Burlew, K. & Smith, L. Measures of racial identity: An overview and a proposed framework. *Journal of Black Psychology* 17 (1991):53-71.

Carlson, R. Where is the person in personality research? *Psychological Bulletin* 75 (1971):203-219.

Cedric X (Clark, now S. M. Khatib), McGhee, D. P., Nobles, W. W., & Luther X (Naim Akbar). Voodoo or IQ: An introduction to African psychology. *Journal of Black Psychology* 1 (1975):9-29.

Coleman, J., et al. *Equality of educational opportunity*. Washington: U. S. Government Printing Office, 1986.

Cross, W. E., Jr. Models of psychological Nigrescence: A literature review. *Journal of Black Psychology* 5 (1978):13-31.

Cross, W. E., Jr. The Negro-to-Black conversion experience: An empirical analysis. In A. Boykin, A. Franklin, & J. Yates, eds., *Research directions of Black psychologists*. New York: Russell Sage Foundation, 1979.

Davidson, A. R., Jaccard, J. J., Triandis, H. C., Morales, M. L., & Diaz-Guerrero, R. Cross-cultural model testing: toward a solution of the etic-emic dilemma. *International Journal of Psychology* 11 (1976):1-13.

DeCharms, R. *Personal causation*. New York: Academic Press, 1968.

Dixon, V. J. World views and research methodology. In L. King, V. Dixon, & W. Nobles (Eds.), *African philosophy: Assumptions & paradigms for research on Black persons*. Los Angeles: Fanon Research & Development Center, 1976.

Fanon, F. *Black skin, white masks*. New York: Grove Press, 1967.

Feyerbend, P. *Against method*. London: Verso, 1978.

Ford, C. S. On the analysis of behavior for cross-cultural comparisons. In C. S. Ford, ed., *Cross-cultural approaches: Readings in comparative research*. New Haven, Conn.: Human Relations Area Files Press, 1967.

Goodman, J. Race, reason, and research. In L. King, V. Dixon, & W. Nobles (Eds.), *African philosophy: Assumptions & paradigms for research on Black persons*. Los Angeles: Fanon Research & Development Center, 1976.

Gordon, R. Notes on white and Black psychology. *Journal of Social Issues* 29 (1973):87-95.

Gordon, V. V. *The self-concept of Black Americans*. Washington, D.C.: The University Press of America, 1977.

Guthrie, R. V. *Even the rat was white: A historical view of psychology*.

New York: Harper & Row, 1976.

Hilliard, T. O. Personality characteristics of Black student activists and nonactivists. In R. Jones, Ed., *Black psychology* (1st ed.). New York: Harper & Row, 1972.

Jackson, G. G. The emergence of a Black perspective in counseling. *Journal of Negro Education* 46 (1977):230-253.

Jackson, G. G. The roots of the backlash theory in mental health. *Journal of Black Psychology* 6 (1979):17-45.

Jencks, C. *Inequality*. New York: Basic Books, Inc.

Jensen, A. R. 1969. How much can we boost I.Q. and scholastic achievement? *Harvard Educational Review* 39 (1972):1-123.

Jones, E. E. Black-white personality differences: Another look. *Journal of Personality Assessment* 42 (1978):244-252.

Jones, R. *Handbook of tests and measurements for Black populations*. Hampton, VA: Cobb and Henry Press, in press.

Kambon, K. *The African personality in America: An African-centered framework*. Tallahassee, Fl: Nubian Nations Publishers, 1992.

Karon, B. P. *Black scars*. New York: Springer Publishing Co., 1975.

Khatib, S. M. & Nobles, W. W. Historical foundations of African psychology and their philosophical consequences. *Journal of Black Psychology* 4(1977):91-101.

King, J. R. African survivals in the Black American family: Key factors in stability. *Journal of Afro-American Issues* 4 (1976):153-167.

King, R. URAEUS: From mental slavery to mastership, Part III. *Uraeus* 1, 3 (1978):

King, R. Black Dot the Black seed: The archetype of humanity, Part II. *Uraeus* 2, 3 (1982):4-22.

Kuhn, T. S. *The stucture of scientific revolutions* (2nd ed.). Chicago: University of Chicago Press, 1970.

Ladner, J. *Tomorrow's tomorrow: The Black woman*. Garden City, N.Y.: Doubleday, 1971.

Linville, P. W. & Jones, E. E. Polarized appraisals of out-group members. *Journal of Personality and Social Psychology* 38 (1980):689-703.

McCullers, J. C. & Staat, J. Draw an ugly man: An inquiry into the dimensions of physical attractiveness. *Personality and Social Psychology Bulletin* 1 (1974):33-35.

McGee, D. P. Psychology: Melanin, the physiological basis for psychological oneness. In L. King, V. Dixon, and W. Nobles (eds.), *African philosophy: Assumptions & paradigms for research on Black persons*. Los Angeles: Fanon Research & Development Center, 1976.

Moss, M. K., Miller, R. M., & Page, R. A. The effects of racial context

on the perception of physical attractiveness. *Sociometry* 38 (1975):525-535.
Moynihan, D. P. *The Negro family: The case for national action.* Washington, D.C.: U. S. Government Printing Office, 1965.
Moynihan, D. P. Benign neglect for issue of race? *Wall Street Journal*, March 3, 1970, p. 20.
Myers, M. & Thompson, V. Africentricity: An analysis of two culture specific instruments. *Western Journal of Black Studies* 18, 4 (1994):179-184.
Nobles, W. W. African philosophy: Foundations for Black psychology. In R. Jones, ed., *Black psychology* (1st ed.). New York: Harper & Row, 1972.
Nobles, W. W. Psychological research and the Black self-concept: A critical review. *Journal of Social Issues* 29 (1973):11-31.
Nobles, W. W. African science: The consciousness of self. In L. King, V. Dixon, & W. Nobles (Eds.), *African philosophy: Assumptions & paradigms for research on Black persons.* Los Angeles: Fanon Research & Development Center, 1976a.
Nobles, W. W. Extended self: Rethinking the so-called Negro self-concept. *Journal of Black Psychology* 2 (1976b):15-24.
Ogletree, K. Internal-external control in Black and white. *Black Books Bulletin* 4 (1976):26-31.
Royce, J. R. Toward a viable theory of individual differences. *Journal of Personality and Social Psychology* 37 (1979):1927-1931.
Ryle, G. *The concept of mind.* London: Hutchinson & Co, 1949.
Semaj, L. T. *Afrikanity, cognition and extended self identity.* Unpublished manuscript, University of the West Indies, Kingston, Jamaica, 1980.
Semaj, L. T. The Black self, identity, and models for a psychology of Black liberation. *Western Journal of Black Studies* 5 (1981):158-171.
Semmes, C. E. Foundations of an Afrocentric social science: Implications for curriculum-building, theory, and research in Black Studies. *Journal of Black Studies* 12 (1981):3-17.
Semmes, C. E. Black Studies and the symbolic structure of domination. *Western Journal of Black Studies* 6 (1982):116-122.
Simpkins, G., Gunnings, T., & Williams R. L. What a culture a difference makes: A rejoinder to Valentine. *Harvard Educational Review* 41 (1971):535-541.
Smith, P. M., Jr. Let's psyche 'em? *Journal of Black Psychology* 1 (1975):42-52.
Toldson, I. & Pasteur, A. Developmental stages of Black self-discovery: Implications for using Black art forms in group interaction. *Journal of Non-White Concerns in Personnel and Guidance* 44

(1975):130-138.
Tounsel, P. L. & Jones, A. C. Theoretical considerations for psychotherapy with Black clients. In R. Jones, ed, *Black psychology* (2nd ed.). New York: Harper & Row, 1980.
Triandis, H. C. *The analysis of subjective culture*. New York: John Wiley & Sons, 1972.
Triandis, H. C. *Variations in Black and white perceptions of the social environment*. Urbana: University of Illinois Press, 1976.
Ugwuegbu, D.C.E. Racial and evidential factors in juror attribution of legal responsibility. *Journal of Experimental Social Psychology* 15 (1979):133-146.
Valentine, C. A. Deficit, difference, and bicultural models of Afro-American behavior. *Harvard Educational Review* 41 (1971):137-157.
Welsing, F. C. The Cress theory of color-confrontation. *Black Scholar* (May 1974):32-40.
White, J. Guidelines for Black psychologists. *The Black Scholar* (March 1970):52-57.
White, J. Toward a Black psychology. In R. Jones (Ed.), *Black psychology* (1st ed.). New York: Harper & Row, 1972.
Williams, J. E. & Morland, J. K. Comment on Banks' "White preference in Blacks: A paradigm in search of a phenomenon." *Psychological Bulletin* 86 (1979):28-32.
Williams, R. L. Abuses and misuses in testing Black children. *The Counseling Psychologist* 2 (1971):62-73.
Williams, R. L. The death of white research in the Black community. *Journal of Non-White Concerns in Personnel and Guidance* 2 (1974):116-132.
Williams, R. L. *The collective Black mind: An Afro-centric theory of Black personality*. St. Louis: Williams & Associates, 1981.
Williams, R. L. & Kirkland, J. The white counselor and the Blacck client. *The Counseling Psychologist* 2 (1971): 114-117.
Wright, B. J. & Isenstein, V. R. *Psychological tests and minorities* (DHEW, Publication No. ADM 78-484). Washington, D.C.: Government Printing Office, 1978.

Chapter 13

Toward Curriculum Development in Black Psychology

Charlyn Harper-Browne

Overview

Although the academic relevance, utility, and substantiality of the discipline called Black Psychology are often challenged and/or ignored, the need for Black Psychology is self-evident: Black people exist, thus Black Psychology exists. It is necessary, then, to continue the contemporary formalization of the discipline through curriculum development. The process and products of curriculum development will contribute (a) to the resolution of unsettled issues within the discipline (e.g., definition, models, etc.); (b) to the institutional credibility of the discipline; (c) to establishing standardized/core subject area in "General Black Psychology"; (d) to the development of specialized courses within the field (e.g., "The Psychology of African American Women"); and (e) to redesigning, and therefore enriching, currently prevailing psychology curricula.

INTRODUCTION

Approximately fifty-five years after the American enslavement of African people was legally abolished in the United States, scholars who were descendents of enslaved Africans first published research (circa 1920s) to refute prevailing ideas of Black racial inferiority and pathology (cf., Guthrie 1976, 1980; Jackson 1982; White 1984). About fifty years later (circa 1970s), descendents of the descendents of enslaved Africans began conscientiously to conceptualize, elaborate, debate, expand, publish, and defend a system of thought they called "Black Psychology" (cf., Jackson 1979, 1982; Jones 1972; Nobles 1972; 1986; White 1972, 1984). Within the last twenty years, various definitions, conceptual orientations, models, and schools have been suggested (cf., Akbar 1984; Baldwin 1976, 1986; Cook and Kono 1977; Fairchild 1988; Karenga 1982; Myers 1988); many articles and books have been published (e.g., Haskins and Butts 1973; Jenkins 1982; Jones 1972, 1980, in press a, in press b; Pasteur and Toldson 1982; Pugh 1972; Smith, Burlew, Mosley, and Whitney 1980; White 1984; Wilcox 1971); controversial theories have been postulated (e.g., Akbar 1981; Azibo 1989a, 1990, In press; Baldwin 1976, 1985; Bulhan 1985; Cross 1971, 1978; Hayes 1972; Nobles 1972, 1986; Welsing 1970; Wright 1980, 1985); innovative research methodologies have been advanced (cf., Azibo 1988a, 1988b, 1989b; Boykin 1977, 1977-1978; Boykin, Franklin, and Yates 1980; Jackson, Tucker, and Bowman [in press]; Jones [in press b]; King, Dixon, and Nobles 1976); the *Journal of Black Psychology* has flourished; and numerous courses have been developed (cf., Fairchild 1986; Harper 1982; Jones 1978)—all under the rubric of *Black Psychology*.

AXIOM I: "BLACK PEOPLE ARE, THUS BLACK PSYCHOLOGY IS"

Notwithstanding an extensive and accessible body of sound theoretical and empirical literature, the academic relevance, utility, and substantiality of the discipline of Black Psychology, like other Black Studies disciplines (cf., Butler 1981; Jackson 1982; Karenga 1982), is still challenged and/or ignored. Many psychology curriculum review boards cry "It does not apply to general audiences." Academic psychologists suggest "It lacks academic rigor." Undergraduate psychology majors claim "It won't help me pass the GRE."* Critics of Black Psychology, for example, attempt to reduce it to "minstrelism," that is, White/Western/conventional/ "real" psychology in blackface, whose purpose is to provide Black psychologists with an opportunity to "create an area of expertise which gives them preeminence in some aspects of the general discipline of psychology" (Nobles 1986:17).

Assertions such as these are often made without *a priori* examination of Black psychological research. Assertions such as these also emanate from thinking encapsulated by the view of a single human norm in a culturally diverse world. Thus, by definition, differences are perceived as deviances and deficiencies. This frame of reference, then, precludes the questions asked, the answers obtained, and the inference made. Baldwin's (1986) position further reveals the inanity of challenges to the legitimacy of Black Psychology and serves as a caveat to Black psychologists to avoid becoming trapped in such an inherently ignorant discussion:

> It should be clear that given the basic fact of cultural relativity across African and European populations . . . surely African (Black) Psychology needs no more a justification of its existence than does Western Psychology. . . . In so much as African people exist, in fact preexisted Europeans as a distinct and independent cultural entity apart from European people, so does African (Black) Psychology, irrespective of when and how Black social scientists actually formalized it in Western society.(236-37)

Thus, the academic relevance, utility, and substantiality of Black Psychology are regarded here as axiomatic. The purpose of this article, then, is to focus on the need for curriculum development within this discipline and to identify pertinent subject matter. It is suggested that the goals of curriculum development in Black Psychology are (a) to achieve consistency (and ultimately standardization) in the numerous courses broadly labeled as Black

* GRE is an acronym for the Graduate Record Exam that must be taken for admission to graduate school in the United States.

Psychology; (b) to develop specialized courses within the discipline (e.g., "The Psychology of African-American Women" [cf., Harper 1985]); and (c) to redesign and improve undergraduate and graduate psychology curricula by incorporating Black psychological research.

TOWARD CURRICULUM DEVELOPMENT

There exists a significant body of literature which has been labeled as Black Psychology because it falls into one or both of the following categories: (a) research about Black people which is psychological in nature and which is authored by either Black or non-Black scholars and (b) research by psychologists who are Black which is informed by several different conceptual orientations. Currently, central debate within the discipline (cf., Baldwin 1986; Jackson 1979) is that of identity and definition: Is Black Psychology whatever Black psychologists study, regardless of their conceptual or operational orientation? Is Black Psychology only that body of psychological research on Black populations which is informed by an Africentric conceptual and operational orientation, regardless of the ethnicity of the researcher? That debate will not be settled here. The process and products of curriculum development, however, will contribute to movement toward resolution of this and other unsettled issues in Black Psychology.

An extremely vital component of curriculum development is an analysis and synthesis of the vast literature generally labeled as Black Psychology. An analysis and synthesis would lay the foundation for the determination of the essential features or the common core of Black Psychology, particularly with respect to delineation of the subject matter within a course in "General Black Psychology." A common core in General Black Psychology would, at once, delimit the parameters of the discipline and further the development of the discipline. A common core is necessary because there currently exists extreme, and potentially damaging, disparity in the content, goals, and focus of courses labeled as Black Psychology. A common, standardized core would establish a baseline of knowledge for all students of the discipline. Moreover, a common, standardized core in General Black Psychology would promote (inter)national institutional credibility for the discipline.

An analysis and synthesis of the vast literature in Black Psychology would also enable the various definitions and conceptual orientations, recommended methodological approaches, debatable theoretical perspectives, and extensive research findings to be viewed and studied as a complex whole and not simply as interesting ideas which are peripheral to "real" psychology. Furthermore, an analysis and synthesis would assist academicians in redesigning—and thus enriching—currently prevailing (i.e., "basic") psychology courses by mainstreaming research by and about Black people into the undergraduate and graduate curricula. The ideas and approaches which evolve from Black Psychology are of value to both Black and non-Black students. By overcoming the invisibility of Black psychologists and their work, psychology would become a field which is more reflective (and more respectful) of cultural and political realities.

SUGGESTED TOPICS IN A BLACK PSYCHOLOGY CURRICULUM

The following list of suggested topics within a Black Psychology curriculum is offered to highlight the current range and scope of theoretical and empirical research within the field, as well as under-researched areas. Furthermore, the list is offered to highlight the fact that the discipline of Black Psychology is analytical, comprehensive, and integrative. Selected topic areas from this list could serve as the core of a General Black Psychology course, while others could be developed into specialized courses and/or incorporated into existing psychology courses (e.g., Developmental Psychology, History and Systems, Abnormal Psychology, Professional Issues, etc.).

SUGGESTED TOPICS

1. Rationale for Black Psychology
2. Definitions and Conceptual Models/Orientation in Black Psychology
3. Western Psychology as an Instrument of Scientific Racism
4. The Eurocentric Conceptual Orientation

5. History of the Development of the Association of Black Psychologists
6. History of the Development of the Discipline of Black Psychology
7. Black Psychologists—Names and Contributions
8. Research Methodologies with Black Populations
   —Critique of Comparative Studies
   —Survey Strategies
   —Experimental Black Psychology
   —Ethnographic Techniques
9. Black Psychology as Revealed in Black Literature: Novels, Biographies, and Autobiographies as Case Studies
10. The African Foundation of African Reality
11. The Africentric Conceptual Orientation/The African World View
12. The Relationship between African Religion and Philosophy and Black Psychology
13. The Relationship between History, Culture, and Personality
14. The Psychological Legacy of Slavery
15. Black Self-Concept, Self-Esteem, and Identity Development
16. Black Personality Development
17. Black Psychopathology
18. Psychological Intervention and Treatment with Black Clients
19. Black Psychological Wellness
20. Media Images and Back Identity
21. Names and Black Identity
22. Racism—Definitions, Types, Effects
23. Prejudice, Discrimination, Bigotry, Ethnocentrism, Oppression
24. Black/White/Other Ethnic Group Relations
25. Black Success *vis-à-vis* Black Cultural Oppression
26. Intelligence/Intelligence Testing in/with Black Populations
27. Black Cognitive Development Issues
   —Styles
   —Ebonics
   —Language Development
28. Neuropsychology and Black Psychology
   —Melanin Research

—Psychopharmacotherapy with Black Populations

29. Black Families
30. Black Male Issues
31. Black Female Issues
32. Black Child Development
    —Parenting
    —Individual Potential Development
    —Motor Precocity
    —Growing Up in a Racist Society
33. Black Adolescent Issues
34. Issues of the Black Aged
35. Sexuality in the Black Community
    —Homosexuality
    —Miscegenation
    —Incest
    —Adolescent Sexuality
    —Male/Female Issues
    —Sexual Dysfunctions
    —AIDS and the Black Community
36. Sexism in the Black Community
37. Antisocial Issues in the Black Community
    —Drug Abuse
    —Disrespect
    —Crime
    —Family Violence
38. Black Community Traditions and Rituals
39. Religion, Spirituality, and Black Psychology
40. The Psychology of Black Leadership
41. Research Directions in Black Psychology
42. Forensics/the Criminal Justice System and Black Psychology
43. The Black Psychologist
    —Training Issues
    —Professional Issues
    —Licensure Issues
    —As an Expert Witness
44. The Black Student as Psychologist

CONCLUSION AND COMMENCEMENT

This article began *in medias res*, that is, in the middle of the history of Black Psychology. Black Psychology is, at once, an ancient and a contemporary discipline. Its ancient roots can be traced to ancient African civilizations formalized in the context of Egyptian philosophy, religion, and mythology (Akbar 1985; Cedric X, McGee, Nobles, and Weems 1976; Myers 1988; Nobles 1986). As current efforts evolve to formalize Black Psychology, via curriculum development and curriculum improvement, it will become clearer that Black Psychology—in its ancient form—is the archetype of psychology, and—in its contemporary form—is the prototype for comprehensive study and understanding of human beings.

REFERENCES

Akbar, N. Mental disorder among African-Americans. *Black Books Bulletin* 7, 2 (1981):18-25.

Akbar, N. Africentric social science for human liberation. *Journal of Black Studies* 14, 4 (1984):395-414.

Akbar, N. Nile Valley origins of the science of the mind. In *Nile Valley Civilization—Proceedings of the Nile Valley Conference, Atlanta, September 26-30, 1985*, ed. I. Van Sertima New Brunswick, N.J.: LTD, 1985:120-32.

Azibo, D. A. Personality, clinical, and social psychological research on Blacks: Appropriate and inappropriate research frameworks. *Western Journal of Black Studies* 12, 4 (1988a):220-33.

Azibo, D. A. Understanding the proper and improper usage of the comparative research framework. *Journal of Black Psychology* 15, 1 (1988b):81-91.

Azibo, D. A. African-centered theses on mental health and a nosology of Black/African personality disorder. *Journal of Black Psychology* 15, 2 (1989a):173-214.

Azibo, D. A. Pitfalls and some ameliorative strategies in African personality research. *Journal of Black Studies* 19, 3 (1989b):306-19.

Azibo, D. A. Advances in Black/African personality theory. *Imhotep: An Afrocentric Review* 2, 1 (1990):22-47.

Azibo, D. A. *Liberation psychology: An introduction to the African personality construct.*

Trenton, N. J.: Africa World Press [in press].

Baldwin, J. A. Black psychology and Black personality: Some issues and consideration. *Black Books Bulletin* 4, 3 (1976):6-11, 65.

Baldwin, J. A. Psychological aspects of European cosmology in American society: African and European cultures. *Western Journal of Black Studies* 9, 4 (1985):216-23.

Baldwin, J. A. African (Black) psychology: Issues and synthesis. *Journal of Black Studies* 16, 3 (1986):235-49.

Boykin, A. W. Experimental psychology from a Black perspective: Issues and answers. *Third conference on empirical research in Black psychology*. New York: National Institute of Education, 1977.

Boykin, A. W. Black psychology and the research process: Keeping the baby but throwing out the bath water. *Journal of Black Psychology*, 4, 1 & 2 (1977-1978):43-64.

Boykin, A. W., A. J. Franklin, and J. F. Yates. *Research directions of Black psychologists*. New York: Russell Sage, 1980.

Bulhan, H. A. Black Americans and psychopathology: An overview of research and theory. *Psychotherapy* 22, 2, Supplement (1985):370-78.

Butler, J. E. *Black studies: Pedagogy and revolution*. Washington, D.C.: University Press of America, 1981.

Cedric X, D. P. McGee, W. Nobles, and L. Weems. *Voodoo or I. Q.: An introduction to African psychology*. Chicago: Third World Press, 1976.

Cook, N., and S. Kono. Black psychology: The third great tradition. *Journal of Black Psychology* 3, 2 (1977):18-28.

Cross, W. The Negro-to-Black conversion experience. *Black World* 20 (1971):13-27.

Cross, W. The Thomas and Cross models of psychological Nigresence: A literature review. *Journal of Black Psychology*, 5, 1 (1978):13-31.

Fairchild, H. A. Teaching Black psychology. *Western Journal of Black Studies* 8, 1 (1986):55-60.

Fairchild, H. A. Curriculum design for Black (African-American) psychology. In *Teaching a psychology of people: Resources for gender and sociocultural awareness*, ed. P. Bronstein and K. Quina, 134-41. Washington, D.C.: American Psychological Association, 1988.

Guthrie, R. *Even the rat was white: A historical view of psychology*. New York: Harper & Row, 1976.

Guthrie, R. The psychology of Black Americans: An

historical perspective. In *Black psychology*, ed. R. Jones, 3rd ed. New York: Harper & Row, 1980.

Harper, C. A. Evaluation of Black psychology syllabi. *Black studies curriculum development and course evaluations—Conferences II: Culture and social analysis*. Atlanta: Institute of the Black World, 1982.

Harper, C. A. Themes in psychological and sociological research on African-American women. *African women's studies series: African women's studies in the United States*. Vol. 4. Atlanta: Atlanta University, 1985.

Haskins, J., and H. Butts. *The psychology of Black language*. New York: Barnes and Noble, 1973.

Hayes, W. A. Radical Black behaviorism. In *Black psychology*, ed. R. Jones, 51-59, 1st ed. New York: Harper & Row,1972.

Jackson, G. G. The origin and development of Black psychology: Implications for Black studies and human behavior. *Studia Africana* 1, 3 (1979):270-293.

Jackson, G. G. Black psychology: An avenue to the study of Afro-Americans. *Journal of Black Studies* 12, 3 (1982):241-60.

Jackson, J. S., M. Tucker, and P. Bowman. Conceptual and methodological problems in survey research on Black Americans. In R. Jones, ed., *Advances in Black psychology*, Vol 2. Hampton, Va.: Cobb & Henry, (in press).

Jenkins, A. H. *The psychology of the Afro-American: An humanistic approach*. New York: Pergamon Press, 1982.

Jones, R. L., ed. *Black psychology*. 1st ed. New York: Harper & Row, 1972.

Jones, R. L., ed. *Sourcebook on the teaching of Black psychology*. Vol. 2. Washington, D.C.: The Association of Black Psychologists, 1978.

Jones, R. L., ed. *Black psychology*. 2nd ed. New York: Harper & Row, 1980.

Jones, R. L., ed. *Black psychology*. 3rd ed. Hampton, VA.: Cobb & Henry (in press [a]).

Jones, R. L., ed. *Advances in Black psychology: Vols. 1, 2, & 3*. Hampton, VA.: Cobb & Henry (in press [b]).

Karenga, M. *Introduction to Black studies*. Inglewood, CA: Kawaida Publications, 1982.

King, L. M., V. Dixon, and W. Nobles, eds. *African philosophy: Assumptions and paradigms for research on Black persons*. Los Angeles: Fanon Center, 1976.

Myers, L. J. *Understanding an Afrocentric worldview: Introduction to optimal psychology*. Dubuque, Iowa: Kendall/Hunt, 1988.

Nobles, W. W. African philosophy: Foundations for Black psychology.

In R. Jones, ed., *Black psychology*, 1st ed. New York: Harper & Row, 1972:18-32.

Nobles, W. W. *African psychology: Toward its reclamation, reascension, and revitalization*. Oakland, Calif.: Institute for the Advanced Study of Black Family Life and Culture, 1986.

Pasteur, A. B., and I. Toldson. *Roots of soul: The psychology of Black expressiveness*. Garden City, N.Y.: Anchor, 1982.

Pugh, R., ed. *Psychology of the Black experience*. Belmont, Calilf.: Wadsworth, 1972.

Smith, W., K.Burlew, M. Mosley, and W. M. Whitney. *Reflections on Black psychology*. Washington, D. C.: University Press of America, 1980.

Welsing, F. C. *The Cress theory of color confrontation*. Washington, D.C.: C-R Publishers, 1970.

White, J. L. Toward a Black psychology. In R. Jones ed., *Black psychology*, 1st ed. New York: Harper & Row, 1972:43-50.

White, J. L. *The psychology of Blacks: An Afro-American perspective*. Englewood Cliffs, N.J.: Prentice-Hall, 1984.

Wilcox, R., ed.*The psychological consequences of being a Black American: A sourcebook of research by Black psychologists*. New York: John Wiley, 1971.

Wright, B. E. Bobby E. Wright: The man and his mission. Atlanta Chapter of the National Association of Black Psychologists, 1980 (Videotape).

Wright, B. E. *The psychopathic racial personality and other essays*. Chicago: Third World Press, 1985.

Chapter 14

Africentric Pedagogy in Psychology: The FAMU Model

Kobi K. K. Kambon*

OVERVIEW

The Psychology Department at Florida A & M University (FAMU) has adopted a unique Africentric program framework, such that virtually all of its curricula and extra curricular programming and activities as well as its physical environment reflect this distinct thrust. Having achieved its stability around 1985, the department now offers an African/Black Psychology emphasis at both the undergraduate and graduate levels of training. The program also includes ongoing Africentric colloquia and symposia, Africentric student organizations and projects, and a week-long university-wide special African/Black Psychology festival (fair/celebration, etc.), featuring nationally and internationally renowned Africentric

*Credit is given to the following colleagues at Florida A & M University for their collaboration on this project: Drs. Yvonne R. Bell, Raeford Brown, Juanita Williams, Seward E. Hamilton, and Aubrey M. Perry.

psychologists and scholars. The program is here described in detail and plans/suggestions for future expansion are discussed. It is recommended that psychology departments at all historically Black colleges and universities (HBCUs) adopt this training model, either in whole or in part, for their own programs.

INTRODUCTION

For well over half a century, Black scholars and leaders have advocated the recognition of and respect for the indigenous cultural ethos that pervades all dimensions of the psychosocial reality of people of African descent (Blyden 1884; Du Bois 1902, 1933; Woodson 1933; Jones 1972, 1980; Nobles 1986). The past two decades have witnessed many contemporary Black scholars proposing that one of the primary means by which this recognition could be achieved is through the institutionalization of the discipline called African/Black Psychology (Akbar 1976; Asante 1980; Baldwin 1976a, 1986, 1989; Jones 1972, 1979a, 1980, 1990; Nobles 1986; Williams 1981). Although the clarion call for Black/African Psychology curricula in HBCUs was first sounded in the 1940s (Canady 1939), it was not until the late 1960s and early 1970s that such courses began to appear on the American educational scene. During this period, some of America's colleges and universities gradually began to institute courses in African/Black Psychology within their psychology and/or Black/African studies curricula (Hicks and Ridley 1979; Jones 1979a), particularly where Black faculty trained in psychology were present in these settings. This trend has occurred most frequently in Black/African studies departments and only occasionally in psychology departments. Ironically, however, the HBCUs have lagged behind in this movement (Baldwin and Lovett 1990; Harper 1982; Hicks and Ridley 1979; Jones 1979a, 1979b), particularly throughout the southern region of the country (where the majority of HBCUs exist). This problem has begun to rectify itself somewhat as a consequence of the growing influence of the Association of Black Psychologists [ABPsi] (Jones 1979a, 1979b; Williams 1974). Nevertheless, the HBCUs are still lagging far behind in these developments (Baldwin and Lovett 1990).

The author argues that the Department of Psychology at Florida

A & M University (FAMU) has begun to play an increasingly major role among HBCUs in the advancement of Black/African Psychology programming in American higher education. Hopefully this trend will expand to other similar institutions as a result of this exposure. Toward that end, this paper will describe the unique approach to integrating African/Black Psychology curricula and emphases into the training program of a traditional psychology department. These developments have taken place over the past ten to twelve years in particular, under the leadership of three Black psychologists: Joseph C. Awkward, Jr., Department Chair 1956–1978; Aubrey M. Perry, Department Chair 1978–1982; and Joseph A. Baldwin, Department Chair 1985–present.

BLACK/AFRICAN PSYCHOLOGY CURRICULA AT FAMU

The first course in Black Psychology was offered at FAMU in 1978. Joseph C. Awkard, Jr., a founding member and past president of ABPsi (1979–1980), and the first ABPsi newsletter editor (1974–1977), instituted a course entitled "Black Psychological Perspectives." Joseph A. Baldwin, also a past president of ABPsi (1982–1983), joined the FAMU psychology department in 1980 and changed the title of the course to "Black Psychology." In 1982, Baldwin introduced a second undergraduate-level course entitled "The Psychology of Racism and Prejudice" as well as a graduate-level course entitled "Advanced Seminar in Black Psychology." At this same time, the Black Psychology and the Advanced Seminar in Black Psychology courses became required courses for all majors at their respective levels of study, and the Black Psychology course was also instituted as a requirement for psychology minors as well, along with the traditional general psychology course. After Baldwin became department chairman in 1985, the Black Psychology course became a regular offering in the psychology curriculum every semester. (Initially it was offered only one semester per school year.) A few years later it became a multiple sections offering.

During this same period, other courses offered in the department also began to incorporate Black Psychology content wherever possible. This had been especially the case with the introduction to psychology (general psychology) course, the history and systems course, and the developmental, personality, social, abnormal, educational, and community psychology courses at the undergraduate level and in virtually all of the graduate level courses. In addition to these curriculum changes, the psychology department intensified its commitment to exposing students to the discipline of African/Black Psychology by initiating in 1981: (a) an ongoing colloquium series each academic year featuring noted local and nationally renowned Black psychologists and scholars, and (b) an annual week of African Psychology symposia, panels and workshops, media, student presentations, and African cultural exhibits and displays.

THE AFRICAN/BLACK PSYCHOLOGY COLLOQUIUM SERIES

The Department of Psychology has operated a viable Black Psychology colloquium series over the past ten years. While most of these programs have been under the sole sponsorship of the department, some have been conducted in conjunction with other campus entities and/or the North Florida Chapter of ABPsi. The colloquia have been designed to expose psychology majors and the campus community to local, national, and international Africentric scholars, community activists, and professional practitioners serving the African American community's psychological, social, educational, and health/medical needs. These programs run throughout the academic year and, depending upon the availability of relevant speakers, some years are more active than others. There had also been a very successful African/Black Psychology support program within the department.

THE BLACK PSYCHOLOGY THEME WEEK PROGRAM

As an integral part of this model, the department instituted a week-long program called "Black Psychology Theme Week" in the Spring of 1981. This program has been conducted annually during the spring semester of each year. It's purpose is twofold:

A. To expose the FAMU student body, faculty, and staff as well as the surrounding African American community to the critical importance of African/Black Psychology for an understanding of the African American experience within the context of its own

African cultural integrity

B. To demonstrate the fundamental potential for African community empowerment of this vital discipline through its African nationalist/cultural consciousness-raising and Africentric mental health preventive-intervention thrust

The activities undertaken during Theme Week are scheduled in and around class meetings in order to touch the largest audience of students. A typical Theme Week schedule includes the following activities: (a) a Keynote Address by a nationally or internationally renowned Africentric scholar; (b) orientation class sessions during the first two days of Theme Week on the history of African Psychology and the Association of Black Psychologists within the framework of the broader African liberation movement; (c) guest lectures, symposia, and workshops on topical issues in African Psychology presented by nationally and internationally renowned Africentric scholars and by guest speakers who are local African American scholars and community activists; (d) African mental health workshops and participatory sessions with students; (e) films and tapes of Africentric scholars; and (f) various African history and cultural exhibits, displays, and presentations highlighting the contributions of African people to world civilization.

The first evening of Theme Week usually is comprised of the Keynote Address. The first two days of classes during Theme Week follow the orientation format mentioned above. The Keynote Speaker also holds an informal session with students sometime during the first or second day of the week. The second evening may involve either a film presentation and discussion or another major presentation by an Africentric scholar. Panels and workshops on African American mental health issues conducted by local activists, scholars, and practitioners as well as media (videotapes and audiotapes) presentations by renowned Africentric scholars comprise the remaining days and evenings of the week. One evening during the week is also devoted to an Africentric presentation by the Psychology Honor Society, Psi Chi. The last Friday of the week is usually regarded as "Alumni Day," where returning alumni of the Psychology Department provide panels and workshops on successfully traversing the graduate school process and on career options for Black psychologists. The culminating event of the week includes an early evening Alumni Reception followed by the Annual Psychology Awards Banquet for both the psychology department and the North Florida Chapter of ABPsi. A major address is delivered at the banquet, and achievement and scholarship awards are presented to the students (both undergraduate and graduate). Recognition and achievement awards are also given to professionals at this time.

Although students had always participated in the Theme Week planning process from its inception, a special student contest to select the theme for the Black Psychology Theme Week program was instituted in 1982 and has been continued on an annual basis. Following is a listing of the themes and speakers comprising the first decade of the program:

1. *The First Annual Black Psychology Theme Week.* 20-25 April 1981. *Theme*: Black Psychology and the Liberation of the Black Mind. *Keynote and Guest Speakers*: Bobby E. Wright, Ph.D., Na'im Akbar, Ph.D., and Joseph A. Baldwin, Ph.D.
2. *The Second Annual Black Psychology Theme Week.* 12-15 April 1982. *Theme*: Black Psychology: The First Step Toward Liberation. *Keynote and Guest Speakers*: Wade W. Nobles, Ph.D., Charlyn Harper-Browne, Ph.D., David Terrell, Ph.D., Na'im Akbar, Ph.D., Joseph A. Baldwin, Ph.D., and Louis A. Ramsey, M.A.
3. *The Third Annual Black Psychology Theme Week.* 21-25 April 1983. *Theme*: Black Psychology: The Wright Path to the Liberation of the African Mind. *Keynote and Guest Speakers*: Na'im Akbar, Ph.D., Joseph A. Baldwin, Ph.D., Yvonne R. Bell, Ph.D., Raeford Brown, Ph.D., Adib Shakir, Ph.D., Louis A. Ramey, M.A., and Emmit Hunt, M.A.
4. *The Fourth Annual Black Psychology Theme Week.* 2-6 April 1984. *Theme*: The Physical, Mental, and Spiritual Implications of Black Psychology for Black Mental Health. *Keynote and Guest Speakers*: Na'im Akbar, Ph.D., Anika Fields, Ph.D., Adib Shakir, Ph.D., Elizabeth A. Holifield, Ph.D., and Herbert Alexander, Ph.D.

5. *The Fifth Annual Black Psychology Theme Week.* 25-29 April 1985. *Theme*: Blacks in Psychology: From Confrontation to Transformation. *Keynote and Guest Speakers*: Robert V. Guthrie, Ph.D., Joseph C. Awkard, Jr., Ed.D., Aubrey M. Perry, Ph.D., Joseph A. Baldwin, Ph.D., and Raeford Brown, Ph.D.
6. *The Sixth Annual Black Psychology Theme Week.* 31 March - 4 April 1986. *Theme*: Black Psychology: An Expression of Self-Affirmation. *Keynote and Guest Speakers*: Asa G. Hilliard, Ed.D., Na'im Akbar, Ph.D., Anika C. Fields, Ph.D., Dallas Williams, Ph.D., and Amos Bradford, Ph.D.
7. *The Seventh Annual Black Psychology Theme Week.* 6-10 April 1987. *Theme*: Black Psychology: A Reconstruction of Values in African-American Life. *Keynote and Guest Speakers*: Gerald C. Jackson, M.A., Aubrey M. Perry, Ph.D., and Joseph A. Baldwin, Ph.D.
8. *The Eighth Annual Black Psychology Theme Week.* 4-9 April 1988. *Theme*: Black Psychology: Building a Strong Future through Knowledge of Our Past. *Keynote and Guest Speakers*: Frances Cress Welsing, M.D., Na'im Akbar, Ph.D., James G. Brown, Ph.D., Juanita Clay, Ph.D., and Dana O. K. Dennard, Ph.D.
9. *The Ninth Annual Black Psychology Theme Week.* 3-7 April 1989. *Theme*: Blacks in Psychology: Designing Methodologies to Combat Racism in the Twenty-first Century. *Keynote and Guest Speakers*: Dona Marimba Richards, Ph.D., Yvonne R. Bell, Ph.D., Dana O. K. Dennard, Ph.D., Sharon Ames-Dennard, Ph.D., E. Ann Holifield, Ph.D., and Seward E. Hamilton, Ph.D.
10. *The Tenth Annual Black Psychology Theme Week.* 2-7 April 1990. *Theme*: Black Psychology: A Decade of Reclaiming Our African Way at FAMU. *Keynote and Guest Speakers*: Jacob H. Carruthers, Ph.D., Na'im Akbar, Ph.D., Seward E. Hamilton, Ph.D., Valorie E. Smith, Ph.D., Theodore Hemmingway, Ph.D., and Joseph A. Baldwin, Ph.D.

THE PSI CHI HONOR SOCIETY: AN AFRICENTRIC MODEL

The Psi Chi National Honor Society in psychology at FAMU was modified in philosophy and approach as a result of the Black Psychology Theme Week Program. Under the creative advisorship of Professor Yvonne R. Bell, Psi Chi at FAMU adopted an Africentric approach shortly after she assumed this post in 1983. This approach has been particularly effective in the establishment of an Africentric Psychology Study Group as part of the initiative process. This process culminates during Theme Week, whereby each initiate must give a major presentation before the department reflecting his or her perspective on the significance of Africentric psychology and articulating his or her commitment to its principles and standards in their development and professional careers. The initiation ceremony is Africentric in format, content, and style. The initiates wear kinte cloth and other traditional African attire for the ceremony. It begins with a Libation to the Ancestors and also includes the so-called "Platonic Oath", redefined (corrected) Africentrically. This occurs during a very moving segment of the program where the appropriate credit due our ancient Ancestors is finally "reclaimed" by these young psychology "warriors."

THE PSYCHOLOGY ALUMNI PROGRAM

One day near the end of Theme Week is devoted exclusively to presentation and workshops by returning alumni of the Psychology Department. In these panels and workshops, the alumni share their graduate school and/or work experiences with the students, as well as their expertise. They also discuss the relevancy of their training at FAMU to their experiences after graduation. This program has proven to be extremely beneficial in providing information and inspiration to the students who will attempt to follow in their footsteps. As was also noted, a formal reception is held for all returning alumni immediately preceding the annual Theme Week Awards Banquet.

PSYCHOLOGY DEPARTMENT AWARDS PROGRAM

The Department of Psychology offers some five categories of awards to its students. These awards cover the areas of academic achievement, leadership, and community service. The following awards are presented by the department:

1. *The Joseph C. Awkard, Sr., Psychology Scholarship Award*: This award is sponsored by Dr. Joseph C. Awkard, Jr., in honor of his late father. It is a certificate and monetary scholarship award in the amount of $500. It is presented to the graduating senior with the highest cumulative grade point average (GPA) in the department who has been accepted to a graduate program in psychology (master's or doctoral level program).

2. *The Psychology Scholastic Award*: This award certificate is given to all psychology majors who maintain a minimum cumulative GPA of 3.00.

3. *The Psi Chi Service Award*: This certificate and name inscription on a perpetual plaque award is given to the graduating senior with a minimum GPA of 2.50, who has been active in the Psi Chi organization and has demonstrated exemplary leadership.

4. *The Psychology Club Service Award*: This certificate and name inscription on a perpetual plaque award is given to the graduating senior with a minimum GPA of 2.50, who has been active in the Psychology Club and has demonstrated exemplary leadership.

5. *The Bobby E. Wright Community Service Award*: This award is in honor of the late President Elect of the Association of Black Psychologists (1981-1982) and outstanding scholar in African (Black) Psychology. It is a certificate and name inscription on a perpetual plaque award. It is given to the graduating senior with a minimum GPA of 2.50, who has demonstrated significant involvement in the university and/or broader African American community (i.e., volunteer work, organizational membership, service in leadership positions, etc.).

The local (North Florida Chapter) Association of Black Psychologists also provides an annual monetary scholarship award to one or more of the graduating seniors from the department. These awards are presented to the students during the Annual Psychology Awards Banquet closing out the Black Psychology Theme Week Program.

THE STUDENT ALLIANCE FOR CULTURAL DEVELOPMENT

Another FAMU student organization adjunct to the Psychology Department's Africentric thrust is called the *Student Alliance for*

Cultural Development (SACD). This organization was founded in 1981 by Joseph A. Baldwin and a small number of undergraduate students, both within and outside of the major, who had been influenced and inspired by Baldwin's Black Psychology course and the first Black Psychology Theme Week Program. The purpose and objectives of SACD have been to stress the African cultural foundations in providing programs and activities for FAMU students to supplement their deficient curriculum experiences in this vital area. Some examples of programs and activities sponsored by the organization include: (a) an African cultural exhibit in the annual homecoming parade, (b) an annual Kwanzaa program near the end of the fall semester, (c) regular Africentric colloquia, symposia, and workshops for developing students' cultural/political consciousness, (d) an annual Black History Month program, (e) an annual African Heritage Week festival near the end of the spring semester, and (f) regular study group meetings to cultivate students' knowledge of African history and culture. Africentric rituals and practices form the basic programmatic procedures for all SACD activities, and membership is open to all Black students at the university. Two psychology professors serve as co-faculty advisors for the organization.

CREATING AN AFRICENTRIC-VALENCED PHYSICAL ENVIRONMENT

The Psychology Department also contains a number of permanent Africentric exhibits and displays to provide a physical ambiance that reinforces its basic philosophical thrust. For example, the main corridor of the department contains a long (24 x 4.5 ft), glass-encased, three-sectional bulletin board with three exhibits. The larger, center exhibit emphasizes Africa as the cradle of civilization and the Nile Valley civilization as the world's first highly developed culture. Prominent in this exhibit is a red, black, and green color scheme, a large silhouette map of Africa in green felt with a red and black outline, and numerous photographs of artifacts and prominent personalities from Nile Valley culture. One of the end section exhibits features enlarged photographs of the early Black psychologists from Robert V. Guthrie's classic book (1976), while the other features outstanding contemporary Black psychologists, including the three departmental chairs mentioned earlier. Other special displays in the two departmental classrooms and reading room/library involve photographs, collages, art work, and symbols on walls and bulletin boards featuring a) the Association of Black Psychologists, b) the Nguzo Saba, and c) ancient Kemetic and West African cultures. Faculty offices also reflect this Africentric ambiance.

CONSIDERATIONS FOR INSTITUTING AN AFRICENTRIC EMPHASIS IN PSYCHOLOGY TRAINING PROGRAMS

The success of the Africentric emphasis in the psychology training program at Florida A & M University can be attributed to the unique combination of a number of important factors and conditions operating both within and outside the boundaries of the Psychology Department. Perhaps only in an environment similar to that of FAMU's Psychology Department could a program such as this one be successfully institutionalized. Although, ironically, the Afro-American Studies program at FAMU has traditionally been a rather weak program, the general environment of the campus includes several other departments offering courses emphasizing the African/African-American experience, such as history, sociology/social welfare, political science, English, art, music, and journalism.

Central among the other critical factors that have facilitated the success of this program has been the support from the university's administration. The Department of Psychology, obviously, has benefited tremendously from the fact that the Dean of the College of Arts and Sciences is a psychologist and former chairman of the department. This, of course, has facilitated budgetary support for the various activities and special needs of the program. Naturally, student support is also critical. The department not only encourages students to participate fully in the curriculum but also encourages participation in the other departmental activities, either by requiring it as part of course requirements, through special class assignments, and/or by offering extra credit course points.

Finally, a successful program of this type also requires, of course, effective and dedicated leadership and a dedicated and committed nucleus of faculty in support of the program. A critical mass of faculty must be committed to the addition and growth of the Africentric emphasis in the basic programmatic offerings of the training program. The Africentric research thrust of a nucleus of the faculty also contributes significantly to defining the overall departmental commitment to Africentric programming.

There is little doubt as well that the Psychology Department at FAMU has also benefited a great deal from the influence and support of the North Florida Association of Black Psychologists. The NFABPsi chapter actively participates in the department's colloquium program and the Black Psychology Theme Week Program by providing speakers and other resources. The chapter also provides financial support through the sponsorship of some Theme Week activities and other departmental activities.

THE FAMU MODEL IN PERSPECTIVE

The Africentric training model at FAMU has indeed become an integral part of the overall psychology training effort. This model has been successful for the following reasons:

A. Dedicated and committed leadership within the departmental faculty to establish and maintain a psychology program based on the Africentric paradigm

B. An institutional recognition of the need for Black/African studies in psychology

C. An institutional commitment to the continuation of the program through the allocation of financial and other resources to support its success

We in the Department of Psychology at Florida A & M University recommend that this type of program, preferably in whole but at the very least in part, be adopted by psychology departments at HBCUs as part of the general curriculum (or curriculum enhancement) effort. While we readily acknowledge that this program is certainly not as developed as it could be and ultimately must become in order to represent a full-fledged Africentric training program in psychology, it represents the only such organized program of its kind to date. Future developments of this model should include the establishment of a Black Psychology (student) club and the addition of many other Black Psychology courses to the curriculum. Such courses might include a History of Psychology course devoted to ancient Kemetic/African contributions, a course devoted to African-American personality and the critical process of child development, one focusing on mental health and Africentric preventive-intervention models, the family, the female and male experiences, and courses on the pineal body-melanin-African spirituality connection, to name a few. Other program expansions would include the addition of a master's degree specialization and eventually a doctoral level specialization in African/Black Psychology. These developments should also include the establishment of an Africentric research-mental health center (think tank) adjunct to the department. Some of these developments are in fact already in progress, while others are more long term projects. However, the department is committed to incorporating as many of them as possible in its future expansion activities.

In conclusion, this approach provides a beginning model for the establishment of an Africentric cultural emphasis in the training of Black psychologists. Such an emphasis at the present time is conspicuously absent in the programmatic thrust of most HBCUs' psychology departments (Baldwin and Lovett 1990). If we are to begin to truly train African-American psychologists (Baldwin 1976b) to effectively confront and develop solutions for the complexity of psychological and physically destructive problems characterizing African communities in the United States, in Africa, and throughout the world, programs such as this one must become institutionalized at all HBCUs (Baldwin 1976b, 1979). Can such institutions and psychology departments legitimately justify their existence on any other grounds?

REFERENCES

Akbar, N. BBB interviews Na'im Akbar. *Black Books Bulletin* 4, 3 (1981):34-39.

Asante, M. K. *Afrocentricity: The theory of social change*. Buffalo: Amulefi Publishing, 1980.

Baldwin, J. A. Black Psychology and Black personality: Some issues for consideration. *Black Books Bulletin* 4, 3 (1976a):6-11, 65.

Baldwin, J. A. Black students, psychology and the graduate school process. Typescript, 1976b.

Baldwin, J. A. Education and oppression in the American context: A psychological analysis. *Journal of Inner City Studies* 1, 1

(1979):62-85.

Baldwin, J. A. African (Black) Psychology: Issues and synthesis. *Journal of Black Studies* 16, 3 (1986):235-49.

Baldwin, J. A. The role of Black psychologists in Black liberation. *Journal of Black Psychology* 16, 1 (1989):67-76.

Baldwin, J. A. and M. Lovett. The status of psychology training at HBCUs: A fifty-year follow-up study. Typescript, 1990.

Blyden, E. W. *Christianity, Islam and the Negro race*. London, 1884.

Canady, H. G. Psychology in Negro institutions. *West Virginia State Bulletin* 3 (June 1939).

DuBois, W. E. B. *The souls of Black folk*. New York: Fawcett Press, 1961.

DuBois, W. E. B. The field and function of Negro institutions. In *The Black experience*, ed. C. Young, Pasadena, Calif: Black Lines Press, 1972.

Guthrie, R. V. *Even the rat was white: A historical view of psychology*. New York: Harper and Row, 1976.

Harper, C. An evaluation of Black Psychology course syllabi. Atlanta Junior College. Typescript, 1982.

Hicks, L. H. and S. Ridley. Black studies in psychology. *American Psychologists* 34 (1979):597-602.

Jones, R. L. *Black Psychology*. 1st ed. New York: Harper and Row, 1972.

Jones, R. L. *Sourcebook on the teaching of Black Psychology*. Vol. 1. Washington, D.C.: Association of Black Psychologists, 1979a.

Jones, R. L. *Sourcebook on the teaching of Black Psychology*. Vol. 2. Washington, D.C.: Association of Black Psychologists, 1979b.

Jones, R. L. *Black Psychology*. 2nd ed. New York: Harper and Row, 1980.

Jones, R. L. *Black Psychology*. 3rd ed. Berkeley: Cobb and Henry Publishers, 1990.

Nobles, W. W. *African Psychology: Towards its reclamation, reascension and revitalization*. Oakland, CA: Black Family Institute, 1986.

Williams, R. L. A history of the Association of Black Psychologists. *Journal of Black Psychology* 1, 1 (1974):9-24.

Williams, R. L. *The collective Black mind: An Afrocentric theory of Black personality*. St. Louis: Williams and Associates, 1981.

Woodson, C. G. *The miseducation of the Negro*. Washington, D.C.: Associated Publishers, 1933.

Contributors

NA'IM AKBAR, Ph.D. is an internationally renowned orator and scholar. As one of the leading theoreticians in African Psychology, Dr. Akbar has authored or co–authored several of the field's foundational works. He is a former President of the Association of Black Psychologists and is a member of the psychology faculty at Florida State University.

DAUDI AJANI YA AZIBO, Ph.D. is an Associate Professor of Psychology at Florida A&M University. He is the author of *Liberation Psychology: An Introduction to the African Personality Construct* (Africa World Press, forthcoming) and several parameter–setting and discipline–shaping articles in Black/Africana Studies as well as in the African Psychology field on methodology, African personality theory, and mental health. The Association of Black Psychologists awarded him its Scholarship Award in August 1989 and named him one of its "Distinguished Psychologists" in August 1993. He serves on the Editorial Board of the *Journal of Black Psychology* and has served as a faculty consultant for the National Council for Black Studies Summer Institute.

CHARLYN HARPER-BROWNE, Ph.D. is Institutional Researcher and Associate Professor of Psychology at Atlanta Metropolitan College. She has developed courses in African Psychology and African Women's Studies and received funding to conduct an evaluation study of African Psychology courses taught throughout the United States. Her interests are adolescence, adolescents, and curriculum development in the African Psychology/discipline. She has served as Treasurer of the Association of Black Psychologists.

JACOB H. CARRUTHERS, Ph.D. has been a founder and an executive officer in several Africentric scholarly organizations. A few are the Association for the Study of Classical African Civilizations, the Kemetic Institute, and the Center for Inner City Studies in Chicago. He is a leading scholar of Medu Neter (hieroglyphics), ancient Nile Valley civilizations, "multiculturalism" in education, the African worldview, and classical and contemporary European thought. A scholar's scholar and contemporary sage, two of his classic works are *Essays in Ancient Egyptian Studies and The Irritated Genie: An Essay on the Haitian Revolution.*

DOROTHY GRANBERRY, Ph.D. is a professor of psychology at Tennessee State University. She has conducted research on African American issues, student academic achievement, academic testing, conflict resolution, and the public life of women. She has published on African American education, conflict resolution, social support, issues in desegregation of higher education, and systems intervention and numerous other issues germane to African Americans.

KOBI K. K. KAMBON, Ph.D. (also known as Joseph A. Baldwin) is Chairman of the Psychology Department at Florida A & M University. He is a former President of the Association of Black Psychologists and one of African Psychology's foremost scholars. Presently he conducts an active research program in the functioning and assessment of African (Black) personality and serves on the Editorial Board of the *Journal of Black Psychology*. He is the author of *The African Personality in America: An African–centered Framework.*

OLOMENJI is a social worker at the Bobby Wright Community Mental Health Center in Chicago. He has a long history of community activism and extensive consulting and work experience in community mental health.

FREDERICK B. PHILLIPS, Psy.D. is the Executive Director of the Progressive Life Center, Inc., in Washington, D.C. He has served as director of the Association of Black Psychologists' grant for AIDS education and training. He will assume the Presidency of the Association of Black Psychologists in August 1996. As a practicing clinical psychologist, he has interests in Africentric psychotherapy, family therapy, rites of passage, substance abuse, and AIDS.

RASHAD K. SAAFIR, Ph.D. is a Chicago–based clinical psychologist in private practice. He is a consultant to community based organizations on program development for children, adolescents and adult populations and a former Chairman of the Department of Psychology, Norfolk State University (1977–78). His research interests include stress management, stress in children, and Africentric approaches to the prevention and treatment of alcohol and other drug abuse.

LEACHIM TUFANI SEMAJ, Ph.D. is affiliated with the University of the West Indies, Kingston, Jamaica, where he is a celebrity known as "the Night Doctor" (a very popular late night radio talk–show host). He has done provocative and precedent–setting work in Black male–female relationships, African personality theory, and racial identity development in African children.

NEFERKARE ABENA STEWART, Ph.D. is a practicing clinical psychologist, a former adjunct faculty member of the School of Ethnic Studies at San Francisco State University, and Director of Consultation Services for the Extended Family Institute in Oakland, California. She is a melanin scholar and an executive officer in the KM WR Association that sponsors the annual melanin conference. She is the author of a forthcoming book entitled *The Gift of Melanin and Afrikan Infant Development.*

AMANI NA UWEZO YA UKOMBOZI (also known as Michael McMillan) is a clinical psychologist. He has served as Director of Employee Treatment for the city of Chicago as well as private corporations. He has been active in the movement for reparations and has served as a consultant to African community groups opposed to forced integration of school systems. He has published articles on the "doll studies" subject.